The Elegant Inn
The Waldorf-Astoria Hotel, 1893–1929

The
Elegant Inn

The Waldorf-Astoria Hotel, 1893–1929

By Albin Pasteur Dearing

Lyle Stuart Inc.   *Secaucus, New Jersey*

Portions of Chapter 9, "The Inn of the
Golden Dragon," appeared previously
in *Smithsonian* magazine.

Library of Congress Cataloging-in Publication Data

Dearing, Albin Pasteur.
  The elegant inn.

  Bibliography: p.
  Includes index.
  1. Waldorf-Astoria Hotel (New York, N.Y. : 1897–1929)
2. New York (N.Y.)—History—1898–1951.   3. New York
(N.Y.)—Social life and customs.   I. Title.
TX941.W33D43   1986   647'.94747'101   85-25030
ISBN 0-8184-0376-4

Published by Lyle Stuart Inc.
120 Enterprise Ave., Secaucus, N.J. 07094
In Canada: Musson Book Company
A division of General Publishing Co. Limited.
Don Mills, Ontario

Queries regarding rights and permissions should be
addressed to: Lyle Stuart, 120 Enterprise Avenue,
Secaucus, N.J. 07094

Manufactured in the United States of America

To
Conrad Nicholson Hilton
1887–1980
Foremost of the World's Great
Innkeepers

There is no private house in which people can enjoy themselves so well as at a capital tavern. Let there be ever so great plenty of good things, ever so much grandeur, ever so much elegance, ever so much desire that everybody should be easy, in the nature of things it cannot be. There must always be some degree of care and anxiety. The master of the house is anxious to entertain his guests; the guests are anxious to be agreeable to him. And no man, but a very impudent dog indeed, can as freely command what is in another man's house as if it were his own. Whereas, at a tavern there is a general freedom from anxiety. You are sure you are welcome. And the more noise you make, the more trouble you give, the more good things you call for, the welcomer you are. No servants will attend you with the alacrity which waiters do who are incited by the prospect of an immediate reward in proportion as they please. No, Sir, there is nothing which has yet been contrived by man by which so much happiness is produced as by a good tavern or inn.

—Samuel Johnson
The Inn, Chapel-house
Oxfordshire
1776

Acknowledgments

*H*istorians are not writers, they're rewriters. The long months and wide distances devoted to creating this work have been pleasantly shortened and helpfully narrowed by a host of earlier chroniclers, as perhaps they in turn were guided by generous predecessors. The Elegant Inn on Fifth Avenue was just weeks away from its demise when, as a teenager, I knew it. Its successor, and its owners, have become familiar precincts and valued friends. With gratitude I thank them, as well as Henry Collins Brown, Dixon Wecter, Lloyd Morris, Oliver Herford, Albert Stevens Crockett, Frederick Lewis Allen, Michael Millgate, Robert Schackleton, Allen Churchill, Mary Cable and a host of New York newspapers and periodicals, notably *The New York Times, The World, The New York Herald* and the *New York Journal,* all, excepting the first, long since passed into limbo. I am indebted as well to the cheerful librarians of the New-York Historical Society, the Library of Congress, Florida Atlantic University at Boca Raton and their most helpful colleagues in the public libraries of West Palm Beach, Fort Lauderdale and Miami. *The Elegant Inn*'s title was the suggestion of my much valued friend, Agnes de Mille.

Without the encouragement, confidence and tireless efforts of my dear critic and colleague, Carmelinda Blagg, *The Elegant Inn* would never have seen the light of day.

Albin Dearing

Perugia, Italy
1986

To a homeless man, who has no spot on this wide world which he can truly call his own, there is a momentary feeling of something like independence and territorial consequence, when, after a weary day's travel, he kicks off his boots, thrusts his feet into slippers, and stretches himself before an inn fire. Let the world without go as it may; let kingdoms rise or fall, so long as he has the wherewithal to pay his bill, he is, for the time being, the very monarch of all he surveys. The arm chair is his throne; the poker his sceptre, and the little parlour of some twelve feet square, his undisputed empire. It is a morsel of certainty, snatched from the midst of the uncertainties of life; it is a sunny moment gleaming out kindly on a cloudy day; and he who has advanced some way on the pilgrimage of existence, knows the importance of husbanding even morsels and moments of enjoyment.

—Washington Irving
The Red Horse
Stratford-on-Avon
1819

Contents

Whoe'er has travelled life's dull round,
Whate'er his various tour has been,
May sigh to think how oft he found
His warmest welcome at an Inn.

—William Shenstone
Henley-on-Thames
1775

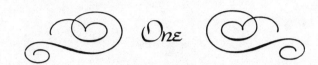

One

All for Charity. . . . and Society

*I*t was raining, a cold, marrow-chilling wetness when on Tuesday evening, March 14, 1893, with its entire 33rd Street porte-cochère and sidewalk canopied under awnings, the world's most luxurious hotel, the Waldorf, every light ablaze, formally opened its doors. Despite the weather, a fatal accident, a kitchen workers' walkout and other contretemps of great launchings, the evening proved an unqualified, joyous success.

Charity, sweet charity, in that special way it has served hotels over the past century, gave a generous assist. At a late hour sponsorship of this grand opening was subtly shifted so that it became St. Mary's Free Hospital for Children, not the hotel, which would profit from the event's generous revenues. That inspiration—having a benefit concert instead of a ball—came from London, it was deferentially announced, and provided a useful maneuver for hurdling the difficult barriers imposed against social functions during Lent, then strictly observed by many churchgoers. Moreover it rallied to the aid of George Boldt, the new hotel's proprietor, an impressive committee of Society leaders and their contemporaries from Boston, Philadelphia and Baltimore. These two objectives set the tone and scope of America's most distinguished hotel for life.

As that day's damp cold enveloped the city, if Society belles complained because the weather would prevent their wearing something new and exciting instead of a gown already seen in that season's ballrooms, neither their demeanor nor the splendor of the occasion would reflect it.

George Boldt and his pretty wife individually welcomed each guest at the door. Thirty-seven-year-old Oscar Tschirkey, destined to become famous as Oscar of the Waldorf, a reputation pre-eminent among major domos worldwide, stood at Boldt's elbow.

A corps of male socialites quickly ushered the guests to the main ballroom where fifteen hundred chairs had been set up. Rain briefly delayed the concert, but just minutes after nine Walter Damrosch lifted his baton and the New York Symphony leapt into Franz Liszt's lively *Festival Sounds*. Some two hundred late arrivals were shunted off for a delightful tour of the Palm Garden whose impressive marble columns had been quarried in Russia, to the nine magnificent private dining rooms, to the sumptuous state suites, the handsome oak-panelled restaurant, the serenely decorous green card rooms. They inspected the staff of trim, starched housemaids, the platoon of brass-buttoned young bell-hops. They admired the hotel's unique pneumatic tube system, which sent a visitor's card from the lobby to any guest's room in forty seconds. They lingered to admire palms, ferns, thousands of American beauty roses, tulips, mignonettes and orchids—its "Dainty Veils of smilax," rapturously wrote one reporter.

In the hotels of that day, special suites were on the lower floors because of their quicker accessibility. Thrown open for this gala audience's enthusiastic inspection was a bedchamber of 15th Century France, authentic to the smallest detail, whose $38,000 furnishings included a superbly carved bedstead with a canopy of figured mahogany. Spontaneous oohs and aahs greeted each of the nine private dining rooms, already set for supper where all were to dine as Mr. Boldt's guests. "Three surpass anything of the kind yet seen in this city in tasteful elegance," said *The Times* writer. "One was an exact reproduction of the dining room of the old Astor mansion with much of the Astor furniture and service, enveloped in dominating linen, lace, and floral tones of pink." Only fourteen guests might be served here, the others in no less splendid dining rooms or the restaurant below. For seats in these stunning rooms, whose dominant colors were blue, green, and bright red accented by a profusion of roses, there seems to have been any amount of good-natured competition.

Private suites with ornate baths gained the approval of Mrs. Alva Smith Vanderbilt, whose predilection for eighteen-karat gold bathroom fixtures was well known. "You don't have to clean them you know," said she, earning the prize for household hints.

Guests inspecting the handsome hotel register would note that Abner Bartlett's daughter and son-in-law, Mr. and Mrs. Jonas B. Kissam and their daughter Grace had been first to register, having jumped the gun a bit and moved in the previous Thursday just moments ahead of the Robert Garretts of Baltimore. Oscar recalls that when Kissam appeared, gladstone bag in hand, the bellboys whom Oscar had so scrupulously drilled for this precise climactic moment, just stood and stared, struck dumb and motionless. The Waldorf's first guest had to carry in his own bag.

While the latecomers drifted from one exciting new revelation to another the Symphony, provided by the generosity of Mrs. William Kissam Vanderbilt, was rendering three complete selections from Bizet's *Carmen,* followed by Max Bruch's "Cello Solo," competently played by Joseph Hollman. Then Vieuxtemps' "Solo for Violin; Ballad, and Polonaise" by another New York concert favorite, Johann Wolff, now Messrs. Wolff and Hollman together rendering Rossini's "Mirais Bianca Luna." As applause subsided, Mrs. Vanderbilt dispatched Oscar with a scribbled note to Damrosch: " 'Brown October Ale' please, in honor of a guest, Mrs. Reginald De Koven, the composer's wife."

Hundreds of newspapers' rapturous reports of the Waldorf gala opening were carried across the land. Correspondents described to the last detail the "Birth of Venus" ceiling painted by Will Low in the Marie Antoinette Ladies Parlor, the Turkish Smoking Room with its low divans and shining exhibit of silver armor, the Great Ballroom in gold and white, its handsome music gallery of treasured Louis XIV furnishings, the nepenthean Cafe's handsome ceiling coffers of English oak and its spacious open hearth where waiters baked potatoes to order, the brilliant Palm Court's five hundred electric lights flanked with azaleas, hydrangeas, Easter lillies, crocuses and palms. One reporter even interviewed Emile, proselyted from the Gebhard family, presiding now as the first Waldorf chef. Society belles of Chicago and San Francisco, Pittsburgh and New Orleans, noting what everyone wore, learned of the new "Watteau fall," a jet coif embellishment, and the stylish new jewelled embroidery. One fancies hearing them say: "My dear, I simply must have my next gown made with a Bertha. Did you read how many women wore them to the Waldorf?"

At eleven-forty Miss Katie McNeary, 23, servant, took an elevator to the eleventh floor. As she stepped from the elevator her dress caught. Richard Cliff, the elevator boy, let go the controlling rope for an instant to disengage Katie's skirt. Instantly the car bolted upward dragging Katie across the floor and over the edge of the open shaft. For one terrible eternity Katie, screaming, dangled beneath the car suspended by her dress. In abrupt spasmodic jerks the cloth ripped free, plunging Katie headlong down the black shaft to its depths. Hurriedly volunteers carrying lamps climbed down into the pit. Frantically, someone summoned the house physician.

The body they found was mangled and broken. Ropes and ladders were fetched to hoist it up onto the wine room floor. Loving hands wiped away the blood. Katie was dead. In the kitchen pandemonium reigned. With loud Irish lamentations thirty-five of Katie's friends grabbed up their belongings and walked out.

Nothing that John Doyle, the assistant steward, could say or do could persuade them to stay. Katie's death was an evil harbinger. These needed the safety of their homes and their rosaries. John Doyle put on his overcoat and hurried out in the night, recruiting helpers wherever he could. Soon he had matters in hand, the kitchen functioning.

In the tradition of great hotels, no word of this would reach the ear of any guest.

Two

The Opulent Era

$\mathcal{W}$hen William Waldorf Astor opened the doors of his luxurious new hotel, New York City could boast eight families whose wealth was multiplying faster than any in history. In several sumptuous Fifth Avenue residences a hundred guests could be served a six-course banquet on one hour's notice. At these the hostesses might appear in gowns costing $40,000, wearing diamonds, emeralds, rubies, sapphires and pearls valued at three quarters of a million. In one such mansion seven Rembrandts were displayed on the walls of a single room. Five family fortunes exceeded two hundred million dollars which even at six percent simple interest would have fetched you $22.45 in the fifty seconds it has taken you to read this far—or $1,347.37 per hour every hour of the day or night, awake or asleep. Forever. And in dollars having ten times the power of today's.

America's Opulent Era was also its magic Age of Science. Automobiles, mostly steam and electric, were appearing. As recent beneficiary of Mr. Edison's marvellous electric lamp whose illumination equalled that of one hundred candles, and of Mr. Bell's telephone whose threadlike lines carried the human voice as far west as Omaha, Wall street, cash in hand, searched far and wide, eager to back even the wackiest scientific cerebrations. Anything was possible, even likely. Thirty-five thousand New Yorkers, confident of talking with the dead, subscribed $1,170,000 to hold hands around tables in darkened seances, to see frothy ectoplasm take the shape of some loved one and get answers to questions through a medium, to hear anguished voices or mysterious rapping noises while furniture flew about the room.

Despite the tailspinning stock market that ten months earlier had plunged one-third of the nation's railroads into bankruptcy, America was robust. Uncle Sam's muscles bulged with inexhaustible coal and ore deposits, new lodes of gold, silver, copper, lead and zinc; acres of new textile

[25]

and sleepless steel mills, endless expanses of timber stands, bottomless wells of petroleum and natural gas, burgeoning hydroelectric plants, hundreds of new labor-saving devices, its fleet of cargo ships on all Earth's seven seas.

One thousand new immigrants were arriving every day contributing to the widening cleavage between restless America's impatient growth and her laggard social conscience. Slavery had been abolished thirty years earlier but on this same March day of 1893 in Fayette, Missouri, one George Winn, black, having been found guilty of vagrancy,* was "sold on the block" for $20 to one H. S. McCampbell of Glen Eden Springs, for whom Winn must toil in total bondage for six months. Nearby in Caddo, Indian Territory, Elias Loraine, Choctaw, who'd been readied for the firing squad then reprieved by a last minute grant of a new trial simply took off. "That being the second Indian to have fled his fate, a revision in the law will probably result," ruefully added a *Times* stringer.

The Nineties were yet a time of chivalry, a time when a gentleman would be as promptly reproached for uttering the word adultery in the presence of a lady as for committing it, a time when books by women authors were not shelved in public libraries alongside those of men. Wrote Stephen Crane, busily revising *Maggie* for her hard cover reappearance, "I have carefully plugged at the words which hurt and it seems to me the book wears quite a new aspect from very slight omissions." Curse words such as "What deh hells deh matter wid yeh" offended the proper 1890 reader, and Crane was required to dispense with a number of "damns," convert "hell" to "h—ll" and politely say, "I'll paste ye" instead of "I'll club hell out of you."

Chivalry would manifest itself in far more vigorous ways than displays of good manners and decorous literature. That same March day, across the river in Newark, Miss Mary Elmenworth, hiding a rawhide horsewhip in the folds of her skirt, lay in wait for one Mr. Thorne who earlier had promised to marry her and then postponed the event with pleas of financial distress. To these a tearful Miss Elmenworth consented, although she had already bought her trousseau, even loaned Thorne three dollars for a new pair of pants. Then one evening, returning from church, who did she see

*"VAGRANT—One who strolls from place to place."—Webster.

[26]

lurking in the shadows? And kissing another girl! Now, clutching her whip, Mary was going to let him have it. As well she did, to the vast satisfaction of bystanders and thousands of newspaper readers. "A broken heart makes an irresistible appeal to the chivalrous mind," notes Ellen Glasgow. And to juries. In that year the courts of New York heard 1,431 suits for breach of promise and made 920 awards, all to the fair plantiffs.

For a Baltimore bride that March day life was kinder. Standing before the altar of St. Ignatius Church, radiant in her gown of white satin, joyous Mary Ellen McCrary cared not to remember that the last time she had been before this very altar was for a funeral. Her own. Yes, just weeks earlier, following a brief illness, Mary Ellen had died. Grief-stricken, her loving relatives had bathed, dressed and borne her here in a satin-lined casket banked with flowers. After last rites were said came the moment for shutting and forever bolting the casket. One mourner's tear-dimmed eyes lingered lovingly on Mary Ellen's exquisite features. "What the. . .!" He went suddenly faint, grasping a pew for support. "Look! Her eyelids fluttered! She is smiling! Her eyes are open!" Alleluia! A miracle! Indeed Mary Ellen wasn't dead at all. "But," insisted the doctor, "her heart had stopped beating . . ." And that ended the matter, for then much in the practice of medicine was perfunctory pathology, often guesswork. Not that an amount of folklore did not linger, but doctors were no longer prescribing heroin for opium addiction and large doses of whiskey for tuberculosis.

What else was taking place across the American landscape these Ides of March, 1893? At Nitta Yuma, near Memphis, a mob of five hundred stormed the jail, overpowered the sheriff, seized his prisoner, one Lee Walton, a murder suspect, hanged him and filled his body with buckshot. Unusual, a lynching? Yes, to be sure, Walton was black. But so was the murder victim. And so was the mob!

Closer to home, prominent New Yorkers infected by the doctrine of "Manifest Destiny" which had wrested Texas from Mexico, were meeting to demand the annexation of Cuba, Hawaii and Canada. Support for this, if muted in Canada, was here both vigorous and vocal. As for Cuba, newspaper dispatches from correspondents purportedly stationed there described Cuba's Spaniards as impatient for American annexation "to escape the excessive taxes of Spain." In Tampa, Florida, General José Martí calmly cooled his heels, waiting, he publicly explained, for the U.S. North Atlantic Squadron to leave Key West so his *Cuba Libre* revolutionaries could invade their homeland without U.S. interference. In Hawaii the annexationists hadn't done so well. Funded by U.S. sugar interests and helped by a free-wheeling American minister, they pulled off a bloodless palace revolution which dethroned Queen Liliukokaleni. But so clumsily, the plot backfired. President Cleveland raged. "An act of war committed by a representative of the United States without authority against a feeble and friendly and confiding people," he called it, promptly cashiering his errant diplomat and flatly refusing to submit the usurper government's treaty of annexation to the Congress for ratification.

A stickler for propriety, Cleveland's political acuity shone elsewhere brightly when he announced that he was setting aside two hours each Monday, Wednesday and Saturday for any and all visitors, "persons having no business who just wanted to drop in at the White House for a chat"; when the White House telephone rang, Cleveland himself answered it. The Waldorf opening, however, he had to miss, offering to send an appropriate representative, perhaps his popular vice-president, Adlai Stevenson. Another invitation, the opening of the new, fashionable ladies Colony Club on Madison Avenue, the president dismissed out of hand. "A woman's best club is in the home," he intoned. Gratuitous? Perhaps. Such remarks, politically suicidal today, were reasonably discreet in 1893 when not only were women unliberated, but could not vote.

Congress, surviving the numbing realization of organized labor's massive clout in the aftermath of America's first nation-wide strike, was focusing its concern on the growing popularity of divorce, "dispatching its two investigators to New England to study causes." Tucked away somewhere the Navy found an unspent $200,000 and was busily constructing its first underwater "torpedo boat." The Army, momentarily at peace with the Indians, was busily at war with renegade Kansans trying to beat the gun on the Cherokee Outlet and stake out claims in Oklahoma. Alarmed that the shift of immigrant flow from Western to Eastern Europe was bringing in another half million each year "unadaptable to the American way of life," Rena Atchison's Immigration Restriction League was vigorously lobbying Congress, but only earning for itself charges of anti-Catholic bias. Rena and her League seemed not to comprehend that many immigrants fled Europe for their lives. For many the quality of American life in the ghetto was scarcely an improvement on what they had left behind.

Two years earlier, an 1890's census shows, twenty-six percent of all New York boys ages ten to fifteen and ten percent of its girls in this age group were gainfully employed, that being the highest point child labor in America was suffered to reach. To the tragic plight of children New Yorkers were not indifferent; New York was the first to enact child labor laws. And enforce them. Militant agents of Elbridge Gerry's Society for the Prevention of Cruelty to Children regularly roamed Gotham's streets stopping and questioning children. Faced by heavy fines and prison, sweatshop operators were quick to conform. More slowly to congeal was public support for decent housing.

This movement's tireless champion was Jacob Riis, erstwhile reporter, who one day had discovered a father, mother, twelve children and six boarders all crammed into two tiny tenement rooms. Thanks to Riis there would be no new construction of these unheated, ill-ventilated, badly lighted six-story firetraps. Some buildings housed as many as forty families, sardining each into suffocating, three-room warrens comprising a living and dining-kitchen area ten feet by fourteen, and two "bedrooms" not half that size. New York, already the third largest German city in the world, contained more Irish than Dublin, more Italians than Venice, with only Chinatown supplying an ethnic neighborhood of respectability and cleanliness. Quipped Riis, who but a few years earlier had himself arrived in steerage from Denmark, "The Irishman is the true cosmopolitan immigrant. All pervading, he shares his lodging with perfect impartiality with the Italian, the Greek, and the 'Dutchman' yielding only to sheer force of numbers. And objecting equally to them all."

Still smarting under the *Times* lash that had driven out Boss Tweed, after a short-lived reform New York's city government was once again the secure fiefdom of Tammany Hall. Its new ruler was the ruthless, teetotaling and pitilessly pragmatic Richard Crocker, who would soon forsake it for Ireland and the next world, leaving behind his Cherokee Indian wife with tidy sums and a Palm Beach villa to closet her three hundred pairs of shoes.

On a visit from England, professing shock at New York's affinity for "bossism," Herbert Spencer chided a Delmonico's gathering. "Americans," he said, "retain the forms of freedom but so far as I can determine

[29]

there has been a considerable loss of its substance. . . . Those who framed your Constitution never dreamed that twenty thousand voters would go to the polls led by a boss."

Public order was in the hands of gigantic policemen in knee-length blue coats, mud-splattered and wrinkled, wearing gray helmets that seemed several sizes too small, who, except when street fights broke out, appeared perpetually idle. Even then these were called "New York's Finest," but a visitor might readily be convinced of the newspaper charges that these 'Tammany cops" on average were as dishonest as the criminals whose villainy they would suppress. Witnesses to their misdeeds dared not to testify lest the police abuse, club or imprison them on trumped up charges and perjured testimony. Police corruption, in spite of indictments for graft and brutality, would prevail for more than a decade.

New York's public sanitation, which like much else in civil administration swings from periods of neglect to years of commendable efficiency, in the early Nineties was back on the filthy side. Trash, kitchen refuse, human and animal excrement was piled too high in many thoroughfares to permit the passage of a peddler's pushcart, a situation little improved in the half century since Charles Dickens's visit when pigs were allowed to roam the streets as a practical means of garbage disposal. Horsecars plying many thoroughfares, and everything else animal drawn, made it almost impossible to keep the streets clean. Travellers on the Madison Avenue car automatically covered their noses against the suffocating stench during the ten-minute Park Avenue tunnel passage.

More refined if no less soiling transit was provided by hundreds of hansom cabs that stood in long ranks around Madison Square and other parkways in the nicer parts of town. After dark the more ancient hackneys, "prowling nighthawks," plied the streets or parked under elevated stations waiting for couples fancying a ride up to Claremont or romantic Central Park. Should a young man be allowed to take his girl to the theater without a chaperone, or in a party of four, he had to hire a four-wheeler, commonly called a "hack." Fashionable livery stables prospered by renting coupés, broughams, landaulettes or victorias. Bicycles, darting in and out through traffic, were a continual menace to pedestrians. "Safety" bicycles, one with both wheels of the same size, had been around only five years. They were becoming the rage in New York with a new bicycle path in Brooklyn and would soon take over Western Avenue slanting from Central

Park to the Hudson. Said Stephen Crane in the *Sun,* "On these gorgeous spring days they appeared in the thousands. All mankind is awheel apparently and a person on nothing but legs feels like a strange animal. A mighty army of wheels streams from the brick wilderness below Central Park and speeds over the asphalt. In the cool of the evening it returns with swaying and flashing of myriad lamps."

The city's frantic growth, and street congestion a natural consequence, inevitably meant plans for rapid transit—on the surface, trestled overhead or tunnelled below. First, the horsecars, drawn over tracks along all avenues except Fifth and Lexington, with three connecting cross-town lines. Soon Third Avenue and Sixth had elevated trains—steam engines, not yet electric—the Sixth Avenue Line scheduling 420 round trips a day between five-thirty in the morning and midnight with its coal-stoked locomotives creating incessant din, showering cinders on the sidewalks below and squirting oil through the open windows of homes. Often it did not stop at some stations. Braver passengers scrambled on and off at their peril. At street level, an addition to track-bound "cars" and the "stages," a 'Nineties innovation was the "bobtail," a new type horse-drawn public conveyance with no conductor. On boarding, a passenger would drop his fare in a box and if change were needed (for the two dollar bill only) he would pass the bill up through a slit in the roof and the driver handed back a sealed envelope containing that amount in coins. From this the passenger dropped a nickel in the box, a receptacle so positioned that the driver peeping down from his perch on the roof could make sure that everyone paid. Those not paying immediately upon stepping aboard heard angry raps on the roof and suffered the scorching stares of fellow passengers. When a passenger wanted to get off he simply pulled an overhead strap which ran up through the roof and was tied to the driver's knee. A gentle pull suggested a lady passenger for whom the driver might steer the vehicle to the curb; too vigorous a yank doomed his passenger to be dropped to fend for himself in the maelstrom of traffic.

Hackneys were the taxis of the street. These were big family coaches and pairs with seats for six. They hired out at a dollar an hour with negotiable rates for shorter lifts. The smaller brougham, the two-wheeled coupé for couples, did not appear until later. Marked progress came with the Greenwich Street Elevated built to connect Yonkers down Ninth Avenue with the Hudson River depots at Thirtieth Street. This was a cogwheel affair which exploded abruptly into motion and stopped with a violent jerk, so violent, in fact, that on its inaugural run official ceremonies had to be halted while President Ackerman of the line, thrown off his feet, retrieved his false teeth.

Up beyond Sixty-Fourth Street lay an expanse of open country. Here the train rolled through shantytown settlements where the impoverished lived in caves or makeshift shelters of packing boxes and discarded junk. For another six miles, all the way to the Harlem River, stretched acres of potatoes, cabbages and lettuce.

Useful as these steam trains were for transporting passengers, the great bulk of New York's freight and passenger travel still depended on the horse. How total was that dependency became cruelly apparent one terrible summer's day when mysteriously all horses were struck down by an affliction identified simply as the epizootic. During that one day 200 animals died in the sweltering heat. For the next four weeks handcarts and strong backs alone would move street commerce. Had it not been for Henry Bergh's Society for the Prevention of Cruelty to Animals, opposed with much hostility by teamsters, there probably would have been many more deaths; the poor beasts were simply overworked and underfed. Bergh's group went about building horse troughs, then provided special ambulances to remove stricken animals to shelters where they could be cared for. They also produced straw hats to protect the animals from the merciless sun.

Before construction of the elevated train, the tortuous trip up Manhattan through traffic took fully half an hour. By far a more popular route was by boat, trim little white steamers plying the Hudson between Peck Slip and One Hundred Thirtieth Street where other boat connections made Fordham, Highbridge, Morris Dock, Kingsbridge, Marble Hill, Ft. George and Spuyten Duyvil along the Harlem River. Sunday picnickers would enjoy the shaded nooks and pleasant groves along the East River or take Starin's Glen Island Boats for even wider adventure.

Mr. Eastman's wondrous Kodak Number Two, "You Press the Button, We Do the Rest," which did not require returning the entire apparatus to him for developing, was just on the market, recruiting photography fans by the thousands.

Eventually steam and horses would give way to electric cars. A major step forward for vertical transportation was the building elevator of Frank Julian Sprague, an associate of Thomas Edison. Despite his illustrious mentor's advice that he was wasting his time, Sprague persisted; Manhattan, corseted by rivers, would go up as well as out. As habitations, apartments rather than single family houses were becoming popular, dating from Rutherford Stuyvesant's Irving Place Flats, cozy self-contained units, some having an intriguing bed which upended and closeted itself when not in use. Virtually all newlyweds and many small families inhabited boardinghouses. Most new private homes were constructed of wood, Dutch limestone, or timbers and stucco, but fashionable upper middle class New Yorkers now flocked into brownstones inspired in part by the two handsome Fifth Avenue Astor residences at 33rd and 34th streets soon to be demolished to make way for the Waldorf.

In words of the conservative press, the brownstones, of a reddish-brown sandstone, were "unique"; the disapproving called them freaks. Faced with Philadelphia pressed brick, their window trim, cornices, rustic columns and stoops of Nova Scotia freestone, the brownstones gave an aura of wealth, dignity, and gracious living. They quickly became the rage. In less than a decade burgeoning New York would become a city of brownstone fronts. Soon houses were being advertised with no other recommendation than their brownstone front. Whatever the rest of the structure, the front had to be stone, had to look like a stone building. "Fifth Avenue," wrote a contemporary English newspaperwoman, "where are congregated the much coveted brownstone fronts is, in front, a very handsome street, the rich color of the stone being itself a beauty unrivalled by any building material yet in use. If New York were built of that stone entirely, as Aberdeen is of granite and Bath of whitestone, it would indeed be superb. But the houses behind the stone fronts were mere shells."

Most of the city's great residences reflected an owner's extravagant indulgence of his architect. Magnificent Norman castles, Loire chateaux, Gothic, Tudor, Roman, Moorish, Byzantine, Baroque villas, faithful copies all, rose side by side; hybrid dwellings displaying vulgar plagiarisms from each. Turrets, cupolas, gables, pilasters and portcullises adorned massive caravanserais numbering from twenty-five to ninety rooms. Some were pleasantly landscaped with sunken gardens, labyrinths of boxwood, gracefully sculpted metal gazebos, gingerbread or oriental teahouses, byzantine cloisters, heated greenhouses, stone-columned arcades with massive, intricately figured iron gateways guarding their impressive entry. A hefty pull on a brass knob here would summon the gatekeeper or footman.

Interiors featured vaulted-ceilinged reception halls leading to balustraded stairways of marble. Walls might be frescoed, or panelled with teak, fruit or nutwoods, or covered above a dark wood dado with silk, damask or brocade and hung with gold-encased paintings and Aubusson, Gobelin or Bayeaux tapestries. Ornamented ceilings exhibited gracefully sculpted moldings or bold coffers of wood and metal, many delicately painted in the fashion of Venice and Tuscany. Massive, scintillating chandeliers bearing hundreds of multi-faceted Bohemian crystals dominated large reception areas and ballrooms, mirrored by floors of tile mosaics, or parquetry oak and teak. Cut stone was popular, polished to the patina of marble and overlaid with treasured carpeting from Turkestan, India, China, Turkey, Persia, the Caucasus or the cushiony broadlooms of Erastus Bigelow. Long flat textured bell-cords were at hand for summoning servants.

For the less wealthy homebuilder the Nineties ushered in the era of the scroll saw, a miracle worker in wood. All America felt its presence in exteriors of gingerbread or scroll-patterned furniture embellished with mother-of-pearl or whalebone scrimshaw. The device unloosed a swirl and loop orgy Gaudi might have relished if indeed he had not inspired it.

Windows need not be rectangular. They might as well be round or trefoiled or scalloped or fan-shaped, even lined up to resemble the portholes of a ship. Exteriors need not be wood or stone or brick or stucco alone, sometimes several of these textured together or all four in combinations. This was the age of Joseph Cleveland Cady and Stanford White, of Richard Morris Hunt and the Waldorf's Henry J. Hardenburgh, architects whose illustrious works may yet be (dimly) seen, thriving in a metropolis which only forty years earlier had no professional architects, for not until 1853 was architecture even considered a profession.

Primitive central heating was just coming into its own: gravity flow hot air piped up through cavernous metal ducts large enough for a man to crawl through, or steam drafted up to cold room radiators from a massive basement furnace. The crackling open fireplaces in every room, in addition to their gift of instant cheer, rendered remote chambers habitable on very cold days, adding the need for vast cellars for storing coal and cordwood whether or not the furnace be gas fired. If these today seem primitive, they become startlingly innovative when one realizes that but fifty years earlier New Yorkers' homes got their heat from wood alone, their illumination from whale oil.

Americans of the Nineties were forensically at odds with plumbing and sanitation. Opposing daily baths was Mary Baker Eddy; once a week was enough, she said. Respected journals such as the *North American Review* deplored the rush of home builders to install bathrooms and flush toilets: "In Washington the sanitary defects in the White House . . ." it warned, "are believed to have contributed to President Garfield's death. In one new splendid New York mansion having a bathroom in the center of the house and no ventilation except through a transom opening into a bedroom, the occupants of that bedroom died of typhoid fever."

Nevertheless, upper-class and wealthier homes installed bathrooms, some as many as four or five. Bathtubs were usually of galvanized zinc, some plain roofing tin simply rimmed with a varnished oak, depressing six-foot-long troughs without hot water or shower requiring an hour to fill from an uncertain single thin pipe. Hot water was fetched from the kitchen. There were no special bath soaps—a brownish bar of smelly laundry soap sufficed—and no dental talcum. Cleaning one's teeth was by no means a universal practice. Toilet tissue hadn't been around but twenty years.

Essential to the less-affluent homeowner was a sitting room or parlor with its "cozy corner." This, occupying the room's best angle, was a tent-like affair hung about with varied weaponry–spears, butcher cleavers made to look like battle-axes, blades from Bowery pawnshops intended to resemble Toledo steel, swords from Damascus (Pennsylvania), scimitars, daggers and other trappings of a Baghdad caliph. Inside was heaped a mound of burnt leather cushions, satin-faced pillows, crazy quilts, flowing scarves aglitter with stars and crescents, piled in profusion on top of an old army cot to effect its conversion to a divan in a Turkish harem. On gala occasions pseudo incense would burn to heighten the mysterious effect. In home décor Americans (Europeans, Asians) traditionally harbor an *idée fixe;* the homemakers' obsession of the Nineties was the rubber plant, which always had the place of honor in the bay window of the front parlor, the "best room" used only for company and for funerals. Its shiny green leaves were a patent of nobility, irrefutable evidence that in this house abided Culture and Refinement.

Funerals were a tribal rite, mourning an institution which confronted families far oftener in the Nineties than today, the funerals of children outnumbering those of adults. The etiquette of mourning was the province of the "mourning warehouse," whose woeful representative arrived bearing bolts of black crêpe, black waxed floral pieces, dresses, mantles and millinery. Black wreaths went onto the front door. Black crêpe draped the mantle and a prominently displayed picture of the loved one. Widows wore black for at least a year, other members of the family perhaps more briefly. A widow's card was heavily bordered in black and her social life cloistered. After a suitable lapse of time, deep mourning tapered off to half-mourning, a gown of cream Indian crepon trimmed in black velvet and Irish guipure.

The gilded rolling pin was an inevitable wall-hanging in the middle-class homemaker's decoration scheme. This symbolized that the family no longer made its own bread but was financially able to purchase ready-baked loaves, and thereby launched into the realm of the affluent.

Other interior decorations followed bizarre conformity: piano legs inevitably tied with wide, baby-blue sashes, coal scuttles inevitably painted with landscape and floral patterns, and whisk brooms inevitably and inconsequentially decorated. Lambrequins and chenile curtains were a must. These hung from the mantlepiece, hung from the piano, hung over the backs of chairs, hung just about everywhere they could be hung. Walls displayed all-but-forgotten imitations bought as "French masters," Currier and Ives farm and sporting prints, marriage certificates, diplomas, resolutions of the United Order of Woodmen.

Elaborate testimonials of bold calligraphic sweep and colorful illumination must be framed in a cluster of pine cones. Of course, American greats in sculpture—La Farge, Ryder, Ward, Saint-Gaudens, Chase, Gifford, Hopkinson Smith—were each creating valued works, but in thousands of homes the sculptured groups of John Rogers, portraying American life with sentiment, humor and pathos, clearly owned the hearts of the Nineties and for several decades to follow. "Weighing the Baby," or "The First Ride," or "Going for the Cows" and "Coming to the Parson" were favorites among seventy-three subjects from Rogers' prodigious production of one hundred thousand pieces. With "The Foundling" and "The Charity Patient" he vigorously indicted social injustice. Other statuettes dealing with the freed Blacks dramatized Rogers' concern for the underprivileged as movingly as had the gifted pen and brush of Winslow Homer, erstwhile *Harper's Weekly* illustrator on Civil War fronts, elected to the National Academy at twenty-nine.

Horsehair sofas, ornamented upholstered chairs cushioned with velvet or damask or petit-point, extravagantly ornamented by some virtuoso of the fret saw or inlaid with mother-of-pearl, set the furniture motif. Electricity not universally available, most homes depended for illumination on gas. Beaded lamp shades, the leaded colored glass of Louis Tiffany, wall fixtures resembling inverted tulips, crystal chandeliers and great brass columnar student lamps were as essentially a part of this parlor clutter as tasseled portières, sombre Brussels carpets, wide varnished doors intended to slide back into the walls, paired ottomans, petit-point-covered footstools and a chaste marble-top table with its huge gilt-edged Family Bible, illustrated with tribal necrology and engravings from Genesis to Revelations and seldom opened except by children to look at the pictures. The piano was rosewood, square, massive and rarely played by any but young ladies up to the time of their marriage. Absolute *pièce de résistance,* "the bright, particular star of the entire Victorian Renaissance," Henry Collins Brown calls it, was the plaster cast replica of Venus de Milo with an eight-day clock in her tummy.

Houses of the Nineties slavishly succumbed to a blue glass affliction. Blue glass windows brought into the house healthful, analeptic rays, therapy for every complaint from dyspepsia to the d.t.'s. Every house had to have one blue glass window, more if the householder could afford them. Many built special solaria inclosed wholly with blue glass. Another cult would supply recruits to the widely advertised electric shock treatments of Dr. Woodbury, a flamboyant, widely admired pathologist whose carriage was drawn by a team of matched elk, whose obesity treatments enlisted both President Cleveland and heavyweight champ Bob Fitzsimmons. However else they may have been beneficial, Fitzsimmons went to a pauper's grave owning only the diamonds set into his teeth—and for even these would his (fourth) wife seek the court's permission to dig him up.

There were yet few home telephones but every residence had a bell for calling messengers, the streets ever populous with armies of messenger boys hurrying hither and thither delivering important notes. Where a telephone had been installed it was considered ill-mannered to use it to invite guests to one's home; or if the telephone was so used, etiquette dictated that the invitation be followed by one in writing.

Though the sitting room (from which parents fled when marriageable daughters received their friends) might contribute to wooing, with its cozy corners' titillating seductiveness, its effect was set to nought in marital bliss by New York decorating firms now advocating a scandalous innovation. Extending their influence to the bedroom, these would abolish the sacramental double bed and replace it with twin beds! Public outcry was prompt. In frontal collision were masculine resentment and feminine determination to be modern. Husbands, even those no longer young and more metaphysically than physically uxorious, battled to retain the ancient hallowed symbol of wedded happiness. Twin beds would weaken the holy bonds of matrimony, clergymen predicted, they would become a social menace. Physicians argued that the old-fashioned double bed was unsanitary, that undisturbed sleep was therapeutic. Because of the fast pace and tensions of New York life, women were becoming increasingly nervous, these said. To wives, innocently bent upon decorative innovations, such medical opinion often imputed undeserved symptoms of hysteria. Brides, by tradition free to choose the furnishings of their future homes, opted for twin beds, and the younger generation, always a little wiser than it cares to appear, refused to concern itself with what the fuss was all about. Why should two steps across a carpet floor prove any obstacle to bliss?

The Opulent Era indulged itself in other idiosyncracies and superstitions. In the realm of infant care these were numerous. If a baby survived its second summer it would survive normally; for some forgotten reason every well regulated infant was supposed to bid this dreary world farewell in its second summer. If daddy had neglected to carry the infant up a flight of stairs the day of its birth it would grow up to be a bank robber, but if on that day baby raised its right arm and howled, you had an embryo Napoleon on your hands and papa's blunder was revoked. If baby's first fingernail cutting was with scissors he'd turn out to be a lawyer, but if bitten off by mother that catastrophe was averted. If baby fell out of bed before eleven months it would be a fool at maturity. When infants cried excessively there was Mrs. Winston's soothing syrup and other opium-laced remedies, abundantly effective, sold by every druggist, all of which today would be against the law. There were no baby foods. Mother's milk was the one and only, and bereft mothers possessing a supply were in steady demand. The wet nurse might otherwise prove useful. On his deathbed, eighty-five-year-old John Jacob Astor, grandfather of the Waldorf's builder, could only be sustained by breast feedings. And then be tossed in a blanket.

To have a male physician in attendance at childbirth was unutterably immodest and engaging foreign midwives of no intelligence as substitutes probably accounts for the high infant mortality, just as their proliferating numbers provided the bulk of abortionists. There was no defined practice called obstetrics; doctors venturing into that zone were marked as sissies.

The ideal female figure of the Opulent Era was an eighteen-inch waist, a high, voluptuous, palpitating bust, and a pair of wide aggressive hips. For those not naturally endowed there were numerous bust forms of padded cotton, inflated rubber and woven wire. Sometimes during a "spooning" party, when the boys would squeeze and kiss the girls, the rubber kind would collapse with a muffled bang to the mortification of its wearer and the hilarious merriment of others. The best bust form belonged to the bustle, a combination of braid and thin hoop iron attached to a gently sweeping flounce then known as the Grecian Bend. For girls imitating their elders bustles were shorter, stuffed with newspaper. When the buttoned back of the skirt, called the plaquette, accidently flew open exposing to the vulgar gaze of the public how the faultless figure had been achieved, tragedy ensued. Women wore only white cotton stockings. First attempts at coloring them introduced circular stripes like a barber pole in red, green, blue and purple. Dyes for these were not fast and the legs of the fairer sex might take on fetching stripes.

Black stockings, next in vogue, offered relief from the monotonous white but black dye was not fast either. When at length the dyeing problem was licked, out went the white. Both male and female wore nightgowns. The lady's, a voluminous affair, was made of Fruit of the Loom sheeting, high cut to the neck with ruffles at the cuffs.

Bedroom slippers were of carpeting or homemade knitted yarn with a thin leather sole and lined with fuzzy cotton, not too lovely but warm, especially during that moment of truth on near zero mornings when one must detroglodyte, come out from beneath a mountain of quilts and blankets, close the window, then strip and dress. Most devised their own teeth-chattering way for accomplishing this, either replacing the nightgown with layers of clothing while still under the bed covers or enduring

[39]

spartan exposure in the raw, pulling on layers of day wear from overhead even as nightwear slipped to the floor; either method joyless. Both sexes of the elder generation still clung to the linen nightcap.

House dresses were seersucker, percale, eiderdown and cotton flannel, and women attached to their girdle a chatelaine, often of beautiful chased sterling. This contained a place for a thimble, needles, thread, pocketknife, pencil, memo pad, pincushion, scissors, smelling salts and scent bottle.

It was fashionable to faint, and smelling salts that would revive a box-fighter were always within reach. Mother Hubbards and shirtwaists came in with the Nineties. The "best dress" in every wardrobe would usually be heavy black silk, crisp enough to stand alone and expected to last a lifetime. Shoes of very high uppers, halfway to the knee, came in two widths, narrow and wide. There were no such thing as legs; it was thought even "fast" if a man referred to them as limbs.

Shoes buttoned up the side with a heavy steel hook or laced up the front over a long tongue. The most popular model was called "the common sense." It featured broad, flat toes, flat heels and heavy soles, comparing in grace and style as a paratrooper boot to a ballet slipper. Yards of skirt trailed to the ground and on wet days dragged into the house a collection of sidewalk trash. Waists buttoned up to the neck, with whalebone collars reaching to the ears, and sleeves came to the knuckles, insulation about as virtuous as any wearing apparel short of armor. In gratifying contrast to the balloon leg-o-mutton sleeves was a skin-tight woolen top known as the Jersey. Of solid color, red being favored, these were popularly worn with a pom-ponned tam-o-shanter. "On an Aphrodite or a Venus," Henry Collins Brown wistfully remembers, "the effect was spectacular!"

Fashion, like love and the stock market, "has its reasons which reason cannot know." One historic wet day Miss Daisy Miller appeared on the street with no bustle, no hip pads and a skirt three inches above the ground. Heads turned, smiles, then laughter followed her. Daisy, dauntless, explained simply that her dress was made for rainy day wear. Hence, for utilitarian reasons, the short skirt was reluctantly accepted. Soon hundreds, then thousands of "Rainy Daisies" appeared in good weather and bad. The bustle was out. A tight-fitting tailored skirt followed, tighter, ever tighter, to become the hobble skirt. Eventually the skirt was slit up the side and the world discovered that women wore hose.

When the Waldorf opened in 1893, inverted coal scuttle bonnets of the Eighties were still in vogue, festooned with pom-pons, nodding plumes or flowing ribbons. Most were made of straw with garden and orchard decorations; red cherries formed from glass, purple grapes stuffed with sawdust, American Beauty roses of pink velvet and morning glories of calico. Collectively, these made a pretty lid, one usually requiring steel lances called hat pins to hold them in place.

Bathing suits were extra heavy blue flannel in two pieces, trousers and skirt: waist trousers to the ankle, the skirt waist lengthened below the knee, joined with a heavy belt, the whole completed with long cotton stockings and shoes. The bather's hat was straw, precisely like those that Mr. Bergh's kindhearted people were putting on horses, the holes through the brims for the horses ears used by milady for tying it on with a wide piece of velvet braid. Such garments weighed a ton in the water and bathers inevitably puddled buckets wherever they stood for a decorous after-dip chat. Few actually swam; so virtuously weighted, how could they?

Men dressed much the same except they refused to wear stockings and bare feet were the dependable means of telling male from female on the beach. Eventually a tiny bit of white braid piping around the collar band and edges of the waist evolved, the first concession to styling in beach wear. From this to the bikini was only a matter of time (three-quarters of a century!). Beach parties with sandwiches, pie and coffee were solemn affairs providing the first acceptable co-mingling of the sexes. Imagine, actually bathing together in the same ocean!

Tennis, just in from England (which got it from Asia as sphairistike) obviously could not be played in 18-inch corsets, bustles, bosom pads and pom-pon hats. Accordingly, along came a tight-fitted gown, flounced from the knees and buttoning up the back literally from ankles to neck, with several petticoats underneath, Leghorn hats—plaited straw from Tuscany—and the inevitable nodding plume, sent milady decorously into the thick of volleys, lobs and base line drives. Actually it all had little to do with sport. Like bicycling, bathing and picnics, tennis provided another grudgingly permitted opportunity for young ladies to escape their chaperones and share some companionable pastime with their male admirers.

Men wore flannel coats in loud and strident stripes, long gray trousers, natty little peaked caps to match their coats. *Daisy Bell* ("A Bicycle Built

[41]

for Two") had become an instant hit but bicycling presented another costuming problem. The net result was that as more ladies went cycling skirts went higher, and piano sales lower, the latter plummeting by forty-five percent, to be precise.

A woman's hair was her crowning glory. A familiar store window attraction advertising a hair grower were the Seven Sutherland Sisters, with hair to their knees. Huge rolls of horse hair called a "rat," together with structures called "switches," "waterfalls," "chignons," "pompadours," braids and rolls, were all part of a woman's coronal adornment. Bangs and spit curls were thought "cute." There were no beauty parlors, but before long a few hairdressing parlors began to appear. Care of the hair was an exhausting experience and there were no shortcuts; it meant waiting hours for the hair to dry after washing it in rainwater sequestered in rain barrels or cisterns installed exclusively for this purpose, then combing out the snarls and tangles.

Face powder was widely used but lipstick and cold cream unheard of. A sunburn tan was considered "common," a mark of association with the lower orders. On every occasion veils were worn to protect pink and white complexions; hardly any woman who would ever be thought respectable went out on the street in daytime without a veil. There were no manicurists—the word itself did not exist—and any young lady wearing deep red nails would have been requested to leave any proper gathering.

Styles in men's clothing seemed more susceptible to change. Waistcoats were multi-colored and multi-patterned. One season trousers would be narrow and tight, the next the reverse. The Prince Albert was worn as formal evening dress; there were few swallow tails, mostly at balls and weddings. The tuxedo, or dinner jacket, came into existence contemporaneously when George Griswold saw such a coat in a Water Street window and ventured to wear it to Pierre Lorillard's fashionable new Tuxedo Country Club. Tuxedo rather than its first bold wearer would give the jacket its name and, unlike Daisy Miller, George's brief meteor of fame sputtered into obscurity.

The present practice of keeping a crease in one's trousers was bad form in the Opulent Era; it was a dead giveaway that you bought your clothes ready made. As a matter of fact, almost everyone did, but would prefer to have others believe that they were made to order and not taken from a pile of others in a store. The first thing to do was iron out all telltale marks of the ready made.

Headgear ran to many diversified shapes. Derbies were at first so low crowned as to be almost flat, then swelled up into a small-sized top hat. Straw hats were black and had narrow brims; even when the yellow straws came in there were no colored hat bands. Colored bands identifying the wearer's guard regiment, club or alma mater came thirty years later. High hats made of gray felt were popular. Black silk "toppers" were rare, and the collapsible opera hat did not appear until a decade later. Soft felt hats were called "slouch hats," worn only while puttering around the house or off fishing. Gentlemen did not invariably remove their hats indoors in public establishments.

Shirts had stiff bosoms and were uniformly white. Originally they opened in the back only, then for a period they opened front and back, finally deciding to open only in the front. A hundred-and-eighty-degree turnabout over ten years. The front-only opening was proudly announced as the "coat shirt." Coats and vests were worn summer and winter. The men's shirtwaist, today's sport shirt, created quite a stir and aroused no little hostility. Hot weather saved it; comfort reigned and the opposition dried up. Promptly upon the approach of cold weather came refuge in the "medicated" red flannel underwear. In some strange and reasoning manner, faith in the efficiency of this peculiar garment was total, its wearer protected from colds, asthma, even fallen arches and dandruff.

There were no safety razors in those days and the general custom was to patronize the local barber twice a week. For the regular customer the barber provided a special mug with his name in shiny gilt letters on the outside. Some went so far as to add a symbolic sign indicating the nature of the customer's vocation or profession. If, for example, you were a plumber, you were shown mending a gas leak; a butcher, with both hands on the counter gazing ecstatically at a large piece of meat. If you kept a saloon (there were four at almost every New York City intersection), a foaming bucket of beer would be on the reverse of your mug, these little touches doing much to create the friendly atmosphere, the camaraderie of the barber shop, a man's inviolable province, where one brush, a towel and the same soap did for all.

A great sensation was created when one shop advertised "A Clean

Towel for Every Customer," a move promising it financial suicide, said its rivals. While waiting your turn you perused such ripe reading as the *Police Gazette* and the *Day's Doings,* with *Puck* and *Judge* displayed as camouflage culture for those unregenerate "pink sheets." The barber shop was usually run by a German who invariably kept a canary. It was a sort of social center, an atmosphere heavily scented with asceptic oils, heavy pomades, brilliantine and bear's grease. When you left you not only had all the latest neighborhood scandal but your visit was proclaimed for at least the remainder of that day by your special aroma.

The streets of New York were filled with itinerant musicians, organ grinders with their little uniformed dancing monkey companions stretching tiny paws for your penny and delighting children with the polite doff of their caps. "Dot Leetle Cherman Bant" was sure to be performing in the parks and squares. There were talented Negro whistlers, occasionally a solo tenor of tremendous virtuosity. Henry Collins Brown best remembers a pair of genuine southern Blacks who whistled "Listen to the Mockingbird," with "Old Black Joe," "Way Down Upon the Swanee River" or "My Darling Nellie Gray" for encores, the last a marching song favored by troops in the war with Spain and preempted by British Tommies marching off to fight the Boers. Whistling was popular entertainment. A Mrs. Shaw who gave whistling performances at halls and private parties in the Nineties afterwards sailed to London for even greater success. When by ordinance itinerant musicians were banished from the streets the children of the poor who customarily gathered around the smiling Italian, dancing and playing games like "Little Sally Waters" or "London Bridge Is Falling Down," lost a great source of pleasure.

New York of the Nineties harbored a great many more amateur musicians than today. The harmonica had returned to popularity and was a favorite instrument of the street performer. The violin another. The accordian and the concertina's dulcet lilt floated over backyard fences for the benefit of all. Many mechanical music devices such as the hand organ and Swiss music box became familiar parlor attractions, heightened when the paper roll of the hand organ appeared in combination with the upright piano. The most famous renditions required only vigorous pumping of broad, flat pedals and a tight grip on the stool to keep from being upset by one's exertions. Favored were Offenbach overtures and nostalgic airs such as "I'll Take You Home Again Kathleen," that young man's promise to return his homesick sweetheart to her native Ireland.

The music box appeared in relative degrees of pretentiousness, sometimes a child's toy looking like a sardine can and rendering "The Sweet Bye and Bye" as you turned the handle, sometimes an elaborate rosewood-cased mechanism that played an extensive repertory indexed on an illuminated cardboard beneath its lid. Others assumed the shape of a cart or wagon and played as its wheels turned. There were also a large number of musical toys on the market: zithers, xylophones, pianos, drums, trumpets. And there was a great sale of whistles, some attached to riding crops, to popguns, to baby cribs, one invariably to a white cord lanyard encircling the squared collar of a small boy's new sailor suit.

Like all great cities of the world the streets of New York nurtured their own unique repertory of street vendor cries: the melodious pan pipes of the scissors sharpener trudging along with his great grindstone slung across his back, or the flower vendor, the sooty coal and coke wagoneer, the fruit pushcart peddler, the fishmonger, the ice man. One could set one's watch by the shrill cry of "Wuxtra! Wuxtra!" preceding the avalanche of newsboys pouring out of Park Row. An insistent bell would mean the paddy-wagon or an ambulance, shrill whistles the patrolman, sirens the fire engine, and at all hours the gentle clippity-clop of horses, silenced only when snow carpeted the streets. Winter brought its own delectable sensations; the aroma of roasting chestnuts, the merry jingle of sleigh bells, the dinner bell rung by a sad-faced Salvation Army Santa reminding holiday shoppers to drop coins into the kettle to provide Christmas dinners for the poor.

Baseball, known elsewhere across America as "the New York game," surprisingly had not yet asserted its popularity in New York. Cricket clubs thrived. The New York League that 1893 season scheduled 135 games from Boston to Pittsburgh to Philadelphia and Baltimore with exhibition games even in the West Indies. Every other sport, spectator or participant, from pit bull fights to horse racing, croquet to the prize ring, recruited its special devotees. Basketball, invented two years earlier by James A. Naismith, had just reached New York's Y.M.C.A. and was played with half-bushel fruit baskets and a soccer ball, with a ladder handy should anyone score a basket. Few did. Two nine-men teams in an hour's furious contest scored only one. In winter there was ice skating and sleigh-ing, even tobogganing for a select few. At Tuxedo Park, that exclusive 6,000 acre sylvan retreat where, as mentioned, today's familiar dinner jacket first appeared, part of Pierre Lorillard's $2,000,000 investment went into a mile-long toboggan run, electric lighted at night and with coaches waiting below to convey guests back to the summit for another thrilling descent.

For Society, summer meant Saratoga, Newport or the spas of Ger-many, and winter Aiken, Palm Beach or the Riviera. Between seasons the unanimously favored weekend rendezvous was Tuxedo. From its hand-some rustic keeper's lodge to its spacious Tudor clubhouse, complete with ballroom and theater, to its stylish cottages with liveried servants, to its gamekeepers in cords and leggins, Tuxedo was an English ducal estate to incite the envy of Britain's most affluent gentry. Tuxedo's theater was for amateurs. Indeed, excepting the sensational Mrs. James Brown Potter, no professional actress ever managed to get beyond its gates; even that celebrated Society beauty was refused a return engagement after abandoning her husband and child for a scandalous European tour with Kyrle Bellew, her leading man.

For the upper middle class, one rung below Society, Saratoga and Newport translated Richfield or Sharon Springs. For those suffering from too rapid passing of the bottle, there awaited Lebanon Springs and Massena Springs, revered "drying out" spas once frequented by Daniel Webster and Henry Clay.

In September 1893, six months after the Waldorf opening, the Duke of Argyl arrived with his intrepid *Thistle* to challenge *Volunteer* for the America's Cup, providing one of those opportunities when some contestant from these young United States could prove his mettle against the best of other lands, preferably Britain. Bursting with pride, all America eagerly awaited news from Newport's great event. The outcome was never in doubt; from the starting gun *Volunteer's* victory was a walkaway. Cheers resounded across the land. "Westward the Star of Yacht Building Takes Its Way! The Scotch can beat the English but America, Never!" headlined the *Times* loading its entire front page and three-quarters of page two with descriptions of that spectacular victory. As the actual race progressed, enthusiastic crowds gathered before bulletin boards outside newspaper plants in Boston, Philadelphia, Chicago, San Francisco, even as other crowds were doing in Glasgow, Liverpool and London. "Police reinforcements on hand were not needed," gloated the *Times* man in London; "The crowds were too disgusted even to form a syndicate to put the *Thistle* into canal service." It was indeed a great day. As reports came in and cheers filled the air, trading was interrupted on both the New York Stock Exchange and the Produce Exchange. Irreverent Wall Street wags, clerks, runners, traders—a breed apart—posted their own bulletin board burlesquing the race as taking place on the lake in Central Park: "The British contender now leads as they reach 94th Street. . .!"

Later, from London, Stephen Crane would write, "If you ever get on speaking terms with an Englishman he says, 'If the Cup once gets over here you'll never get it back.' It was cried out in the coffee rooms of hotels, in clubs, in buses, everywhere people could meet. The last stroke arrived yesterday when a lady looked at me over her teacup and said, 'If the Cup once gets over here you'll never get it back.' I assented at once. I knew enough to assent at once. She didn't know a yacht from a motor car but she had been given the password by her husband who had said to her: 'If the Cup once gets over here they'll never get it back.' So she said to me, 'If the Cup once gets over her you'll never get it back.' "

New Yorkers promenading on Fifth Avenue—a daily ritual in fine weather—generally walked downtown in the mornings as far as Mr. A. T. Stewart's impressive white marble mansion at 34th Street, and uptown in the afternoon, with Central Park and its mineral waters programmed for Sunday.

Every afternoon, the weather fair, brought Society out for a drive down Fifth Avenue to Washington Square then back to 49th Street. Nowhere on this continent could be seen such an impressive procession of beauty and fashion. Regularly admired were the shiny, sleek victorias of the rich and fashionable, their female occupants displaying their newest and smartest frocks, usually adorned with an immense corsage of violets, this being the day when popularity might be reckoned by the largest cluster; pedestrians, equally on display, never doubted that the violet bouquets had just been received from devoted admirers.

Sunday in Central Park saw a parade of landaus, broughams, surreys, traps, tandems, phaetons, the smart new "C-spring" barouche, most with smartly uniformed drivers and cockade-hatted footmen. But in the carriages of the Belmonts, the Goulds, the Vanderbilts and Logans, the proud owners themselves took the reins. In winter Society paraded in sleighs. Traditionally a magnum of champagne awaited the first sleighing party to arrive over the season's first snowfall at the Widow McGown's Tavern (1746), a setting today for hardy perennials in Central Park's Conservatory Garden.

In summer, fashionable parties often drove all the way down to Coney Island to see the sights and perhaps enjoy hot buttered corn on the cob or that brand new Coney Island specialty, the hot dog. Coaching, the thrilling spectacle of handsomely matched four-in-hands, first became popular in the Seventies, providing the glamorous and joyous exhibition of prancing animals, glistening lacquered coaches, trumpeting coachmen, handsome top-hatted gentlemen with, of course, their fabulous women—many recruited from the stage, some even from the street, but all breathtakingly beautiful.

Founded by Colonel William Jay, Leonard Jerome and Delancey Kane, another grandson of John Jacob Astor, the coaching clubs were governed by inflexible rules that fastidiously stipulated even how the driver's apron must be folded when not in use, precisely how artificial flowers must be affixed to the throat-latch of every horse. The driver bore the title of "whip" and being Gentleman Whip was the most envied cachet of New York's socially elect. Customarily, the Coaching Club turned out on certain announced days each spring and autumn, its inevitable route through Central Park, thence over to Riverside Drive and up to Claremont Inn on the present site of Grant's Tomb to cap the gala occasion with a splendid bird and game dinner. The Coaching Club made Society's only public display. Hundreds lining their route lustily cheered their vast approval.

One of the more appealing qualities of New York City has been its endless opportunities for fun. As far back as Dutch and British colonial times, among seafarers Fun City was rated "The Pearl of the Atlantic Seaboard," unique among ports of call for a roistering good time. During its century and a half of colonialism New York had been spared the suffocating religious piety of Puritan Boston or Quaker Philadelphia, nor had its social ordering known the rigid stratification of Baltimore,

Charleston, New Orleans and Savannah. Indeed, excepting perhaps Paris, no metropolis matched New York's reputation for liberality and tolerance. "The city has to be tolerant," said E.B. White. "Otherwise it would explode in a radioactive cloud of hate, rancor and bigotry."

Everything New York does has always been done on the grand scale, everything good, everything bad. It is a fact of American commercial life that unless an idea or a product has captured New York it has not captured America. This is notably true for those seeking recognition in the creative and the performing arts; a performer big in Dallas is a big Dallas performer; a performer big in New York is a performer big in America.

In the Gay Nineties many New York religious leaders were no less shrill than in the Seventies when the Rev. Henry Ward Beecher and Victoria Woodhull had jousted in scandalous exposés, when Anthony Comstock's reformers were raiding respectable precincts such as the Knoedler Gallery for exhibiting paintings of nudes, when a Virginia woman who posted a volume of Balzac was arrested for sending obscene literature through the mails.

The Nineties' unrelenting foe of vice and venality was Dr. Charles Henry Parkhurst. From his pulpit in Old Madison Square Church and in the press Parkhurst courageously exposed collusion between the police, Mayor Grant and District Attorney Nicoll. They were all linked, he said, "in an administrative criminality that was filthyfying our entire municipal life, making New York a hotbed of knavery, debauchery and bestiality." Discredited by a grand jury, Parkhurst disguised himself as a Bowery bum and with a hired detective to serve as guide toured chinese opium dens, five-cent flop houses whose transient guests regularly became Tammany voters on election day. Parkhurst gave lurid descriptions of "tight houses" where the women wore nothing but tights, homosexual brothels where painted men, calling each other by womens' names, spoke in high falsetto voices, saloons that sold pint bottles of whiskey to children.

It would take another ten years before the corrupt police establishment was chastened. Nor would it be done by clerics, but enterprising newsmen like Stephen Crane. In the celebrated Becker-Dora Clark brutality case, ventilated by Crane's persistence, Police Captain Becker protested with righteous indignation any connection with Officer Becker, and the vigilant Commissioner Theodore Roosevelt sustained him. Officer Becker was later arrested, tried, convicted and sent to the electric chair as an accomplice in the murder of Herman Rosenthal. He was the first New York City policeman to be sentenced to death.

Tastes change, minds broaden, sights are elevated, manners and morals shift, reforms move in cycles. A scant thirty years earlier the works of William Shakespeare were not permitted on the campus of Harvard, much less studied there. And for all its scandals and reforming pulpiteers New York of the Opulent Era also had spiritual leaders of great stature.

Widely admired was Bishop Henry C. Potter. Sister Francesca Cabrini became the first American canonized by Catholics. Immensely popular was amiable Dr. John Hull, pastor of the Presbyterian Church at Fifth Avenue and 55th Street who every Sunday "preached to $250,000,000."

Immigrants by the thousands were rapidly expanding New York's Jewish population, vastly strengthening its influential rabbinical tradition that dated back to 1654. But the religious event making greatest impact that summer of the Waldorf opening was the Christian Endeavor Society world convocation filling the 17,000-seat Madison Square Garden from morning to night for one solid week. *The Times,* caught up by the conventioneers' infectious enthusiasm, brought out a ten-page special edition. Never for long dormant among Calvinists, the Temperance movement was again militant; newspapers described as "thunderous" the applause awarded the Ohio delegation's rousing

O-hi-o
We won't go
To the World's Fair
If liquor's sold there
No! No! No!

thereby dooming Chicago's forthcoming World Columbian Exposition to get along without them. All in all, however passionate its love of religious revivals or its transient fervors for reform, New York of 1893 differed little from New York of 1697, when then-Governor Dongan said of it:

> Here be not many of the Church of England; few Roman catholicks; abundance of Quakers preachers men and women especially; Singing Quakers, Ranting Quakers, Sabbatarians; some Anabaptists, some independents; some Jews; in short of all sorts of opinions there are some, and the most part of none at all.

"Standing heads" in New York newspaper composing rooms of the Nineties included: Duels, Divorces, Defalcations, Murders, Frauds, Elopements, Pedestrianism (foot races) and Balls. Duels were becoming less common, although two ladies, one French, one American, after an acerbic argument about the relative merits of American versus French surgeons, had at each other with sabers.

Of balls there were many: decorous, dignified and extravagant affairs whose attendance cut across the whole social spectrum. Annually scheduled were the regimental balls, those of the boat clubs, the French Cooks, the Sangerbund, the Liederkranz, the fashionable Patriarchs and Junior Patriarchs, New York Mannechor, Foresters, Purim, Iphetonga of Brooklyn, the Firemen, the Colored Sporting Club, the Cooks and Pastry Cooks. More exclusive, the French Chefs did their own thing at the Metropolitan Opera House competing with magnificent sculptures from their ovens which brought into view the gastronomic genius of Delmonico's, Rector's, Sherry's, Hoffman House, the Fifth Avenue Hotel, the Brevoort, the St. James, the Windsor, the Sturtevant, the Leland, the Gilsey and the Brunswick.

New York's forty-five legitimate theaters, music halls (these numbered only twenty-four scarcely four years earlier), and its concert stage prospered with importations of the world's great. The Metropolitan Opera, founded after William Henry Vanderbilt had been repeatedly denied the social distinction of owning one of the eighteen boxes at the Academy of Music, now ten years in its new home, squeaked through another season stubbornly managing to keep its preponderantly Wagnerian repertory solidly on the boards. Carnegie Hall, which had opened two years earlier with Tschaikowsky conducting the Philharmonic, now confessed the need of an all-night liquor license to augment its income. "After the Ball Was Over" sold its ten millionth copy and recruited for the booming sheet music industry scores of salesmen who had been selling corsets. Variety shows had a huge following both along the Rialto and down the lower East Side; Hubert's 14th Street Museum was featuring "Two Tons in Tights," a fat woman's bicycle race, and Mr. Barnum was announcing the formation of a circus partnership with Mr. Bailey. American artists and sculptors, under heavy economic competition from importations, merged the National Academy of Design with the Architectural League of New York to create the Art Students League and were impressively ensconced in their new American Fine Arts Society building at 215 West 57th Street.

One day young Stephen Crane, who had earlier lived in a garret above the old studios the artists formerly occupied on East 23rd Street, made a nostalgic pilgrimage back to those once joyous precincts, abandoned now and silent. Crane was in search of inspiration for a newspaper feature. It proved a rewarding quest. Crane found chalked across a ceiling beam and hardly legible: "Congratulate yourselves if you have done something strange and extravagant and broken the monotony of a decorous age." It had been written there and signed by Ralph Waldo Emerson.

Writers then formed no "workshops." However, an eclectic group, the Century Club, long presided over by New York's greatly beloved William Cullen Bryant, regularly foregathered in an old house off Irving Place on 15th Street where set-piece battles raged between the traditionalists and a new cult, those staunch disciples of Emerson, if betimes vague and vulnerable in equations of reality and vulgarity. The Lotos Club at Fifth Avenue at 21st Street would later gather in many of these, the volatile minds assembled around its festive board fusing massive intellectual detonations. The early Nineties marked the apogee of vibrant William Dean Howells, the demise of an industrious Herman Melville, now past seventy and dying, a recluse in his dark, outdated 26th Street home, misunderstood by the uncomprehending, and ever in a desperate contest with time. Before his end Melville had, indeed, completed his great *Billy Budd,* which an unimaginative publisher would let gather dust for thirty years. When finally published it ignited like thermite, first as a novel, then a successful film, finally as inspiration for an affecting Benjamin Britten opera; a very worthy companion to *Moby-Dick*.

The Nineties saw the rise of literary salons. *The* Mrs. Astor, victim of her own boring gatherings, hearing that the Sunday afternoon gatherings of Elsie de Wolfe and Elizabeth Marbury had become the focal point of wit and wisdom, determined to have an *avant-garde* literary gathering of her own. "Yes, I'm having a party, too," she boasted one day to Miss de Wolfe. And whom was she relying upon to supply its bohemian atmosphere? "Why, J. P. Morgan and Edith Wharton," she said.

The Lyceum of Fourth Avenue near 23rd Street, "the drawing room of the drama," with its gifted repertory company, Louis Tiffany décor and a steady output of modern productions portraying New York social life, was Society's favorite. "Society went there," one wit declared, "to learn from actors and actresses how they ought to behave, furnish their homes and wear their clothes."

Why not? Ideas have to start somewhere. A crime writer's whodunit then enjoying a healthy run on Broadway had for its plot a murderer being identified by fingerprint (a hobby of the author). This idea quickly found favor with New York's police who put it to work; subsequently law enforcement worldwide followed suit, standardizing fingerprint classification for criminal identification. Similarly, a chance Lotus Club member's casual suggestion that someone should go to Africa and hunt for the Scot explorer Dr. Livingstone came to the ears of the *Herald's* James Gordon Bennett who at once launched Henry Stanley's highly publicized search which thrilled and delighted millions—everyone except Livingstone, who had no wish to be "found," preferring instead to die in the jungle, which he eventually succeeded in doing.

Greater successes than the Lyceum were blossoming farther east along the Rialto, as then was known all Broadway. This was the era of Lillian Russell, Eleanor Duse, Sarah Bernhardt, Ellen Terry, Edwin Booth, Fanny Davenport, Helen Modjeska, the Florodora Sextette (which, with heavy losses to marriage, actually numbered seventy-three), Mary Anderson. And the incomparable Lillie Langtry!

Wherever Lillie Langtry went crowds followed. What Langtry said Americans quoted. When Langtry performed, every space was sold for months in advance. Photographs of the Jersey Lily, propped against a vase of cattails, were enshrined on lambrequined mantlepieces in cities, towns and crossroad villages all across the continent. Famous men who'd never met her named their ships, mines, their estates after her. Texans named a village for her. America's young women wound their tresses in the Psyche knot that Lily wore and donned the skin tight "jersey" Lily introduced. All of this long decades before the invention of motion pictures, the radio, or the all-pervasive tube.

On the bawdy side, prostitutes in New York flourished, conservative estimates putting their number at 28,000, though admittedly no dependable means existed for making such a count. Gambling, too, thrived. Richard Canfield, James McNeil Whistler's friend, ran New York's tables with the highest stakes, as also he did each summer at Saratoga, when not preoccupied with enlarging his exceptional collection of paintings.

New Yorkers of the Nineties, as New Yorkers of today, loved parades, even if each one left behind four tons of rubbish to be swept up. Visiting dignitaries, national heros, its own handsome mounted policemen, its Seventh Regiment, its Squadron A, its Old Guard, its indestructable Sons of Hibernia were all proudly and lustily cheered. In fact, with the return of the city's cyclical passion for clean streets, Col. George Waring even paraded his Department of Sanitation battalions in crisp gleaming white, shouldering their brooms and shovels and smartly wheeling their carts with West Point precision to the martial music of their own band. Delighted New Yorkers cheered wildly, and showed their ready support by leaving behind another four tons of litter. The 1893 parade calendar, seeming a mite bare that summer of the Waldorf's opening, in a gracious salute to Chicago's Columbian Exposition the New York state legislature met and appropriated $200,000 to bring the great warships of the world's navies to anchor in the Hudson while their crews paraded up Fifth Avenue in a colorful, stirring spectacle that lasted for five hours.

From Walldorf to Waldorf

$\mathcal{H}$otel life in New York had undergone an upheaval during the decade of the Eighties. Until now most hostelries operated under what was known as the American Plan whereby the guest would be charged an inclusive rate for both room and meals. In front-rank establishments like the Hoffman House, the Fifth Avenue Hotel, the Brevoort, guests dined at great long family-sized tables where quite soon all became acquainted. Following dinner there was often dancing—a lancer, a quadrille, a minuet—and before retiring, a midnight supper. In such genteel atmosphere hotel life was pleasant and venturesome, guest stays were lengthier, many new and enduring attachments formed.

For the increasing numbers of commercial travelers this arrangement, however convivial, wasn't always economical. If mealtime found them far from their hotels they'd be nonetheless obliged to pay for meals there. For the great hotels as well, the American Plan could prove disadvantageous. Their dining facilities being almost exclusively for their guests, the excellence of their cuisine remained unknown to many New Yorkers, which meant that restaurants thrived.

Dining out became popular. Smart New Yorkers thronged to Delmonico's and Louis Sherry's. Gentlewomen did not go to Rector's except incognita, although it was sure to provide more excitement, for here one saw both the noted and the notorious of the glamorously enticing life of Broadway. If after the theater a lady of fashion wearing a low-cut gown would sup at Rector's, she must hurry home, change her dress, put on the largest and floppiest hat she owned, then make sure of a table in the darkened part of the room.

New York boasted a dozen or more other fine restaurants, all prospering and collectively denying the hotels this revenue. Consequently, in the years immediately preceding the Waldorf's launching, the American

[57]

Plan had begun to evaporate in favor of the European Plan whereby the guest paid separately for meals and lodging. The effect was at once remarkable; several Fifth Avenue hotels were soon feeding five times the number they slept. Hotel catering services began. Hotel profits rose. Nor did this mean the end of the great restaurants, although those serving as many as a thousand meals per day would soon feel the effect. On the other hand hotels could serve such numbers, and being fortified by guarantees of their guests on hand, proved more resilient both in their menus and their capacity to cope with days of wretched weather.

Over the years New York hotels had built particular and durable followings; Southerners favored the St. Nicholas, circus people the St. Charles, actors and writers the Union Palace. If one were a Wall Street speculator or banker he would most often be found at the Windsor; turf lovers preferred the Hoffman; Republicans, diplomats, Congressional committees patronized the Fifth Avenue. The Democrats preferred the St. James, railroad promoters the Brunswick, while the Gilsey was for mining speculators and the Brevoort, because once their Prince of Wales had stopped there, a favorite of British sea captains. Opposite Grand Central the Rossmore and St. Cloud got most of the overnight transient trade. West Point and Annapolis were loyal to the Sturtevant and the Leland; in fact, once when Congress had been slow to pay our midshipmen and cadets these hotels advanced them credit. With the opening of Mr. Astor's luxurious new establishment at Fifth Avenue and Thirty-fourth Street, such loyalties as these would undergo considerable stress.

As an industry, hotels in America had little awareness of their collective clout. Occasionally when troublesome bills would be presented in the legislature, New York's hotel men might confer to decide a common course of action. For example, in 1887 when Albany had passed a law requiring all hotels to equip every room with a length of knotted rope in case of fire. Prohibition, the *bête noire* of innkeepers, whose gestations were local ordinances prescribing odd hours and strictured circumstances when liquor might be sold, loomed threateningly for hotel and restaurant proprietors fully thirty years before congressional passage of the Volstead Act. By 1893 Kansas, Maine and New Hampshire were dry and sentiment for dry laws spreading. By local options scores of communities had made it a fact; even the bartenders union had voted to have all its members take the pledge!

On other fronts hotel workers were organizing. By the time of the Waldorf opening New York trade unions already had recruited several thousand stemming from the Waiters Alliance, formed to combat the "Vampire System" of hiring. By this iniquitous practice hotel waiters were supplied by certain saloon keepers who would send along their favored patrons then extort even larger patronage from these in return. One evening the waiters' plight had been described to a sensitive, young labor leader who just recently had himself become a bench-worker at Satchelberger's Cigar Factory. He promised to do something about it. He did. His name was Samuel Gompers, and from this conversation began what eventually would become Gompers' monument, the American Federation of Labor. Understandably, hotel unions have remained a solid A. F. of L. constituent.

Important hotel proprietors had other problems. They welcomed the shift in popularity from the American to European Plan that put them into lively competition with the better restaurants. Menus, more *à la carte* then *table d'hote,* meant wider selection, and sharper buying. Larger New York hotels of that day cured their own meats, carried all vegetables in season, often as many as twenty-five varieties of fish. Among vintners and produce houses, this widening demand for food and beverages meant that hotels had greater buying power, even more if they should work together.

Already other areas of cooperation had developed. New York's hotel keepers were exchanging "black-lists" of undesirables: persons owing them money, troublesome guests, confidence men, prostitutes. Should a guest register who had left an unpaid bill at another New York hotel, he might find a discreet reminder of this tucked under his door the following morning. In 1892, the year before the Waldorf launching, hotel men gathered at Saratoga, organized an association and founded an insurance fund. When twelve months later a hundred and fifty members of the Hotel Men's Mutual Benefit Association assembled at Mr. Willard's hotel in Washington, they could note with satisfaction that they now were a thousand strong, that out of their benefit fund they had paid but ten death claims. Feted in that special way a hotel man enjoys when guest of a proud colleague, they listened to inspiring toasts and danced "The Hotel Lancers" and other ballroom figures until the wee hours, but were promptly punctual next morning for the four-block carriage journey to the White House to pay their respects to President Cleveland.

America has no aristocracy. The great bulk of her settlers coming from Europe's middle and lower classes, ingrained in each American school child is the knowledge that the Founding Fathers fought against privileged aristocracy, determined to establish a classless society. America's Constitution canonizes the Common Man, and without the explicit approval of Congress no American may accept foreign honors. "All men are created equal," albeit from the moment of creation a host of prenatal inequalities become operative. Because society is intrinsically selective, the absence of aristocracy brings into play diverse criteria for social differentiation. In some parts of the world persons of little hair discriminate against those having an abundance of it, in others differentiation is by smell; those accustomed to a diet of meat, for example, give off odors that are highly objectionable to those whose diet is vegetarian or fish, so objectionable, in fact, that in some regions the vegetarian can't abide being in the same room with meat eaters.

Hair, smell, color of skin, religious beliefs, the hunters inhabiting the mountains versus the farmer inhabitants of the valley, those possessing many camels or walrus tusks or buffalo hides versus those who have but few, all are distinctions contributing to societal selection. In the American South prior to the Civil War a man's real mark of social distinction was the number of slaves he owned. In America, where no legal preference may be endowed by birth, Society sets about making one. Charleston members of Society are born into it, or may marry into it, rights jealously protected by hereditary membership in its august St. Cecilia Society, a decorous, inviolate temple of ancestor worship. St. Cecilians, however, make no public display of their exclusiveness. They shun public notice, in fact steadfastly forbid newspaper coverage of their annual ball. As a purebred in snobbish America's social order, Charleston ranks alone. At one time New York Society also revered its aristocratic privacy; some small segment of it still does. When Heber R. Bishop gave a dinner which the Waldorf reported to the press, Bishop, enraged, stormed into the hotel, upbraided its manager and vowed never again to darken its doors. Descent from such pinnacles of propriety to social levels where hosts and hostesses are motivated as much by an instinct for advertisement as by a wish to entertain, permits the mutational process of converting a social nonentity into a "Society" figure in terms of wealth. That provided, whether New York, Chicago, San Francisco, the height of one's climb will be in some proportion to the distance in time separating him from

that original grubstaking, hard working, calculating, roughhewn and betimes shady old ancestor who put it all together. Often a social grouping
welded by wealth will clasp to its bosom persons of no wealth but having
other accomplishments—artistic, scientific, scholastic. These amuse them,
supply character and color to a spectrum otherwise displaying a dominant
aura of green. Rules of conduct—often more notable in the breach than
in the observance—cloak the group in respectability and the result is a
distinct social stratum which delights them, and, after all, who cares?
Nevertheless, envied by many because of their celebrity, as the "in" crowd
what these say and do may largely affect the commercial success of certain
business enterprises. For example, an hotel.

John Jacob Astor, founder of the Astor dynasties in America and
Great Britain, was the son of a poor Bavarian butcher whose name was
Ashdor. Astor grew up in the village of Walldorf (yes, two "l's") near
Heidelberg but left Germany as a teenager to work for his brother selling
musical instruments in London until he had enough money for passage
to America. On the morning of his New World arrival young Astor displayed some of the shrewd pragmatism characteristic of his long and successful career. It was the bitter January of 1784 and the vessel lay icebound
in Chesapeake Bay not only unable to get into Baltimore harbor but in
danger of having her hull stove in by the ice. At length the skipper ordered
all passengers to leave their luggage behind and abandon ship. When
young Astor appeared on deck smartly attired in his Sunday best, "Why,"
asked the astonished captain, "are you so dressed up?" "Vell," said Astor,
"ef vee make it I hef on my best suit. Ef vee don't make it, it does not
matter vot I hef on."

He made it. And kept on making it for more than half a century.
During that crossing, Astor, a personable, attractive youth became friendly
with several German fur traders who bedazzled him with tales of great
riches to be made in furs. Astor made it there, too. At the time of his
death he was both America's foremost fur trader and New Yorks largest
landowner, reputedly the richest man in the New World. Along the way
he had become landlord of much of New York City, multiplying his fur
fortune many times through smart real estate transactions. One rule guided
these: never sell, an injunction, however, that, without Astor's sense of
timing, would ruin others holding properties outside Manhattan's pattern
of growth. Astor bought wisely and on those rare occasions when he did

relinquish title it meant an exchange to enlarge other more promising holdings. How well did this pay off? Over the next one hundred years growing America's population multiplied itself sixteen times. But that of New York one hundred and ten times!

The Astors have a long tradition as innkeepers. The first Astor hotel, the original Astor House built in 1830 at Broadway and Barclay Street, was the finest of its day. Its bar, the longest in town, originated the free bar lunch, a widely copied idea universally popular through New York's oncoming century.

Four generations and a hundred million dollars later appeared William Waldorf Astor, son of John Jacob Astor III, an ambitious, intelligent man, remarkably industrious and a thoroughgoing snob. William Waldorf enjoyed being rich but wanted fame as well. He plunged into politics, served one term in the state legislature, then was twice defeated for Congress, the second defeat, doubtless, because Jake Hess, Republican boss in the Astors' "Silk Stocking" district, absconded with the campaign funds. Rejected, Astor sulked until influential friends secured for him a presidential appointment as United States minister to Italy. After a year in Rome, largely spent writing a scholarly history of Italy's illustrious Sforza family, Astor resigned, and returning to New York devoted his attention to completion of his new 220-foot, $800,000 steel yacht. It was during this period that his wife battled, if half-heartedly, with his aunt, Mrs. William Backhouse Astor, as to which would have Society's cachet as *the* Mrs. Astor in Newport.

In the ongoing process of expanding his real estate holdings Astor bought the New Netherlands Hotel. Hotels were profitable in the Astor portfolio, New York was vigorously pushing uptown, and Astor soon announced plans for a great new one, the Waldorf, to occupy his half of the Fifth Avenue block which today exhibits the Empire State Building. His handsome yacht launched, Astor now sailed for England where he secretly planned forever to remain. Restless, he soon bought and merged two London newspapers, then a magazine, combined them and commissioned Swinburne to commemorate their rebirth in immutable verse. Following generous loans to the Conservative Party, Astor was soon elected to the exclusive Carleton Club. All now needed for eternal bliss were a title and an elegant stately family seat. In Shropshire, for $1,250,000, Astor took title to Cliveden, immortalized by Alexander Pope:

Gallant and Gay in Cliveden's proud alcove,
The bower of wanton Shrewsbury's scandals and love.

commemorating an earlier owner, the wicked Earl of Shrewsbury, who, without so much as an if you please, had tossed out his wife and installed that of a neighbor. An oncoming Astor generation would give Cliveden even greater notoriety, this time as rallying ground for "the Cliveden Set," an odd socio-intellectual amalgam of pro-Hitler British sentiment sparked by W.W.A.'s energetic daughter-in-law, Virginia-born Lady Nancy Langhorne Astor.

Cliveden refurbished, Hever Castle was the next acquisition of the now Lord Astor, baronet, who meanwhile had renounced U.S. citizenship though by no means renouncing keen concern for New York's opinion of him, an obsession forever with him. While America vented its displeasure that more than five hundred American women had become the wives of titled foreigners, taking abroad with them upwards of two hundred millions to shore up their noble spouses' solvency, Englishmen were complaining about upstart American millionaires buying British titles. Even had he not this to overcome, William Waldorf Astor had so abundantly developed his propensity for snobbishness even Mayfair would find him objectionable. When one evening a lady guest appeared at an Astor concert escorted by a respectable gentleman with whom she had been dining, Astor met them at the door and ordered the gentleman to leave. Not satisfied with this rudeness, the following day Astor set something of a record for boorish behavior by publishing in his newspaper an item calling attention to the fact that the gentleman in question, Captain Sir Barkeley Milne, had been asked to leave the Astor premises because he had not been invited. Such deliberate affrontery went down poorly with everyone including the Prince of Wales, Astor's sponsor in the Carleton Club. Promptly the club's governors let Astor know that an apology was in order. Obediently Astor complied, and now owning not one but two castles, a villa at Sorrento and a stylish London townhouse, our penitent was elevated to viscount.

Before abandoning New York, leaving construction of his new hotel in the hands of others, Astor had also contracted to build a cream-colored Touraine chateau on the northeast corner of Fifth Avenue and 56th Street. Here would rise Venus from the Fifth Avenue sea of Florentine palazzos,

Victorian mansions and French Renaissance villas. But this Astor sold before ever moving in, concluding that he'd no longer any desire to live in New York. Had not its voters twice failed to recognize his merit? Nevertheless, from London Astor scrupulously continued to solicit New York's good opinion by making sure that reports of his more commendable activities came promptly to the notice of its newspapers.

Whether to influence Wall Street share holdings on which he had taken a short position, or for the puckish pleasure of reading his own obituary, one day Astor faked a cable from London announcing his death. Dutifully, Trinity Church published funeral bans and *The Times,* in two columns on page one, mourned his passing, adding a few days later a reader's letter to its already redundant eulogies. The letter was an enlightening disclosure of Astor's little known military career. It seems that for a while he had been a private in Co. K of the stylish Seventh Regiment, had regularly shouldered his musket as a common soldier and marched around that noble armory's drill floor, "until appointed a colonel on General Shaler's staff." Astor's leap from buck private to colonel seemed no immodest hurdle to the latter-writer, one Captain H. B. Steele, who praised Astor as "a mighty good example for other sons of millionaires who would buy their commissions instead of earning them." From even farther out on a limb Steele continues, "We have in our National Guard two of our wealthiest young gentlemen of German descent who have followed Mr. Astor's example," disclosures which would seem to weight the venerable Seventh more heavily on the side of ballroom than battlefield proficiency. A fortnight later Astor's demise was exposed as a hoax and Park Row's reaction was remarkably restrained. Chuckling at *The Times's* discomfort, *The Herald* stood silently on its earlier obituary: "The death of William Waldorf Astor, though not an event of great and lasting significance either in the world of action or the world of thought, will be generally deplored." Stung, *The Times* brooded for a while, but when a few months later Astor bought the *Pall Mall Gazette,* and appointed two titled friends to run it, *The Times* featured its London man's comment that they were "titled gentlemen who neither know anything about running a magazine or anything else." Later that autumn when Mrs. Astor came home to die, *The Times* obituary decorously commended her great charity and many good works. Briefly beguiled by a new religion then fashionable in London, in New York at least William Waldorf Astor remained a

The original Waldorf-Astoria Hotel between 33rd and 34th Streets at Fifth Avenue. The thirteen-story Waldorf (left) opened in March, 1893, and the sixteen-story Astoria opened in November, 1897. The view is to the southwest, with 34th Street on the right and Fifth Avenue on the left. (Courtesy Waldorf-Astoria Hotel)

Fifth Avenue before the coming of the Waldorf. The view is to the south from 37th Street, with the spire of the Brick Presbyterian Church in the foreground.

The Stewart Mansion, circa 1880, the home of Alexander Turney Stewart, whose fashionable department store was on Broadway at 9th Street. The marble mansion, located on the northwest corner of Fifth Avenue and 34th Street, was the terminus for Sunday strollers along Fifth.

The Fifth Avenue Hotel at Fifth Avenue between 23rd and 24th Streets, circa 1859. The first and most lavish of the uptown hotels until the coming of the Waldorf. (*Harper's Weekly*, October 1, 1859)

The original Waldorf Hotel, circa 1893. The view is to the south; on the right is the home of John Jacob Astor III, which would soon be demolished to make way for the Astoria Hotel. (Courtesy Waldorf-Astoria Hotel)

The original Waldorf, circa 1893. The view is to the west, looking down 33rd Street. (Courtesy Waldorf-Astoria Hotel)

Fashionable Fifth Avenue during the Age of Opulence. On the left is the Waldorf, with the home of John Jacob Astor III just beyond. The spire of the Brick Presbyterian Church at 37th Street is in the center. (Courtesy Waldorf-Astoria Hotel)

The completed Waldorf-Astoria Hotel, circa 1897. The view is to the south, with the white-marbelled Stewart mansion in the center. (Courtesy Waldorf-Astoria Hotel)

The main entrance to the Waldorf on 33rd Street, 1893. (Courtesy Waldorf-Astoria Hotel)

The carriage entrance on 34th Street, 1897. (Courtesy Waldorf-Astoria Hotel)

The stately Peacock Alley, where Society promenaded and flaunted
appearances. (Courtesy Waldorf-Astoria Hotel)

At the opening of the Waldorf in 1893, this room was known as the Men's Cafe. Later, in 1897, when the Astoria opened and the four-sided mahogany bar was installed, this room was used as a reading and writing room. (Courtesy Waldorf-Astoria Hotel)

The dining room, photographed in 1929. (Courtesy Waldorf-Astoria Hotel)

steadfast Episcopalian and the two exquisitely sculptured bronze doors of Old Trinity testify his devotion to his splendid wife.

When the Waldorf grossed four and a half million the first year, Astor saw ample justification for enlarging it by an addition on the northern half of its Fifth Avenue block, the half occupied by the residence of *the* Mrs. Astor. William Waldorf had spoken with his cousin John Jacob Astor about this, but before agreeing to the joint venture, John Jacob, influenced no doubt by his redoubtable ma, demanded certain guarantees. It wasn't that Mrs. Astor objected to being moved; she thoroughly disliked being overshadowed by her nephew's hotel, once threatening to tear down her house and replace it with a livery stable. She was no less annoyed that "Gentleman Jim" Corbett had opened a roisterous saloon just a few doors west along 34th Street. But, said she, any Waldorf annex on *their* half of the block would have to be a separate structure, not built flush against the walls of the present Waldorf but separated by at least thirty inches of air space. Should ever her son and his very unpredictable cousin quarrel, John Jacob could shut off his half from the Waldorf and run it independently. Another stipulation, obvious the dictate of vanity, provided that the towers on John Jacob Astor's annex should rise three stories higher than those of William's Waldorf.

Now, the knotty problem—what to call the joint venture? Hyphens were popular; *The New York Times* would remain *The New-York Times* for several more decades. Indeed, when two Roosevelt cousins married (even as did Franklin and Eleanor) they became Mr. and Mrs. J. Roosevelt-Roosevelt, pretty heady stuff. Some earlier Astor having contrived Astoria as the name for holdings in Oregon and in New York's borough of Queens, Waldorf-Astoria it would be.

Notwithstanding its progenitor's boorish behavior, bad manners and snobbishness, the British branch of the family founded by William Waldorf Astor achieved honors. By 1935 five Astors had served Britain with distinction in Parliament.

The Man Who Made the Waldorf

$\mathcal{A}$s a symbol the Waldorf-Astoria soon epitomized both the opulent power as well as the inexhaustible vitality of New York. It typified the great city whose citizens, driven by an insatiable passion for cultural elegance were pillaging Europe and the Far East.

"Most of all," notes historian Lloyd Morris, "the Waldorf-Astoria spoke eloquently for New York's prodigal extravagance, its delight in costly pleasures, its determination to achieve a state of luxury, a splendor such as men had never before conceived. Like New York itself, the Waldorf-Astoria crystalized the improbable and fabulous. It was a vast, glittering, iridescent fantasy that had been conjured up to infect millions of plain Americans with a new ideal, the aspiration to lead an expensive, gregarious life as publicly as possible. To citizens of Keokuk, Kansas City, or Kokomo it made available for a few weeks or days a palace of more stupefying grandeur than any Vanderbilt chateau. For residents of New York's brownstone East Side, its Harlemites, its Brooklynites, the cliff dwellers of Central Park West, it afforded an opportunity to duplicate the repast being served to members of the Four Hundred at a nearby table or, far more cheaply, to sit and watch their entrance and exit."

Oliver Herford believes the mission of the Waldorf-Astoria was to bring exclusiveness to the masses. "It existed to fulfill a universal American daydream that had never before become articulate. As a cultural institution the influence of the Waldorf-Astoria far exceeded that of the Astor Library."*

"Every successful organization is no more than the lengthened shadow of one man," goes a familiar saying. That a hotel, even one with grandeur built into its cornerstone, has exerted so profound an influence on the

*Provided by a bequest of John Jacob Astor with his friend Washington Irving as executor—now a wing of the New York Public Library.

lives of five generations of Americans setting standards of professional hospitality, dictating modes of dress, entertainment and etiquette—even codifying standards of social merit, qualities that make Waldorf-Astoria a mark of excellence around the world—urgently dispatches us in search of that one man. Whose inherent good taste and soaring imagination first set its sights? Whose leadership and personal example perfected its superb organization? Who, in the face of buffeting economic winds and the inconstant whims of popular fancy held high its goals and steered unswervingly toward them?

Several exceptional men playing unique roles all made durable contributions to the Waldorf's success. William Waldorf Astor's bold concept of the world's first luxury skyscraper hotel was far more than plucky entrepreneurial bravado. After all, it was his money, exclusively; no syndicate, no tax-exempt church organization, no insurance company, no bank, no layered confection of leveraged debts and mortgages. Astor's money, and only Astor's money, built the Waldorf.

From the late E. M. Statler, long America's ranking professional host, we hear that oft-repeated maxim: The three most important factors in the success of a hotel are location, location and location. When in 1890 Astor determined to build at 33rd and Fifth Avenue, the site was not only far uptown but in a neighborhood yet predominantly residential.

Astor realized that the Waldorf would either hasten the transmutation of its environment or become isolated by it and fail. As New York's first landlord, from four generations of landlords, Mohammed would summon the mountain; his hotel would change the neighborhood, not surrender to it. Astor's task is better evaluated when one realizes that Tiffany's elegance was then to be found far down on Union Square; that today's smart Park Avenue was then a narrow, trashy thoroughfare of stalls, second-rate shops and small factories on its lower part, still known as Fourth Avenue.

The Waldorf, the tallest hotel in the world, would also pioneer the concept of vertical habitation; people, food and equipment would be conveyed up and down hoisting shafts called "elevators." Success here meant not only overcoming a popular aversion to heights but everyone's very real fear of fire hazards. From the investor's viewpoint vertical habitations meant greatly increasing the return a landowner might expect from his precious patch on Manhattan's slender strand.

Vertical habitations would accelerate a rapid appreciation of land value, hence a greatly expanded community tax base. In skillful permutations, Henry J. Hardenburgh, Astor's architect, alchemized all this into functional reality. To architect Hardenburgh must also be credited the fine selection, and the sensitive direction of sculptors, painters and decorators—the Lows, the Turners, the Simonses, the Blashfields—selected to adorn his towering fourteen-storied masterpiece.

Abner Bartlett discovered George Boldt and Abner Bartlett successfully conducted the fragile family negotiations that three years later, brought about the Astoria annex. When William Waldorf Astor sailed away he left to another Astor relation, Charles A Peabody, to manage the numerous Astor properties. To Peabody is credited the recruitment of Oscar Tschirky, and Oscar would infuse this handsome, lifeless structure with warmth, friendliness and hospitality.

In any gallery of Waldorf-Astoria greats would hang the portrait of its super sleuth, "house dick" par excellence, Joe Smith, who for twenty-four years kept unblemished the Waldorf reputation. These hallowed walls would also display Nora Foley, housekeeper, who for thirty years supervised 280 maids and a corps of housemen, plumbers, painters, carpenters, cabinetmakers, seamstresses, paperhangers and upholsterers, patiently gratifying the occupants of the Waldorf's 2200 beds, surely the world's most spoiled, pampered and eccentric patrons ever collected under one roof.

If a guest wanted extra blankets or a special lounging chair, these appeared instantly and would be installed for him without asking upon his next arrival at the Waldorf. If a guest wanted pillows that were overstuffed, the contents of three pillows were quickly emptied into one. One guest wanted only new blankets because she liked their smell. Another required extra wardrobes,which were promptly manufactured expressly for her. When another found the chairs too high their legs were shortened. Another required light bulbs of higher wattage. One preferred metal to wicker trash baskets. Another wanted the bathroom floor carpeted wall to wall. A certain guest asked that pictures on the walls display only homey old farm scenes. Another could be contented only with window curtains of Belgian lace. Guests in brass beds wanted wooden beds, those in wooden ones wanted brass. Some wanted linen sheets instead of cotton, others cotton instead of linen. No pillows and lots of towels, or no towels and lots of pillows, whatever it be, the most bizarre request Nora Foley granted without the lift of an eyebrow. Pets are not kept in Waldorf suites, but for two weeks a white donkey was stabled in the hotel basement.

Beside the unflappable Foley, who believed that any Waldorf guest was entitled to idiosyncracies, scores of other Waldorf workers earned great eminence in the hotel industry through a novitiate in Waldorf ranks. Indeed, over the nine decades the collective numbers of fine hotel schools at Penn State, Cornell, Houston and Michigan State have hardly outdistanced the Waldorf-Astoria as training centers for first rank hotel men.

George Boldt did not walk into a great business and make it greater. Nor did he simply breathe life into this fabulous Galatea. Yet more than anyone Boldt changed New York's and then America's concept of hotel life and with it the important role of the hotel in the community.

This robust 1890 America into which the Waldorf was born differed from today by more than the absence of automobiles, airplanes, radio, television and motion picture theaters. Cocktails were then never served in the home, divorces were never acceptable to its society, women did not then smoke and their hemlines were never higher than their calves. Of New York's twenty-four legitimate theaters reputable New Yorkers would not wish to be seen in as many as ten of them. Nightclubs did not exist. There was not so much as a single fashionable cabaret. And a first-rate hotel was a place where a traveler might find palatable food and clean lodging.

Hotels were never considered social centers; one would no more have considered giving a dinner, a dance, a reception, a concert, an after-theater supper at a hotel than at the railway station. New York visitors could expect comfortable beds and good food at the Hoffman House, the Cambridge, the Brunswick, the Albermarle, the Fifth Avenue, the Victoria, the Holland House or the Buckingham, and perhaps elsewhere as well. But these, New York's best, were lodgements, never social centers. Until the Nineties smart New Yorkers did little dining out and then it was either Delmonicos, or Louis Sherry's—that mirrored Versailles of Lucullan delights on Madison Square—and even these were off-limits for unaccompanied ladies of good families.

Earlier noted was New York's fondness for balls; virtually everyone from every social strata in this convivial community attended at least one ball each year. Yet balls were not held in hotels but in private residences, public ballrooms or on an armory drill floor.

The Man Who Made the Waldorf

Except for Cesar Ritz's singular success with the Savoy in London, Europeans no more than Americans thought of hotels as proper environs for dining and dancing. Urban inns, whether in Europe or America, were usually entered through a narrow street-level vestibule, where one passed the reception desk then climbed stairs to parlors and dining rooms. The most desirable room accommodations as well as better private suites were usually located on the second floor. By climbing a third and sometimes a fourth, even a fifth flight of stairs, the traveler obtained rooms at lower prices.

A few New York hotels did operate public barrooms—strictly a man's world—the bar itself being a large rectangular structure, commandingly positioned in the center of the room. One, at least, the Hoffman House, run by gun-wielding Ned Stokes—who did in Jim Fisk and got Josie Mansfield and four years at Sing Sing from which he mysteriously managed nocturnal horseback outings—also served excellent meals. Conversely, Delmonicos and Sherry's provided living accommodations for a modest number of permanent bachelor guests.

George Boldt would change all this. Inspired perhaps by London's Cesar Ritz, Boldt set out to bring New York's first families regularly into his hotel. He would make it their favored rendezvous for lunch, for afternoon tea, for dinner, dancing, and for all private family functions from baptisms, birthday parties, debutante parties, weddings, bar mitzvahs, and golden anniversaries.

Gastronomy Boldt would widen in appeal beyond a small cult of cosmopolites to become the popular pastime of thousands. What hostess in America has failed to offer her delighted guests a Waldorf Salad—chopped celery, raisins, apples and walnuts, generously drenched with mayonnaise, artistically cushioned on a bed of lettuce leaves?

What bridal gift list did not include that delectable novelty introduced by the Waldorf-Astoria, the chafing dish? With this splendid utensil brides could perform three bits of Waldorf magic: chicken-a-la-king, lobster Newburg and Welsh rarebit. Gold prospectors in faraway Alaska were soon demanding "Oscar Sauce," harbinger of an entire new industry of bottled condiments. From dining at the Waldorf or even following the regularly published accounts of its cuisine, popular notions of a "swell feed" became refined, polished, elevated.

All these mutations George Boldt achieved with his hotel. He made it *the* place for concerts, for amateur theatricals, for travelogues, for scientific study groups, for Protestant and Catholic worship services, and a series of Monday morning music lectures which were to run for forty-five years attracting thousands of the most accomplished musicians and all the socially privileged in the Western World.

The Waldorf-Astoria's example was soon followed. Across America other hotels sought to integrate themselves into their community's life, thereby changing the whole character of the industry and bringing to it whopping new revenues and prestige which hotels hitherto had not enjoyed.

That earlier glimpse of Boldt's promotional skill, his adroit shifting of nominal sponsorship of the Waldorf's opening from the hotel itself to Society's pet charity, at once raising the quality of attendance, broadening the impact of its publicity, surmounting an inhibiting religious taboo, presaged a rich repertory of similarly innovative gambits intuitive to George Boldt.

The cognate quantity contributing to a successful organization is often the people factor; recruitment, training, supervision of people, coping with their problems as a group, their personal problems as individuals. However beguiling its general atmosphere of efficiency, luxury and ease, a hotel can be instantly imperilled by a single employee's negligence: slovenly waiter or maid, a discourteous doorman or bellhop, an apathetic clerk, an unsympathetic assistant manager, and another unhappy guest has departed never to return.

"In a hotel the guest is a buyer, the employees of the hotel are the sellers,"said George Boldt. "Buyer and seller are constantly together. For every moment of the guest's stay at the hotel he must be 'sold' over and over again."

Every hotel is a "people business," only as good as its engineers, mechanics, bellmen, housemen, laundresses, valets, housemaids, chefs, bakers, butchers, waiters, busboys, bartenders, security officers, elevator operators, plumbers, electricians, painters, upholsterers, doormen, telephone operators, postal clerks, wine stewards, florists, ticketing clerks, cashiers, bookkeepers, house physicians, dentist (yes, in the case of the Waldorf), and staff photographer. In sum, nine hundred and seventy "hosts" (double that number to man the Waldorf of today).

One wonders where George Boldt may have learned so wide a variety of functions. More to the point, how did he manage to supervise each through his trained lieutenants? And how did he consistently inspire the whole with that essential pride of performance, *esprit de corps,* without which there is no whole but only an array of unassimilated parts?

Others describe Boldt as something of a martinet, a man of mercurial moods. An assistant manager he saw dancing with a guest he fired on the spot. This man had broken a cardinal rule; no Waldorf employee must ever forget his place as servitor. His public firing of Tom Hilliard, a faithful assistant—the one individual Boldt had brought with him to the Waldorf—was an act of uncontrolled temper, and Boldt apologized for it fifteen minutes later when he introduced Hilliard as his probable successor. In such little irrational acts great leaders become human.

"He was not at all the high-pressure executive," recalls Oscar. "He was gentle and mild-mannered, dignified but unassuming. With his long, curly beard, his pince-nez glasses on a black silk cord, he looked like a typical German professor. Nevertheless, for all his quiet charm he was a vigorous executive. An untiring worker himself, he expected all of us to work just as long and just as hard. He was a stickler for detail. It seems to me he was on the job twenty-four hours a day. I know he was on duty from nine in the morning until two the next, for I followed his routine myself and there were many weeks when I saw my wife and children for only fleeting minutes."

George Boldt was born on Rugen, a Baltic island separated from the romantic shores of Germany's Mecklenburg by a narrow strait. Its people were mostly farmers and fishermen, a modest number resort keepers. The Boldt family were of the comfortable middle-class. His father, a government offical, provided his son with the advantages of education, his mother the value of social refinements. Island dwellers either accept their watery confines as encompassing all that is worthwhile or suffer a claustrophobic insularity that sooner or later compels them to sail away. Whether it was a result of young George's ambition or Bismarck's need for troops, Boldt one day decided to sail away, to emigrate to America.

His first U. S. employment was in the kitchen of the Merchants Exchange Hotel at Broadway and Chambers Street, from which he soon graduated to the Arlington Hotel as kitchen helper, then waiter. Now came the lure of the great open spaces—Texas! So quite soon we find young Siegfried in his cabin on a river's bank prospecting for riches. Came suddenly a torrential spring flood and Boldt's cabin with all his earthly possessions was swept away.

Broke, disillusioned, sick of Eldorado's trackless expanse, Boldt made his way back to New York to start all over again, first as an oyster shucker, then waiter, eventually dining room captain in Parker's Restaurant. This was the same Parker's Restaurant which Gentleman Jim Corbett bought and removed from Greeley Square to West 34th Street to the annoyance of *the* Mrs. Astor.

One day some fond patron offered Boldt a chance to run a small hotel at Cornwall-on-Hudson. Another upward shift took him south to Pennsylvania to the staff of William Kehrer as assistant manager of the Philadelphia Club. From this to management of the Bellevue seems but a short lateral. Moreover, it proved the real beginning, not the end, of his lifelong association with Kehrer, for he married Kehrer's lovely daughter, Louise, a woman of rare charm and beauty, perhaps the single individual whose contribution to Boldt's success was greater than any other's. Louise had grown up in the innkeeper's world and she knew every function of it—dishwasher, cook, maid, housekeeper, purchasing, cashier. More important, George Boldt's bride possessed a natural graciousness, charm and wit which combined in her talent for making friends. Of his thousands of Waldorf patrons, Boldt made a great many personal friends, cronies even, and Louise charmed them all.

At their little four-storied Bellevue, Louise was cashier, and it was through her that the Boldts became friendly with Abner Bartlett, a real estate "conveyancer" in the employ of W. W. Astor. Some say that Bartlett's frequent Philadelphia visits were to be with his daughter, others that, like many other New Yorkers, he found Philadelphia a requisite safe distance to enjoy an amount of freedom, to relax from the demands of his difficult boss.

Gossip lingers that Mrs. William Waldorf Astor suffered a nervous breakdown and was quietly sequestered in the Boldt's Bellevue to be nursed back to health by Louise. In any event, one day Boldt told Bartlett of his ambition to return to New York, perhaps to buy the Holland House. This prompted Barlett to reveal William Waldorf Astor's plans for the luxurious new Waldorf. If, added Bartlett, Boldt could raise a hundred thousand dollars to furnish it, Bartlett would be happy to introduce him to Astor as a likely Waldorf lessee. Boldt and Astor soon met, liked each other, and the deal was made.

The agreement provided that Boldt would have complete charge as lessee for which he would annually pay Astor five percent of the cost of the building plus six percent of the value of the ground on which it sat: for these purposes the land's value was set in excess of $2 million. (Two generations earlier John Jacob Astor had bought that property for $20,000 as a modest part of a fifty-acre farm that stretched across Manhattan almost to the banks of the Hudson. Thirty years later other Astors would sell the Waldorf site to the Empire State's builders for $8,000,000 per acre.)

Boldt's impact on the Waldorf was immediate. In meetings with Hardenburgh he quickly revised interior plans for the lower floors. Ladies in that day did not enter hotels through the main entrance, it being thought indecorous for a lady to stand waiting and stared at whilst her husband went through discussions of room preference, a formality of registering. Hotels of quality then had a special ladies' entrance and a private ladies' lounge.

Boldt reasoned that if the main lobby were made attractive with plants, paintings, sculpture, perhaps even an open tea garden, its less-than-lovely commercial aspects would no longer prove objectionable, hence no need for a separate ladies' entrance and lounge.

George Boldt loved flowers. From Philadelphia he brought along his own florist to inaugurate the practice of having fresh flowers on every table of the Waldorf's five restaurants and in all its suites, thenceforth a distinctive Waldorf tradition.

That summer George and Louise Boldt set out on a tour of Europe. They visited palaces and great villas, museums and grand hotels, tirelessly looking, cautiously buying. Surely Arnold Constable helped, but most of the furnishings of the hotel were purchased that summer abroad by these two.

So precise was Louise Boldt's planning that when their purchases began to arrive she could station herself in the lobby of the yet unfinished Waldorf and from the bill of lading on each carton know at once for what particular room its contents were intended.

Similarly, in the selection of drapes, tapestries, vases, lamps, in every guest room was felt Louise Boldt's sensitive, feminine touch; lady guests would need little boxes for their jewelry and packets of needles, spools of thread, pincushions. For the guests' peace of mind every room would have a candlestick and a candle, "just in case the electric lights fail," said Louise, voicing the sentiments of many who distrusted the new electric lights. Hence, candlesticks, and in dainty, crystal patterns.

Men of the Nineties often chewed tobacco. If cuspidors were necessary, these, too, should be elegant, flowered china and clean, not the brass saloon variety. The Waldorf would become the first American hotel to adorn each table of its restaurants with a candelabra as well as flowers. Every inch of their hotel to fall under the public's view, said Boldt, must appear as pleasant as the most gracious home the guest had ever known, or hoped one day to own. Paint, decoration, furnishings were props, prodigal things to be used constantly. "Luxury for the masses" is another line attributed to Boldt. Under the guidance of Louise and George Boldt the Waldorf would soon emerge as the ultimate in gracious opulence.

The public's response was immediate; far more than one guest had made flat offers for the entire furnishings of a suite, thinking to transfer it intact to Atlanta, Chicago, Albuquerque, Denver or perhaps out among the oil rigs and cattle-ranging plains of Texas. As prospective guests, Boldt's first targets were the social elite of New York, their cousins from Boston, Baltimore, Philadelphia, for Boldt knew that the hotel preferred by influential New Yorkers would soon become the hotel most preferred by influential travelers from the hinterland, or from Europe or South America, indeed, from around the globe. The herd follows the bell cow; corral the bell cows.

"I'd rather see Mrs. Stuyvesant Fish enjoying a cup of tea in an all but empty Palm Room than a dozen lesser-known guests there feasting," said Boldt.

Contrasted with the quiet dignity, the serene beauty of the Waldorf, Delmonicos, Society's favorite rendezvous, seemed suddenly tasteless and vulgar. Both Delmonicos and Louis Sherry's hurriedly underwent expensive face-liftings, but alas, too late; by now New York's most discriminating were locked irretrievably into the elegant confines of their splendid Waldorf-Astoria.

A custom familiar to European visitors of having meals served in their rooms was another Waldorf American innovation. Surprisingly, quite as much as the ladies, men guests, too, relished being pampered. For generations of Americans, memories of the Waldorf are delightfully lazy breakfasts in bed. The idea became immensely popular but an expense to the hotel. When higher prices were imposed deliberately to discourage it, the guests paid without a murmur. Hence, Room Service prospered with special portable hot tables, warming ovens, gleaming silver, sparkling tablecloths and, as always, fresh flowers, along with *The Times* or *The Herald Trib,* all conspiring to cheerfully launch a guest on even the gloomiest of days.

"We must make this hotel a haven for the well-to-do," George Boldt told Oscar. "Pad on the luxury and ease of living. There are always enough people willing to pay for these privileges. Just give them the chance. Make the Waldorf so convenient and comfortable they will never go another place."

Had George Boldt said this in 1894 when the hotel financially had turned the corner and become profitable, such boldness would not have meant much. When he did say it was during that first dismal summer of the Waldorf, depression-ridden 1893, so poor its business that one day the hotel could count only forty-eight guests against twenty times that number of employees. Against steadily falling income most businessmen would have viewed the situation differently; few would have had the courage to increase by one dollar any item on any guest's bill. But Boldt, seldom wanting in confidence, knew that he had found the formula for his hotel's success. Luxury!

His lobby having been converted into an elegant lounge with its Palm Garden in full view, here was where he must make things happen. Through glass partitions a visitor arriving by the main entrance looked directly into the Palm Garden. This Boldt would populate with the fashionable set; he needed them on display. Meals in the Palm Garden were exclusively à la carte, and dress for dinner in the Palm Garden was mandatory—not tuxedos, but swallow-tails—unless, as might in an emergency occur, a guest holding top rung credentials had bribed the headwaiter.

Ladies lunching in the Palm Garden soon found it such a pleasant meeting place that they tarried on through tea. Guests arriving for tea would remain for dinner. Soon lines began to form and reservations became necessary. The Palm Garden, Oscar blocking the way with his silken rope, symbolized success. Indeed, a reservation there soon became more sought after than a box at the Metropolitan. And doubtless it cost as much, with a generous gratuity to Oscar for starters.

In those days it was impolite for gentlemen to smoke where ladies were present. A good after-dinner cigar was deemed essential to enjoyment of the meal, so it was the custom for gentlemen to dispatch their wives back up to their rooms while they lingered below and smoked. Boldt's Waldorf would change this.

First an orchestra was brought into the lobby area for a program of light, after-dinner music. Then low coffee tables were placed beside deep comfortable chairs. Now a massive, turbanned Turk and his son, colorfully costumed, appeared pushing a pram of gleaming copper coffee urns maneuvering silently from guest to guest, preparing and serving that acrid, turbid "mokka' which Turks, who introduced coffee to Europe, relish.

The idea proved at once popular. Husband and wife could enjoy this after-dinner tête-à-tête, she sipping from her cup, he contented with his cigar, both spectators to an endless parade of glamorous celebrities. So agreeable a setting naturally proved conducive to an amount of social mixing even as it had only a decade earlier when hotel guests all dined at a single long table. Businessmen now would introduce their wives to business acquaintances, wives would become friendly, often companionable for shopping and sightseeing whilst their husbands worked.

Because of this convivial Waldorf experience it soon became more the custom for men to take their wives on business trips to New York, vacations which wives, finding new friends from faraway places, heartily enjoyed. Imagine the report back home. "Why, Mary, I was sitting with Bill in the Waldorf lobby talking with this very attractive couple from Spokane—he was a railroad president I believe—and who do you imagine I saw? Why there was Mrs. Vanderbilt; you know, the one whose daughter married that duke, and Mrs. Astor and Mrs Stuyvesant Fish. And I'll tell you the truth, Mary, the gown Mrs. Vanderbilt had on was not a bit more stylish than that little blue satin one old Mrs. Banks over on Locust Street whipped up for me to wear to New York . . ."

Another Boldt innovation of far-reaching influence on American hotel operations was his idea of having a branch office receptionist centrally located upon each floor. Selected gentlewomen employed at these posts would greet each guest by name at the guest's every coming and going. Keys, mail and messages were also handed them here. The floor receptionist also checked on housekeeping, room services, the delivery of parcels.

Boldt knew that in so large a hotel personal contact between host and guest all but disappears, the hotel becomes impersonal, the guest feels "institutionalized." So again, out on the lobby floor, in full view, readily available, he installed an assistant manager. With the arrival of each guest a note was placed on this one's desk and copies sped to department heads. At the reception desks guests were asked if they'd care for the same room of their previous visit; if that was not available, asked whether an identical one situated on another floor would be satisfactory. Should the guest demur that a different exposure might mean too great a wind or drafts, from beneath the desk the receptionist produced a small instrument which showed at once the direction and velocity of winds.

Boldt loved gadgets; the pneumatic tubes, the electric bulb carriage calls, the elevators flashing light controls, his network of hushed but authoritative buzzers. Merely exhibiting this front desk wind gauge, fresh from the Realm of Science, reminded the guest of the Waldorf's updated and unfailing solicitude.

The room having been selected, usually an assistant manager would escort the guest to his room, personally inspecting, making sure that it was in order, its appointments satisfactory. When Boldt knew that departing guests were scheduled for an ocean sailing, he saw to it that their stateroom aboard ship welcomed them with a great basket of fruit and wines bearing his card. Rarely did he refuse to cash any guest's personal check or advance needed cash; $100,000 was kept on hand for this purpose.

Even guests unknown to him had some available credit. What traveler at one time or another did not find himself short of cash? No man, he reasoned, would risk disgrace and possible criminal action for any small sum. Thus did the Waldorf become home in New York for thousands of loyal patrons, a family attachment which many, five generations later, loyally sustain. Because of its size and glamor one may not think the Waldorf-Astoria a family hotel. Yet such it became more quickly than any other in New York.

To keep the patronage of New York's first families, Boldt realized that he must stimulate activities of broad family appeal, appeals both esthetic and Lucullan. Comfortable beds, good food and drink mid pleasant surroundings—these were staples, values which might be established in every first class New York hotel of the Opulent Era.

Beyond these, contended Boldt, for whatever activity New York Society was intrigued by, the Waldorf must become the focal point. For those homes which had none, or none now large enough, the hotel must offer its Grand Ballroom with, of course, matchless facilities for private dinners, luncheons, teas and receptions.

But what of Society's more esoteric interests? Why not concerts, recitals, dramatics, lectures? Even spiritualists! And, yes, "Tableaux Vivants," flower shows, fashion shows, a circus! Yes, it would hold Sunday worship services. And parties for children, children of all ages.

Music, to George Boldt, meant German music; art must be French; and literature, if at all, American, largely that from the expatriate pen of Henry James. But it was not for the Waldorf to impose such standards; the hotel's function was to come up with the best of whatever was desired by Mrs. Vanderbilt, Mr. Morgan or Mr. Harry Payne Whitney.

One bright day in 1893 when Albert Morris Bagby walked in seeking a larger auditorium for his Monday morning music lectures, one of the Muses played right into Boldt's hands. Bagby had been holding his meetings at the Rembrandt Studios on West 57th Street but a sudden burst of popularity after his Newport season overflowed those facilities.

Needless to say Boldt was enthusiastic, and for the next forty-five years the Bagby Musical Mornings at the Waldorf topped New York Society's music calendar. Bagby, a one-time newspaperman who had studied piano in Weimar under Franz Liszt, knew a great deal about composition and composers and was an arresting speaker. Initially his friend Arthur Friedheim, pianist, appeared with him to illustrate certain musical passages or render entire selections.

Soon this program format was expanded so that in time just about every musician of note appeared in the Bagby series. First was Nellie Melba, then Emma Calvé, Geraldine Farrar, Amelita Galli-Curci were soon to follow. Now came Jascha Heifetz, Mischa Elman, Rosa Ponselle, Lucrezia Bori, Giovanni Martinelli, Richard Crooks, Claudia Muzio, all great favorites. On seventeen separate occasions Caruso sang. So eminent were these performers, the lecture aspect of Bagby's Musical Mornings was phased out.

What performer arriving in New York hoping to attract audiences to the Metropolitan, Carnegie Hall or elsewhere would not have been immensely pleased to first appear at a Musical Morning at the Waldorf? Not one line of advertising was needed to promote this subscription series, yet every seat in the Grand Ballroom was taken. Seldom did the audience know in advance what artist would appear; it was enough for smart New Yorkers to know that on Monday morning the Waldorf was the place to be. Indeed, no cultural activity in New York history has enjoyed greater prestige nor established so faithful a following as Musical Mornings at the Waldorf.

Another Waldorf musical triumph, also dating back to that first bleak eventful winter, were concerts under the baton of Anton Seidl, erstwhile conductor of great German opera orchestras whose tenure at the Metropolitan dated back to 1885 when Vanderbilt determined to make New York opera succeed on exclusively German fare.

However arguable that view, Seidl, a friend of Richard Wagner, proved to be someone to be listened to both as musician and raconteur. His Waldorf concerts, patterned after the legendary court *musicales* of Hapsburgs and Hohenzollerns, enjoyed immense popularity. Seat prices for a single series ranged from $60 to $300; these latter being regularly held by, among others, Messrs. J. P. Morgan, George Gould, Perry Belmont. Such exorbitant prices caused an out-distanced *Times* editor to scold the promoters for "keeping people away by a ticket that is too high in price for music lovers to jump over." Despite a stubborn economic depression and the *Times* complaint, many did hurdle the expense. There were never empty seats at Seidl's concerts.

Its momentum in the world of music accelerating, the Harlem Philharmonic Society became the next attraction on the Waldorf's cultural calendar. Founded in 1891 by a group of uptown residents who believed that small, exclusive orchestral concerts would be welcomed by people of that community, for forty years this group held concerts at the Waldorf. Similarly, the Rubenstein Club, dating back to the early nineties, brought to the Waldorf Maria Jeritza, Amy Goldsmith, Kathryn Kerin-Child, Emma Redell, and the Hilger Trio. Its principal function was the subsidy of music scholarships for promising pianists and vocalists.

Each Rubenstein season ended with a gala concert and its annual White Breakfast, one such assembling 2,000 guests to hear "The Waldorf-

Astoria March" composed by Rubenstein Club president William Rogers Chapman. Later Deems Taylor conducted the new Manhattan Symphony Orchestra at the new Waldorf, premiering there "Through the Looking Glass," his own composition. Guest conductors of that promising aggregation numbered Eugene Plotnikoff of the Moscow Imperial Orchestra, along with Alexander Aslanoff of Petrograd's Imperial Opera.

In her series of Candle Light Musicales, Helen Schaffmeister delighted listeners crowding the Basildon Room, as did Marion Bauer, composer, lecturer, critic, whose faithful followers regularly gathered in the Astor Club Gallery. The Mendelssohn Glee Club and the University Glee Club of New York were hardy perennials, as were the seasonal appearances of glee clubs from Columbia, Harvard, Princeton, and Yale.

An event on the regular cultural calendar known as the Diaz Tuesday Afternoons featured such performers as the unique Vienna Boys Choir, founded in 1498 by the Emperor Maxmilian, a celebrated group of talented youngsters whose distinguished alumni numbered both Schubert and Hayden. Incidentally, it was at the Waldorf-Astoria that the New York Philharmonic Society won for that great orchestra a lasting lease on life. At a single fund-raising banquet, $500,000 was subscribed, the orchestra showing its appreciation by a performance, its only ever outside a concert hall. Harry Harkness Flagler, the Society's president, permanently established the Waldorf as the Society's headquarters and here for years it continued to reside under the management of Frank H. Berend and Thomas Jefferson Miley.

Boldt's belief that the surest way to get families into his hotel was to stimulate activities there of appeal to the family, all ages and both sexes, included activities for the very young as well. Hence, dancing classes, puppet shows, once even a full-fledged circus. Party-givers, then as now, plumbed their fertile imaginations to come up with new, stimulating ideas for fun. One reads reports of lavish private extravaganzas at the Waldorf, hears whispers of "racy" stag parties with nude beauties popping up out of great centerpiece pies. Of record is a simple little dinner in 1899 for forty guests at a cost per guest of $250.00, perhaps a bit steep because of Oscar's discovery of a pre-French Revolution vintaged wine to crown a menu of roast mountain sheep with purée of chestnuts, ruddy ducks, and oversized blue raspberries which had been hothouse-grown especially for the occasion.

More appealing for family audiences was the "Spielgartenfest" celebrating the hotel's fourth anniversary: During the afternoon *Alice in Wonderland* was performed for the delight of children while the evening's entertainment featured whist played by fifty-two living cards. Setting for this was the Prussian Court of Queen Louise. The game started in the Marie Antoinette Room with a parade of cards. Dressed in costumes appropriate to each suit—hearts, diamonds, clubs, spades—even numbered cards and aces being young ladies, odd numbers young men, each participant carrying a sign telling what suit and number the particular card represented.

E. Vail Stebbins served as joker. In an intricate dance figure the joker shuffled the deck, the last dancer to fall in behind him—which tonight happened to be diamonds—setting the trumps. In view of all sat the players, Dr. Thomas F. Young, Jr., F. D. Winslow, F. H. Bosworth and Berkley Mostyn. As each player called forth the card he wished, partisan cheers rose from the audience. At the close of a tightly contested match, Miss Julia Bradley as ace of trumps was triumphantly crowned Queen of the Cards.

Boldt's ideas of *le grand luxe* soon made the Waldorf-Astoria proprietor of a handsome yacht. Guests desiring to see Manhattan by water needed only to add their names to its passenger list. This outing, if done properly, naturally required a handsome coach and four-in-hand to convey passengers those several blocks to the *Calypso's* Hudson berth.

The yacht excursions proved popular, but even more so the coaching to and fro, so popular, in fact, that Boldt arranged with T. Suffern Tailer to extend these outings to include Woodmanston and Arrowhead, far north on Manhattan's western tip.

When the automobile made its appearance Boldt inaugurated a private motor car service between the Waldorf-Astoria and the new Bellevue-Stratford hotel in Philadelphia. His predilection for gadgetry, for any new manifestation the Realm of Science might spawn, enlisted Boldt among early radio enthusiasts. New York and Philadelphia's first radio broadcast facilities were atop the roofs of the Waldorf-Astoria and the Bellevue-Stratford; first among inter-city radio relays was the Waldorf transmitter linked with one atop the Congress Hotel in Chicago.

Being a family hotel imposes certain obligations beyond supplying decorous atmosphere, proper entertainment, good food and drink. The children brought by their parents or nurses to puppet shows would return before many years for prep school graduation parties, bar mitzvahs, engagement announcement parties, wedding receptions, college formals, debutante balls, testimonial retirement banquets, eventually their own gold and silver wedding anniversaries.

Strict decorum distinguished every activity in the Waldorf's great public rooms. Parents of teen-aged daughters could feel as reassured knowing their child was at a party in the Empire Room as were she receiving in the straight-backed chairs of a boarding school's astringently lighted "dating parlor." How people behaved in its public rooms normally would be of little concern to a hotel unless, of course, such behavior shocked or annoyed other guests. On the other hand, one recalls that Miss Fay Templeton was politely reminded by a Waldorf official that ladies did not smoke in its lobby. No prudery dictated this; Americans of other generations simply set standards of etiquette and ladies and gentlemen respected them.

If a gentleman of the Teens received a lady visitor in his room at the Waldorf-Astoria there would be no complaint from the hotel provided she were properly announced, the hour discreet, and the guest's door into the hall remained open. Not that an amount of hanky-panky may not have budded at the Waldorf-Astoria, only that it would so without the vigilant hotel management's knowledge.

During the Prohibition era young peoples' parties became more difficult to supervise. No liquor could be served anywhere on Waldorf-Astoria property—stern injunction indeed, considering how many other hotels showed popular contempt of both the law and "dry" efforts to enforce Prohibition.

"No," ruled its proprietor. So long as Prohibition was the law of the land the Waldorf-Astoria would uphold it. To the letter. On one occasion security officers keeping an eye on youthful celebrants at a college dance soon noticed several unusually boisterous young males. These were watched closely. None had a bottle hidden under his table. No, the punch wasn't spiked. When, from time to time these absented themselves from the ballroom they were followed. Outside, across the street from the Thirty-Third Street entrance, stood two parked limousines, completely stocked, dispensing bootlegged booze by the drink.

Fortunately, George C. Boldt did not live to suffer the numerous difficulties this absurd law imposed on the hotels. Other manifestations of America's changing life style elicited from him no enthusiasm. The fact that so phlegmatic an attitude would ultimately meet defeat only causes one to empathize with George Boldt; flawless individuals are difficult to identify with!

The hotel's first such contretemps wasn't long in coming. Boldt himself wore a handsome close-cropped beard which he kept fastidiously trimmed. But waiters, he decided, looked neater without beards; that way they'd betray no coffee stains or other food morsels they might have taken a swipe at as they shuttled to and from the kitchens. No problem here. The hotel said no beards, and those valuing their Waldorf employment complied, grudgingly, perhaps, but complied.

When one day Boldt futher decreed that the hackmen who lined the curbing outside the hotel also be clean-shaven, such arbitrary extension of privilege to include those picturesque proprietors of hacks in the public way brought roars of outrage. Word of this quickly appeared in print, and soon war was declared. On one side stood Boldt, defiant, bearded and alone. Arrayed against him were the combined forces of waiters and hackmen, the latter summoning to their cause the entire Liberty Dawn Association of Hack Drivers, a union affiliate of the Knights of Labor.

Public reaction to Boldt's edict was prompt and positive. Editorials quick to raise the banner of personal freedom went after Boldt with a vengeance. "It was undeniably the right of every free man," stormed the *Sun,* "to wear his beard where, when, and in whatever fashion he pleased." In secret sessions the labor leaders described Boldt as contemptuous of the Bill of Rights—perhaps the Declaration of Independence, the Magna Carta. . .!

Trumpteted the *Times:* "The cabmen struck the clearest note of strength in their assertion that if such a hirsuteless system be just then the same rule should apply to the public servants of the people, viz, the Governor of the State, members of the Legislature and other state and city officials."

Tongue in cheek, the *Times* published one-column pictures of Governor Roswell P. Flower both with and without his beard, thus taking the controversy right up on the State House steps. It being an election year, Governor Flower came out on cue, rising quickly to the defense of the cabbies and waiters. Announced this sharp, self-made Watertown wit, "It was not many years ago that I was a servant myself, and I used to wear my beard as I pleased and my hair as long as I pleased. Had any man dictated to me that I should put a French twist to my beard or a Spanish curl to my hair I would have taken it as an insult. I will veto any bill regulating men's beards."

Of course no such bill had been proposed nor even dreamed of but Flower's speech made good copy, the Knights of Labor and the newspapers were delighted, and Boldt forced to beat a hasty retreat; it is one thing to dictate social preferments to Americans, quite another its beards, as more than one academic board has had to learn.

Britain's Royal Navy may permit only its officers to grow beards, which, obversely caused the U. S. Navy to endorse them for all. The Army prescribes the precise width and length of sideburns and moustaches. The Marines insist that a Leatherneck look like a peeled onion, and if Boldt wanted Waldorf waiters without beards, waiters being in plentiful supply, none would argue.

But not the hackmen.

Another troublesome brouhaha erupted in 1905 when Boldt fired Tom Hilliard. He had picked up Hilliard many years before in Philadelphia when Hilliard was working as a porter in Wanamakers. Hilliard he trained and Hilliard learned fast. In time it was Hilliard who alone made certain that the hotel's equipment—electrical, steam, water-powered—all functioned. From $300 a month Hilliard's pay soared to $15,000 a year. So dependable was he, Boldt never was required to have the vaguest understanding of the mechanical functioning of the Waldorf's many machines. Hilliard became responsible for the room operations as well, much as Oscar was for food and drink.

In 1900 when Boldt refused him a salary raise, Hilliard resigned. Before long Boldt was aboard ship for Europe to find Hilliard and persuade him to come back, this time on a five-year contract.

Their final break was again because of money; Boldt's Waldorf profits had grown astonishingly large and Hilliard was convinced he was not getting his share. One day he led a delegation of three top colleagues into Boldt's office with a joint demand for increased pay. Boldt begged for

[88]

time to consider the matter, and finally granted Hilliard's demand for $25,000; after separately placating the others, he waited a few months then bought up the six months remaining on Hilliard's contract.

Seven years later Hilliard was president of the new Hotel Vanderbilt, just three blocks east of the old Waldorf, and proving a small but effective rival. Pressure from new hotels farther uptown had already begun to be felt at the Waldorf. Again Hilliard strode into his old boss's familiar office, this time with an offer—three million dollars for Boldt's lease and the furnishings of the Waldorf plus a salary to Boldt of fifty thousand a year for the use of his name in the management and Boldt's regular appearances in the lobby. Boldt scorned the offer. Six years later Boldt was dead, his Waldorf equities auctioned. What did his lease and the hotel's furnishings bring? Less than one hundred-thousand dollars.

Biographers differ sharply as to Boldt's prowess as a banker, a venture he went into by forming the Trust Company of the Republic. One admirer writes that Boldt's splendid handling of this institution in bankruptcy brought him the friendship of J. P. Morgan, who was often at the Waldorf-Astoria and a visitor to Boldt in his private office. This appears an exaggeration.

Boldt was at the helm of his bank when the Dresser Company's failure precipitated uncontrollable bank runs resulting in near disaster for several trust companies, a panic which Morgan alone was able to stem by quietly assembling the heads of all the trust companies, telling them what to do, and refusing to let them leave his locked library until they agreed to do it. Morgan did not consider Boldt important enough to be among these. On the other hand if his critics accused the innkeeper of presumptuousness for fancying himself the peer of financiers, none could doubt George Boldt's competence in real estate matters.

Although the contrary impression lingered for half a century George Boldt never owned a single share of equity in the Waldorf-Astoria. But he did own other Fifth Avenue real estate; in fact, his sale in 1907 of one building site at Fifth Avenue and 37th Street for $3,000,000 was reported the biggest single New York realty transaction of record. It netted Boldt upwards of one million. Adjacent to this property Boldt built for his Louise a beautiful townhouse but, alas, less than thirty days after its completion Louise was dead.

[89]

Perhaps the manorial edifice he then undertook on Hart Island in upstate Lake St. George was an attempt to assuage his loneliness and grief. But as newspaper pictures even now perennially remind, "Boldt's Castle" would also go unfinished. It stands today, a great Gothic pile, sepulchered against the blue gray Adirondacks; lonely, silent, its stones scarcely visible among savage briars and bracken, the dream castle of an immigrant lad from the distant Isle of Rugen destined to become the greatest professional host in all America.

Perhaps in all the world.

Chicago Comes to the Waldorf

$\mathcal{A}$merica came of age in the year 1893. Not because of the Waldorf's opening, an event of consequence in the lives of but few, but because of Chicago's World's Columbian Exposition, compared to which the Philadelphia Centennial of 1879 would seem a county fair.

Just as Philadelphia's show had exhibited America's Age of Iron even while America's Age of Wood was still running, Chicago's great event would signal America's vast leap into the new realm of steel and electricity. Beginning in the spring of that year the exposition continued through the summer and closed in the fall, an eight month binge making Americans the most vainglorious people on earth. From all across this continent millions came to the fair, other thousands from around the world.

In art, architecture, engineering and construction it was a dazzling accomplishment, radiating concepts of grandeur, of splendor, of achievement later to be translated by scores of architects and builders into astonishing structures, awesome and inspiring to a worshipful world. Contemptuous New York and envious Philadelphia at first spoke slightingly of the enterprise: "An exposition commemorating the 400th anniversary of Columbus's discoveries in *Chicago?* Surely you jest."

But proponents of the Chicago Exposition were not to be thought mere city boosters wishing to extoll their sprawling metropolis of wooden rookeries and unpaved streets. Seeing the fair's imaginative concepts had inspired them with enthusiasm. Carrying them into fruition they did with tireless zeal. Although the exposition's concept was no one man's alone, its dominant influence was Daniel Hudson Burnham, architect of its master plan. Burnham's close associates, New Yorkers would later pride themselves, were Frederick Law Olmstead, America's leading landscape designer, the creator of Central Park, and Francis Davis Millet, a talented artist, writer, architect whose career had begun as a drummer

[93]

boy on the bloody battlefields of the Civil War and ended no less heroically, as did that of John Jacob Astor, co-owner of the Elegant Inn, when the *Titanic* went down. These three levied freely on the greatest artistic talents of the nation. Behind them stood such dependable Chicago stalwarts as Potter Palmer, Marshall Field, Harlow Higginbotham and George H. Davis.

Thanks largely to Mrs. Potter Palmer and her indefatigable female cohorts, both the exposition and the emerging prestige of American womanhood were brought to flower. Entertaining foreign dignitaries was but a modest part of the ladies' assignment; resulting from their efforts the greatest collection of art ever assembled in this nation or elsewhere—the finest work of Italian, Dutch, Spanish, French, and Flemish masters—was brought under one roof.

Never before or since has any exposition wielded wider influence. From near and far, transported to the shores of Lake Michigan and set up on islands dredged up from its bottom, were exhibited the greatest of everything the world had to offer. Giant white buildings, frameworked in steel and covered with "staff"—a wire-molded plaster of Paris and hemp fibreboard—displayed magnificence, grace and beauty to rival the splendid temples of the Pharaohs, the Incas, Babylonia, Greece, India and Rome. These housed great expansion engines, luxurious Pullman cars, the newly patented linotype.

Visitors would see, many for the first time, electric kitchens, farm machines propelled by gas, even trained tigers riding the backs of elephants. Dominating the landscape was its thrilling two hundred and fifty foot Ferris Wheel, each one of whose thirty-six cars carried twenty passengers for breathtaking revolutions and boundless vistas.

Burnham had hoped that from his six hundred and sixty-six acres of canals and lagoons Chicago would retain many small recreational islands, but this was not to be. Preserved were only those valiant ladies' Palace of Fine Arts, which is today's Museum of Science and Industry, and the tree-bordered Midway Plaisance, campus now of the University of Chicago.

Consider for a moment what America represented when Chicago opened her great display. In terms of such commonalities as roads and daily mail, the telephone, the automobile, warmth, light, education, this populace was back in the dark ages compared to western Europe. Most inhabited farms or clustered in widely scattered towns and villages. A sizable majority were illiterate. Civil War devastation had left a third of the population dazed and helpless. More stultifying were the ignorance-spawned prejudices imbedded in the people's psyche, the carcinomatous growth of bigotry.

In communities comprising Protestants and Roman Catholics, Methodist and Baptist preachers regularly denounced the Pope from their pulpits while priests denounced Protestants as heretics. "In an unbelievable number of small communities the only Roman Catholic was an Irishman, and he ran a saloon," notes Albert Stevens Crockett. In the eyes of many Southerners, Blacks, Catholics and Jews were vaguely lumped together as subspecies generally tolerated, rarely cultivated and but grudgingly admired. Impossible for New Yorkers to comprehend were thousands of American towns and villages whose populations were almost entirely English or Scottish, where even Germans were a curiosity and Italians only seen at fruit stands.

For most rural Americans a visit to Wisconsin, where entire communities are Dutch, Swiss, French, German, Russian, or Scandinavian, would have been as fascinating and as enlightening as one's first summer in Europe. Outside the South's and New England's rigid confines several midwestern states offered hopeful glimpses of homogenized but alien societies.

Mr. Morse's telegraph, whose progress a blinkered group of congressmen had blocked for seven years, had been around for half a century but unless a village lay along a railroad, communication with the outside world still depended on the horse. For coastal settlements and those on navigable streams, steam and sail tied them to the nation. An inland village, even one ninety miles from Baltimore or seventy miles from Washington would remain as remote as an Alaskan outpost.

Good interstate roads were generations away. A few hundred miles of macadam highways called turnpikes were owned by private companies exacting tolls. Most thoroughfares were dirt or sand, the first impassable in wet weather, the second rendered almost so in dry. "Corduroy" roads, a narrow carpet of saplings laid side by side, linked many communities across lowland hummock areas, providing a bumpy but satisfactory stagecoach passage; many remained in use far into this century. Wooden blocks were the paving stones of most cities.

In sum, the era of many inventions which gave reality to quick and easy communications, to comfort, to culture, to luxury, was yet well below America's roseate horizon. For most Americans the matter of day-to-day survival was of continuing concern, while for the privileged upper third it was a psychological struggle against the handicap of hideous and futile furniture, artless "art", or the inefficient and cluttersome inconvenience typifying Yankee ingenuity super-imposed upon Victorian taste.

Chicago's exposition heralded the arrival of that "tide in the affairs of men. . ." and many fairgoers came home resolved to take it at the flood. So vigorous was the onsweep of prosperity engulfing this continent in the final decade of the last century that financial reversals which earlier had "panicked" Wall street and delayed for a year the opening of Chicago's fair died aborning. Superior forces of nature and history suddenly combined with ingenuity and enterprise to sweep away all negative portents. In the subsequent onrush of wealth the Middle West and the Far West thrived. Venturesome men overnight became financial giants. Wealth gave them power undreamed of and their newly won eminence made them restless, discontented with their rural surroundings, their suffocating small-town sameness. With money burning in so many pockets, ways must be found to spend it. New York was on the lips of every ambitious outlander; shining there was a magic city where strange and startling adventure lurked beyond each street corner. As a den of sin and iniquity New York regularly received a compelling advertisement from many a rural pulpit. Preachers, not the best of psychologists, seemed not to realize that the lurid pictures they painted only whetted popular interest. Men, women too, yearned to see for themselves.

And so in ever-growing numbers they landed on Manhattan Island to see for themselves the life then passing as cosmopolitan. So delightful did they find it that many of New York's six thousand daily visitors stayed on to edge their way into its midst. The more restless of these spent and splurged and made headlines. Others, surviving the first heady daze of their new wealth studied with fascination the behavior of those accustomed to wealth, saw what they did to fill their lives, observed how they dressed, how they acted and strove to pattern themselves after them. Those of native grace and gentle instincts needed no tutors other than their own discernment and intuition.

A few seasons of New York left these unsated. Europe would become their oyster. It comes as no surprise that robust men for whom the bridge between dollar-a-day labor and immense wealth was but a quick single hurdle should do things in Europe that proved shocking to respectable folks back home. Instead of a limited number of amusements theirs was now the fun of buying anything they fancied. Whatever their rank or upbringing—or want of each—they displayed the same basic appetites at which the prudish, even the young, the less competent, shook their heads. Wine, women and song. And gambling, gambling with stakes only men of great wealth could afford.

How such men or their wives behaved in New York and in Europe often kept their acquaintances and a good segment of newspaper readers in a giggly state of titillation. What were those madcap-millionaires up to now? Bathing nude in the fountains of Rome! Riding horses into the casino at Cannes! Once Europe had awakened them New York failed to chain their enthusiasms.

But all these must depart from New York's piers and come early if they'd be assured of best accommodations aboard ship. Waiting, its arms outstretched, beguiling, beautiful, luxurious, was a foretaste of Old World elegance—the Waldorf-Astoria.

For all Chicago's promise of good things—notably its promise to bring the world across New York's doorstep—New York's immediate benefits from the Colombian Exposition proved disappointing. Token numbers of Europeans and South Americans were attracted to Chicago's great celebration, and there had been the fine flotilla of warships and parade of foreign navies. But in that first summer of its existence the Waldorf experienced many worrisome days.

Not until December with the Bagby concerts underway and holiday parties scheduled would the hotel's revenues show an encouraging upturn. On New Year's Day 1894 the hotel filled for the first time. "Happy New Year!" wrote a celebrating night clerk across the hotel register.

One hour after midnight a guest who was destined to bring an abundance of income and excitement to these cheerful precincts walked in. His one striking feature was a moustache that resembled a parted brown scrubbing brush. In a bold, clearly legible hand he wrote "J. W. Gates, Chicago" across the hotel register's first 1894 page.

This was not "Bet-a-Million" Gates's first appearance at the Waldorf. He'd dropped in earlier and liked what he saw. Three weeks later he was back. Another month again finds him at the Waldorf, this time with his friend Isaac L. "Ike" Elwood, another Chicagoan, coming perhaps to see if the tales John Gates had brought back about this fabulous hotel were true. And so began the Gates-Waldorf nuptials.

Over the next three years Gates and his cronies, Colonel John Lambert, John A. Drake, Charles T. Yerkes and others whose stars were in the Gates constellation all became permanently established at the Elegant Inn. Their favored gathering place was the Men's Cafe, a hospitable, cheerful, wood-panelled lounge comfortably provided with mahogany tables and large overstuffed leather armchairs. A great four-sided mahogany bar attended by eight bartenders dominated the room and its catalog of bar recipes numbered five hundred mixes gathered from around the world. Separate from the bar a "free lunch" buffet displayed Virginia hams, Vermont turkeys, various hot delicacies in casseroles and a tempting assortment of cold meats, olives, gherkins, onions, boiled eggs and cheese.

The Stock Exchange closed at three o'clock and within two hours the Waldorf Men's Cafe became a vibrant Wall Street extension. Patrons traded shares, warrants, sold options, grain or commodity futures, or consolidated components of some projected new "trust." Occasionally J. P. Morgan, "Morgan the Great Financial Gorgon" as a popular song described him, would appear, usually to sit at a table alone, a glowering, grim, red-faced man with restless, dark burning eyes.

Taciturn, enigmatic Henry Clay Frick and "Smiling Charlie" Schwab, associates of Andrew Carnegie, were frequent guests, as was Judge William Henry Moore, a suave, cultivated gentleman who had formed great trusts in minerals, matches and biscuits. Financiers often spoke of another Chicagoan, Judge Elbert H. Gary, a cold, precise, astute corporation lawyer who with John Gates had formed the wire nail trust, linchpin of the great steel corporation. Conversations between these two would begin in the Men's Bar then move up to the elaborate suite for which Gates paid twenty thousand dollars a year, thence to the private dining room where Gates and his pals gambled through the night, sometimes far into the next day.

Mrs. Gates at times lacked sympathy for her husband's amusements, for his unconventional hours. When he reported losses there was apt to be a scene; the next day he must shop for a necklace or a diamond brooch. But when he made a killing Mrs. Gates would cheerfully get out of bed and make coffee and flapjacks on the range in the private pantry Boldt had installed for them.

"Bet-a-Million" Gates he would eventually be called, for John Gates bet on anything, the turn of a card, the speed of a horse, the course of the stock market. Once on a dull, confining day at the Waldorf he even bet a thousand dollars on which of two raindrops uncertainly coursing down the windowpane would first reach the sill. More perhaps then any other, this energetic Chicago super-salesman helped launch the oncoming great American era of Big Business.

Gate's thesis was simply that several competitive manufacturers making and selling the same commodity would profit more by pooling their interests and forming a super enterprise, one with enough clout to fix both the selling price of that commodity as well as the cost of its raw materials and services. Only the bold and grandiose appealed to Gates and this marked him as a symbol of the times.

With the luxurious Waldorf-Astoria as rallying point for big business, and Gates so picturesquely typifying it, the public was finding it hard to distinguish between big business and big gambling. To Gates the relevance of such a comparison might never have occurred. Gambling for stakes higher than ever conceived was both his amusement and his vocation. His robust joviality masked a ruthless will. Crude, sometimes vulgar, his lack of breeding disturbed polite folk, including J. P. Morgan.

Gate's sales career began when Elwood hired him to sell barbed wire which he did, fast and abundantly, the thousands of miles of barbed wire needed where open ranging of cattle and sheep was slowly disappearing. Gates soon founded a manufacturing facility of his own, and ignoring Elwood's patents kept him at bay through a succession of court orders until he'd effectively muscled in on Elwood's market. "If you can't lick'em. join 'em." Strictly as an expedient these two became friends, or at least bedfellows with a swords point agreement on blanket sharing. One verbal exchange between the two, Albert Stevens Crockett records, was more than idle rhetoric.

One Waldorf evening Gates, Elwood and friends were dining as prelude to a vigorous night of poker. Stimulated by good fellowship, those about the table indulged in reminiscence, each telling stories of his life, or significant chapters from it. When Gates's turn came he began, "Before I was into steel . . ."

Elwood interupted. "How do you spell that, John?"

Chicago, too busy with its own burgeoning growth, may have been too preoccupied to pay much attention to Gates and his cronies. Its near Northside and starchy Lakeshore society certainly had not opened its doors to them—not that this might be of the vaguest relevance to what these blades were about or why they preferred New York as seat of operations. New York nonetheless would become aware of them, of their propensity for gambling, of their business cunning, dauntless schemes and insatiable appetite for excitement. No less discriminating, New York Society would not now nor soon take them to its well-bodiced bosom; the spontaneous welcome New York offered Europeans and other glamorous foreigners was rarely extended to hinterland folk. Wall Street nevertheless quickly learned respect for John Gates, for Ike Elwood, Elbert Gary, John Lambert and Max Pam. Indeed, Wall Street was shamelessly soon in bed with them, more chastened than tarnished from the experience.

Gates, born on a farm in Du Page County, Illinois in 1855, had but a grade school education before going to work as clerk in a small hardware store in Turner's Junction. From this came his job with Elwood, and his rapid conclusion that greater profits were to be had from manufacturing and selling for oneself than peddling the wares of another. Gates soon owned two small barbed-wire producing concerns which he merged to form Consolidated Steel and Wire Company. That profitably done he determined to bring aboard the entire wire industry, his first great Waldorf-spawned venture, along with Elwood, L. L. Smith and J.H. Parks, a convivial group whose spare time divided between scheming the creation of some intriguing new stock or commodity speculation and equally devout sessions of poker.

"Mr. Gates and his four companions ate, drank, slept and talked business in relays for ten days without ever stirring out of their rooms," remembers Oscar, discreetly making no mention of poker.

Soon after their mass descent on the Waldorf the Chicago Corsairs would discover a few yards west of the Waldorf-Astoria on 34th Street, what New York Tenderloin families dubbed the "House of the Bronze Doors." And its sculptured bronze portals that gave it daytime respectability by night were an essential part of its defense. The casino's operation was, of course, illegal and if not so fashionable or exclusive as Canfield's, it nevertheless attracted a large, well-heeled clientele. Its proprietors were Frank Farrell and Gottfried Wallbaum, the former remembered as promoter of the Pool Room Syndicate. Aside from its convenience to the

Waldorf, Farrell's establishment appealed to Gates because the stakes were higher than Canfield's. Nor was it necessary to ask the proprietor's permission to raise them. Whether baccarat, faro, klondyke, or the fascinating, unpredictable travels of that little ivory ball tossing aimlessly about the ridges of a roulette disc, the sky was the limit. The House of the Bronze Doors knew numerous tense dramas, stakes which would have quickened the pulse of the most jaundiced Atlantic City, Monte Carlo or Vegas croupier.

No such establishment could for long content the Gates group; their own circle, jousts with each other, they much preferred. For several years their play remained in the private precincts of the Waldorf; what transpired here would not excite newpaper city rooms. Favored setting was that august Astor dining room which had been brought piece by piece, panel by panel, from William Waldorf Astor's former residence. Were this not available there was the State Suite nearby, or one of the club rooms on the fifteenth floor, or perhaps Gates's apartment.

Eyewitnesses to their play maintain that these western millionaires who flocked to the Waldorf toward the end of the last century gambled for the biggest stakes the world has known, a statement hardly susceptible to proof since among all big-time gamblers there are losers and who wants to admit to being one? Sitting in on their games one saw the ante start at $1,000 and, as enthusiasm grew, jump to $2,000, $5,000, $10,000. Winnings and losses in a single evening could range from $75,000 to $150,000 (multiply by ten for today's dollar). Another observer reports that across the United States there were not fifteen or twenty poker players who could sit comfortably in a game with such stakes. Two who could and did were Hermann Frisch, the "Sulphur King," and Gates's old friend, Loyall L. Smith, once a poor Chicago newsboy and now a wealthy New Yorker. Here also would be found Herman Sielcken, the Coffee King, who was to make a fortune for himself and forever saddle a tremendous indemnity on American coffee drinkers by devising Brazil's coffee export price-fixing scheme. Colonel John Lambert was another.

Henry Clay Frick, in his own right America's leading coke producer and later Andrew Carnegie's lieutenant, was a Waldorf regular until completion of his own Fifth Avenue mansion. Frick had leapt into prominence when Alexander Berkman put two pistol slugs and numerous knife thrusts into him as protest against Frick's tough suppression of the bloody Homestead Mines strike; Frick, by the way, was the one individual whom Gates invariably addressed as Mister, a deference Gates did not extend even to J. Pierpont Morgan.

A suspicious man, Frick disdained publicity, assiduously avoided newspapermen and eventually became America's foremost art connoisseur, the only collector who, at Morgan's death, came up with the sums adequate to acquire the great Morgan canvases. Generations of art students, collectors, and connoisseurs the world around have made grateful use of the matchless art reference library which is today housed in that same handsome Fifth Avenue mansion.

Often some visiting oil man might take a hand in the Gates poker game. One popular regular, oddly enough, was an unidentified former Army captain, a player low in financial means but high in skill, whose exceptional card sense provided his convivial, leisurely livelihood. Occassionally Elbert H. Gary was dealt a hand in these games, though Gary was then neither important nor rich; his wealth and reputation as head of Big Steel were yet to materialize. Just now he was the respected, quiet former mayor of Wheaton, Illinois, the one-time Du Page County judge with a blossoming law practice, a matchless reputation for singular trail sense in that legislative labyrinth known as the Sherman Anti-trust Act: "Statutes erected as a wall Gary could turn into an arch," one contemporary writes.

One evening Gary did show up at the door of a fifteenth-floor room where Gates and others were in the midst of a lively session. Chips worth $1,000 apiece were stacked high around the table. "Louis," said Gary quietly to the waiter on duty, "tell Mr. Gates that Judge Gary is here and would like to join him and his friends."

The waiter went inside and quietly delivered the message. Gates, his eyes fixed on his cards, shifted his cigar. "Tell Judge Gary the game is going to be so high it will be over his head," he said.

Quietly the future chief of the great Steel Trust, the man destined to become the most widely quoted authority in the industrial world, turned back down the hall to the elevator.

Perhaps the biggest game in these private Waldorf confines took place in the late Nineties, and was not poker but baccarat. Some believe it to have been the largest single game of chance ever played. Baccarat being limitless in its players so long as new decks of cards are at hand, there were about a dozen players assembled in addition to Gates, L. N. Hueston, a Chicago financier, Loyall L. Smith, Colonel Lambert, Ike Elwood and William Henry Moore.

Dinner was served in the Astor dining room, and the game was played in Room 141 adjoining. Heavy drinking was not characteristic of this particular dinner or during the play, which soon began and continued until five the next morning. At dawn the banker took charge and counted the chips. The total? More than one million dollars!

At times such play might continue for five or six days, the players sleeping in relays. Meals were invariably taken on the spot, what to order left to Oscar or a headwaiter, the dinner as costly as could be reasonably contrived. It might start with Buffet Russe, green turtle soup and terrapin, for an entrée perhaps canvasback duck.

Crêpe Suzettes were Gates's favorite dessert and it was not unusual for fifteen or twenty of these luscious paperthin pancakes to slide down the Gates gullet in the wake of five stevedore-sized courses. Meals such as this with accompanying wines, spirits and liquors would likely have convulsed a normal stomach or chuted its owner neatly beneath the table. With dessert came champagne. Between meals there was Scotch. Yet these were serious gamblers—they knew the need of keen wits and agile minds.

Once the cards were dealt all boozing stopped. Usually. One tale lingers of a newcomer who started off drinking highballs and kept at it. He won. The more he drank the higher his stack; the least valuable chip was $100. At the game's finish he was too drunk to count and had a waiter do it for him. About $60,000. "Aw, hell," he said, half rising, "I thought I'd won a million," and with a sweep of his arm sent the chips flying, then sprawled flat on top of them, out cold. The other players watched in silence, then settled on the figure computed by the waiter.

His predilection for the House of the Bronze Doors meant by no means that Gates was a stranger at Canfield's, which about the time of the annexation of the Astoria behind the Waldorf's hyphen had moved from its Madison Square neighborhood up to 5 East 44th Street. Canfield had the reputation of being a "square" gambler—neither a crooked wheel nor loaded dice ever in his establishment.

In other ways Canfield was an unusual personality, esteemed for his love of art, his paintings, porcelains, bronzes, his warm friendship with James McNeill Whistler. In manners, dress and tastes Canfield was the

"Prince of Gamblers." Big losers might be invited to his private offices to share a consoling pint of champagne, but no consoling pat on the back, no "better luck next time."

Canfield told each loser that his loss was to be expected, that if he played again with the hope of recouping, chances were he would lose even more. Canfield saw no reason to pretend sympathy; his guests would return to the tables anyway. Honesty was the keystone of Canfield's valued reputation. Evidence of this is an interview he gave *The New York Herald,* the hard statistics showing the odds always favoring the house and virtually guaranteeing a profit to its proprietor:

"In business if you or I can lend money at five percent we think we are doing pretty well," said Canfield. "Every time a roulette wheel spins the percentage on a thirty-six-inch wheel levies five and five-nineteenths percent against the player. Therefore, you can say I get an interest on my money of five and five-nineteenths percent every time a roulette wheel is spun. If I have any patronage at all, you can imagine what interest I get on my money in any one night. All the house wants is to have the play last long enough and it will inevitably get all the money any player has."

Canfield's new five-storied casino with its tasteful appointments, its lavish free lunch, pleasant reception rooms and his reputation for fairness were compellingly attractive for well-heeled gamblers wanting a whirl at roulette, baccarat or cards, craps—anything so long as the game be sumptuous and exciting.

As noted earlier, the Canfield house imposed a limit which could only be waived by consent of its proprietor. At Canfield's, Gates won and lost staggering sums at baccarat, one of his favorite games. With the change of seasons Gates would appear at Canfield's summer casino at Saratoga. One remarkable evening Gates was loser by $150,000 before his luck began to change. With Canfield's acquiescence he upped the stakes, played doggedly, proceeded to recoup, emerging eventually $150,000 ahead. Until 1902 when a raid by a crusading young district attorney named William Travers Jerome put an end to Canfield's, Gates was its most faithful patron.

At poker Gates was not always so lucky. *The New York Herald* of March 1900 tells of a game in which Joseph Leiter, son of Chicago merchant Levi Leiter, bluffed Gates with a pair of sevens to the tune of

$80,000, a sum Leiter says was only part of a series of "retributory" poker games in which he took Gates for more than a million. At some point earlier, it seems Gates had muscled in and thwarted Leiter's attempt to bring off a coup in a Chicago wheat speculation; Leiter was out to get his scalp.

When questioned about this years later, a Gates aide could not recall any crippling Leiter attack. "Whatever Mr. Gates may have lost that winter to Mr. Leiter certainly did not pinch. A rise in both Baltimore & Ohio and Union Pacific stocks netted him between three and four million."

When the Stock Exchange closed at the end of its business day, the Wall Street offices of Harris, Gates & Company often became the scene of a stiff card game, sort of a downtown warmup for later Waldorf sessions mainly for visiting Chicagoans. Besides Gates and Ike Elwood, John Drake often would appear with an occasional accomplished New York poker player invited to sit in.

"By the way, what are we playing for?" one such visitor asked.

"One a point," answered Gates.

The visitor, it developed, came out three hundred and thirty points ahead.

"You'll get your check tomorrow, or surely by Monday," Robert Foy, Gates's secretary, told him.

On Monday at breakfast the winner opened an envelope and out tumbled Gates's check for $33,000. He broke out in a cold sweat. There must have been a mistake! He hurried to the Waldorf to question Foy. "You've made a mistake. This check is for $33,000!"

"Not at all," said Foy. "You were three hundred and thirty points ahead at the finish. At a hundred a point doesn't that add up to $33,000?"

"My God. A hundred dollars a point!" the man gasped. "I thought we were playing for a dollar a point!" Not satisfied with Foy's assurances he sought out Gates. "I'm a poor man. If I had lost this sum I might have somehow scraped it together but I can tell you it would have hurt like the devil. I don't feel right in taking this money. I got it under false pretenses," he protested.

"Cut it out," said Gates. "We had the game, didn't we? You won didn't you? You got the check, didn't you? Forget it."

The *Herald* of March 7, 1902, tells of a lemon pie which Gates and friends once ate that netted the pie maker $12,000. A telegraph operator named Kane, employed by the Harris, Gates Company, was permanently stationed at the hotel, his job being to watch the ticker and alert Gates and his associates of any noteworthy change in the market's trend. Kane was given time off for lunch, told to eat in the hotel dining room and charge his meals to Gates. But being a simple man, perhaps thrifty as well, Kane elected to bring his lunch from home. One day at noon, the market quiet, Kane was lunching alone, enjoying a thick slice of luscious lemon pie, when R. M. Rogers, the Harris, Gates office manager, sauntered in. The sight of Kane's pie proved too tempting. Seeing his mouth watering, Kane handed him half.

"That is the best pie I ever ate!" declared Rogers. "Where did you get it?"

"My wife made it."

Rogers had an idea. J. F. Harris, Gates's partner, had invited several important men to lunch the following day at the office. A luscious, home-made lemon pie, thought Rogers, would prove a real treat. "Do you think your wife would make me a pie like this tomorrow if I should send a messenger for it?"

"Sure she would," said Kane.

The next day a luscious lemon pie formed the centerpiece for a lavishly set table. Besides Harris and Gates, guests were L. N. Hueston of Chicago, George Randolph of the B & O and Theodore P. Shonts, later to become chairman of the Panama Canal Commission. Like small boys their eyes widened when they sliced up the pie.

"Just like mother used to bake," was Gates's appraisal.

"Excellent!" agreed Hueston.

"We must do something to immortalize this pie and its maker," said Shonts.

A second luncheon was scheduled for the next day with another pie of Mrs. Kane's making. Sated, happy, the pie satisfactorily tucked behind their generous vests, the guests lolled back in their chairs. Fired with gratitude for Mrs. Kane's culinary gifts they instructed Rogers to buy 100 shares of Northern Pacific to be held in the name of A. G. Pymacher ("a good piemaker") and present the stock to Mrs. Kane. The shares were promptly bought at once for 113¼.

The next day Northern Pacific began its sensational advance and

Mrs. Kane's shares closed at 120. The following day Northern Pacific reached 135 and Kane was getting nervous. After all, it was one fabulous profit for a pie. He spoke to Rogers. "Yes," agreed Rogers, "there is always the possibility that Northern Pacific might take a tumble."

"True," agreed "Mr. Pymacher." "On the other hand, it seems off to a brisk start. I know what I'll do, I'll toss a coin; heads we sell, tails we hold on."

The coin landed heads. The stock was sold and Mrs. Kane netted more than $12,000 for her pie! Our pie story does not end here.

The next day Northern Pacific stock really began to perform. Efforts of short sellers to stem its advance put many in a bind; frantic offers as high as a thousand dollars a share echoed through the Street. Had Kane held on to his wife's stock that wonderful pie would have netted her $87,000!

"The accidental is what occurs, but not always, nor of necessity, nor for the most part. It is obvious why there is no science of such a thing," said Socrates, equating pure chance as accident. Gates and his type, men of massive appetites, liked to gamble, they were stimulated by the thrill of it. But they did not care for pure chance as Socrates defined it.

True, one doesn't know which card may turn; that aspect of poker is pure chance. But a poker player does fathom his adversaries, or strives desperately to. He also knows something of the laws of probability . Skill at cards is in some direct proportion to one's ability to concentrate. Through a run of sheer chance skill at times may go down the drain. Hence the success of Gates's inebriate guest. Bereft of all capacity to concentrate, he wins nonetheless.

Financiers, those imaginative men who put together the great "trusts" of the Nineties, were not all of Gates's stripe. They were not gamblers. Many knew they were putting their money on a sure thing. The Nineties was the Age of Amalgamations much as the late 1960's was an Age of Conglomerates, neither in the long run providing the weal or the woe of capitalist America's economic system. Little businesses still become big, and big ones suffer hardening of the arteries.

Nevertheless, mergers, combines, consolidations, cartels or "trusts" were the order of the day. What Gates had done in forming American Steel and Wire, the Rockefellers with Standard Oil, Frick with the coke ovens of Pennsylvania, William Henry Moore with a series of royal flushes that produced the American Can Company, the Match Company and the National Biscuit Company. Even as rumors were being whispered at the Waldorf of a mammoth steel combine, Judge Moore had just put together his National Steel Company.

Moore, an Amherst graduate who'd served a novitiate of sorts in Wisconsin before moving down to Chicago, became the man with the formula, sort of the Booz Allen & Hamilton of his day. In striking ways Moore differed from many of his contemporaries. Cultivated, cultured, he was also a horse fancier of rare discernment, a fact which opened many social citadels to him in an otherwise rigidly cloistered New York Society.

Two others of consequence to this Waldorf coterie we have passed over lightly were Messers. Daniel G. Reid and William B. Leeds, also Chicagoans, founders of the American Tin Plate Company, another trust. Reid was what newspaperman then called a "high roller," a robust man of strenuous appetites, in tastes and temperament the precise opposite of his partner, William M. Leeds. In Chicago's Loop, dangerously near gossipy newspaper city rooms, flourished two notorious brothels. From time to time Reid would storm back into Chicago and take command of one or the other establishment and in the *patois du quartier,* "buy up the house." Then followed a riotous Bacchanalia, classicly replete with naiads and flute song, often lasting for a week. To top it all off, Reid might then take an ax and smash the piano and whatever else was within reach. Quietly the madam would tote up the damages and Reid, having sinned and now properly penitent, would write a fat expiatory check.

Aware of Reid's reputation as a "sport" and a high roller, suspicious Wall Street withheld from him the celebrity status awarded Gates. One day in 1900 Reid issued "buy" orders to his brokers for 40,000 shares of Chicago, Rock Island and Pacific Railway stock, stipulating that the purchase be geographically scattered among twenty widely separated brokers. Reid's calculated effect was to produce a flood of buying orders, encouraging tipsters to spread the word that a large pool had been formed to boost Rock Island to the rooftops, with not one or two but a hundred brokers apparently taking every share offered. Reid's ploy quickly took on the dimensions of those great bull movements market gamblers are ever on the alert for. Buyers rushed in. Rock Island soared thirty points.

Eventually, momentum gone, as ever, demand slackened, the stock teetered as Reid unloaded, and then started down fast. So rapid was its drop that many margin buyers who had bought on the upside could not cover. Scores were being wiped out while non-margin buyers found themselves in possession of a security they must either sell at a large loss or hold indefinitely in feeble hopes of its someday recovery. Stock Exchange governors promptly ordered an investigation. The only punishable offender turned out to be the dimwitted brokerage firm who had executed Reid's buy orders. It was suspended.

William B. Leeds, Reid's partner in the Tin Plate combine, was a strikingly handsome man whose notoriety was established in quite a different way. Unlike Reid he was not thought a "bad actor," a popular derogatory label for someone too frequently involved in shady deals. Leeds's leap into the headlines came about through his quite guileless purchase of a gift while vacationing in Europe. From its spies in Paris the United States Customs Service learned one day that Leeds had paid Bernard Citroen $360,000 for a magnificent string of pearls. Great care had been taken in selecting the gems, it was indeed a necklace fit for a queen. And now Mr. and Mrs. Leeds were aboard ship on their way home. Hot tips, which the Customs Service took pains to leak the length of Park Row, intimated to newsmen that a big smuggling story would break when the Leeds's ship docked. Ship reporters and photographers, along with an army of customs snoopers, were waiting on the pier.

Affecting disinterest, the customs official examined the Leeds's customs declaration. Aha, no necklace! Quietly inspectors separated the Leeds's luggage and ransacked it. Nothing. The deputy surveyor in charge was in a quandary; his European spies had been hitherto absolutely dependable. In fact, in his pocket was their cablegram stating that the jewels had left France.

Frustrated, the official became nervous. Leeds was a powerful man with many political connections. However much he might wish to strip and search the persons of Mr. and Mrs. William Leeds, such an affront just might abruptly change the direction of his career.

After a hurried, whispered conference, the deputy customs inspector walked over to Leeds and told him just what was on his mind. Smiling, Leeds took a document from his pocket and handed it to the official. It certified that William B. Leeds was purchasing a necklace in Paris from Bernard Citroen, the same to be delivered in New York, duty paid. Red-faced, the customs man apologized. Enjoying the official's discomfort,

Leeds slammed the door of their carriage and the couple headed for the Waldorf. Government sleuths now hunted down Citroen. Passenger lists of other ships were scrupulously examined. Sure enough, Citroen had entered New York two days earlier. Yes, he had brought in a package of pearls which had been examined, the duty paid, the pearls handed back to Mr. Citroen.

Noisily, the government filed suit. Citroen had not declared the pearls as a necklace but had brought them in loose in several containers. By law a necklace of this value would be dutiable at sixty percent whereas the duty on unstrung pearls was only ten percent. Receipts were produced showing that the loose pearls had been appraised at $225,000 on which Citroen had paid duty of $22,500. Had they remained a necklace he would have had to pay $135,000. Fraud! shouted the Treasury Department attorneys. The Citroen pearls should have been appraised as a necklace at $300,000, maybe even $360,000, at which figure the duty would have been $216,000, upping the cost of Mrs. Leeds's pearls, delivered in New York, to $576,000.

Indeed, by any reckoning $75,000 is quite a price for a piece of string!

For two years the newspapers headlined the case against Citroen. Finally, the courts ruled against the government: Citroen had complied with the law. Regardless of whether the pearls had once been a necklace, a tiara, a bracelet, or snugly in the wombs of their oysters, when Citroen brought them into the United States they were merely loose pearls. For years the Leeds pearls were the most famous jewels in America.

An element of mystery surrounds the early days of the greatest of all trusts, the United States Steel Corporation. Not its origins, not the motivations of its founders, not its principles. The mystery? What had prompted J. P. Morgan, taking lock, stock and barrel Gates's idea and Gates's formula, even Gates's companions, to offload Gates? And did that expulsion motivate Gates on to greater achievement, his forming of his Texas Company?

Gates and his cronies enjoyed doing things in *la grande manière;* anything worth doing was worth doing with a bang.

One afternoon John Lambert and Max Pam, lounging in the Waldorf lobby, saw Gates approaching.

"Want to make a lot of money?" asked Lambert.

Absurd question. Oscar, standing by, could hardly restrain a wry chuckle. Gates did laugh.

Lambert was serious. "You could make a lot of money and a great name for yourself, John, by organizing the steel companies."

Gates's smile vanished. He gazed intently from Lambert to Pam, then back at Lambert. He motioned them towards the Men's Bar. "Come. Let's have a drink," he said.

Lambert's question did indeed strike Oscar as funny. Did John Gates want to make a lot of money! The whole financial world knew of Gates's ruthless acquisitiveness. Even Morgan's eyes flickered when Gates's name was mentioned. Morgan had not forgotten that Gates's first Wall Street foray had netted Gates more than a million. None quicker than Morgan would recognize in Gates the cool cunning, the brash daring of the skilled speculator.

Gates also had an aberrant capacity for friendship; he was a man who'd sit all night at the bedside of a sick friend only to destroy him financially the next day. Morgan belived Gates to be totally insensitive, a gambler who would bet on anything—cards, billiards, trap shooting, horses, cotton, grain, coffee. Hadn't the New York Cotton Exchange been several times spun into paroxysms by Gates's speculations? Hadn't Gates's sharp practices in coffee trading twice thrown the Brazilians into panic? Hadn't Gates once structured a successful corner in hops?

On the New York Stock Exchange Gates's thrusts for the jugular had been equally savage. On one notable occasion after Gates had bulled the market for all it would take he intuitively sensed that certain New York banking elements were closing ranks along a hostile front; a sixth sense told him they were going to call his loans. Next morning at the market's opening gong, Gates quietly began unloading, sending the market averages down by more than ten points even though doing so depressed other of his holdings for a paper loss of $8,000,000. Had Morgan secretly been behind the banks' hostility? Why had these two fallen out?

Belief is that J. Pierpont Morgan was more than a little intimidated by John W. Gates.

John Gates was more than a compulsive gambler or reckless speculator. He was a great organizer, a born leader of men. When he put together the Texas Company he displayed for the Rockefellers' benefit considerable understanding of what they would achieve when forming their great Standard Oil combine. Enough to make them jittery. Gates's capture of the Louisville and Nashville Railroad from the Rothschild-Belmont syndicate was even more of a triumph. As an L & N investor, he had secretly had the railroad audited and his auditor's appraisal revealed that August Belmont had shorted its assets by $10,000,000. Quietly Gates went full speed ahead and got control, to the sorrow and unrelenting hostility of the powerful House of Rothschild, August Belmont's European employers.

Back to that conversation in the Waldorf Men's Bar. The drinks poured, Gates listened attentively to Lambert and Pam. What they said made sense. Yes, why not organize the entire steel industry, the whole process from ore mines and coke ovens to finished product—all aspects of it—rails, sheets, pipe, rods, wire, bridges, even the railroads and ore carriers that transported it, put it all together in one gigantic, super corporation! It would be the greatest industrial colossus ever conceived. Yes, he would call it the United States Steel Corporation. Along more modest lines, one fine example of what could result was Andrew Carnegie's successful combine of raw materials, mills and steel fabricators.

The challenge thrilled Gates. He knew at once he would need two things: First, assurance that his own American Steel and Wire stockholders would go along with the project. Second, bringing together interests so vast, far greater than those he commanded, needed the prestige of J. Pierpont Morgan. Gates would lose no time sounding him out.

Morgan found the plan intriguing. He admired many of Gates's associates, especially Judge Gary. Yes, agreed Morgan, the Carnegie combine should be brought in, perhaps first. Morgan confided that he had heard that Andrew Carnegie, wearying of the chase, was eager to retire, to spend his remaining years in the quiet splendor of his castle in the Scottish Highlands, play golf, ride, be serenaded by a private band of kilted pipers.

Carnegie's most trusted deputy was his faithful Charles Schwab, the son of a livery stable keeper who had come up the hard way. Morgan's and Gates's strategy was to beguile Schwab into an "accidental" meeting, sound him out as to the genuineness of Carnegie's wish to retire, and get some idea of Carnegie's price for his vast holdings. Meanwhile, Morgan would do his homework, learn all about steel, leaving to Gates and others details for putting it all together.

At Gates's suggestion Charlie Schwab appeared one day at the Bellevue-Stratford in Philadelphia where Morgan was supposed, accidentally, to run into him. But no Morgan. Instead, Schwab found a message from Gates saying that it had been snowing in New York and Morgan's doctor forbade his going out. Since Schwab had come that far, why not come on up to New York where Morgan would meet him at his library? Schwab went to New York, right into the Gorgon's lair, and he gave Morgan the answer he sought; yes, Andy Carnegie was thinking of retirement. Later, enroute home, Charles Schwab was plagued with worry—had he been indiscreet? How best to report this little unauthorized excursion to his chief? Carnegie might react negatively, even prove hostile.

Concerned deeply about this, when he reached Pittsburgh Schwab decided to resort to his long and valued friendship with Mrs. Carnegie, a friendship dating back to his boyhood when he would saddle up her favorite horse for her at the Carnegie summer cottage. Yes, he would solicit her advice. Mrs. Carnegie, a most agreeable lady, listened sympathetically.

"Why, Charlie," she said, "why not simply invite Andy for a golf game and tell him about it?"

The day for that game loomed anything but hopefully. The sky was overcast, patches of snow streaked the roughs and sandtraps, a typical autumn afternoon at old St. Andrew's. Carnegie heard the thing through, Schwab scrupulously studying his reaction as he explained it. At first the old steelmaker seemed depressed by the idea of retirement and idleness; Carnegie loved business, its unremitting chances for a good fight. Finally he said he would think it over.

The next day the two discussed it further. At length Carnegie scribbled on a slip of paper a figure, the amount of the proposed new Gates-Morgan combine's equities he would accept in exchange for his properties. Schwab hurried back to Morgan.

With only a quick glance at the scribbled figure, "I accept," said Morgan.

Meanwhile, Gary, who headed Federal Steel, had been installed in Morgan's offices and was busily lining up the other constituent companies. Although friendly, Schwab did not admire Gates; Gates to him typified a buccaneer, a totally insensitive, hard-nosed businessman who'd drive prices up through artificial scarcities then bludgeon the consumer. Schwab felt that Gates viewed all business transactions as a poker game where one told one's adversary nothing, in fact, took every means to deceive him, played ruthlessly to win. Schwab, Andrew Carnegie and J. Pierpont Morgan, were men of a different stamp. They played to win, vigorously, but by their code; the ends did not irrevocably justify the means. These three were churchgoing Christians; for all their patrician aloofness and seignorial airs, Morgan and Carnegie were humble men steadfast in their religious devotions.

Knowing this about J. Pierpont Morgan, his reasons for not wanting Gates on the board of Big Steel become less a mystery. He respected Gates's leadership abilities, his cunning, his knowledge of the steel industry. But Morgan feared Gates. Gates lacked those innate personal virtues which Morgan felt happy about. Moreover, even had he wanted to adorn Gates with a director's mantle (and everyone expected that he would), Schwab, ergo Carnegie, would have opposed it. Schwab had devised his own way of saying so.

Before negotiating the Morgan-Carnegie transaction, in a speech at the Manhattan Club Schwab lashed out at corporations who throttled competition by combines and trade agreements to create a monopoly, then jacked up prices to make a fast buck, a rebuke aimed directly at Gates, at Moore, and at several other steel industry promoters whose holding company control permitted them to double and treble prices. Indeed, if Morgan had countenanced such practices, plucky Charlie Schwab's criticism would have landed on him as well.

Gates, on the other hand, had built his huge combination of wire manufacturers by allegedly watering the stock, by closing down thirteen mills, then publishing pessimistic statements about the steel business generally in order to clean up on short sales of his American Steel and Wire stock. In Schwab's view, Gates personified dangerous and predatory influences that, unfortunately, prompted many corporate consolidations of that era.

Oscar, enjoying little more than a worm's eye view, rises to Gates's defense, praising his many private charities. But for philanthropies on the scale of Morgan's, or Carnegie's, or Frick's, or Rockefeller's or a legion of other financiers respected for their good works rather than their capacity to amass wealth, John W. Gates stands alone, if not unique, as one utterly ungiven to giving. If, as Oscar declares, Gates had many private charities, they remain unchronicled. In fact, of their wealthy patrons, other Waldorf-Astoria servitors remembered Gates as extremely penurious when it came to tipping, even below the standard fifteen percent.

As do most legends, What John Gates contributed to the Waldorf-Astoria image, spotlighting it as sanctum of America's greatest captains of industry, as favorite watering place of the Nineties, expanded its significance far more imaginatively than even George Boldt dared hope.

Morgan's affront sent Gates into exile. He left the Waldorf for the Plaza. Years later, during the summer of 1911, he was often seen in Paris, to which he'd migrated from Port Arthur, Texas, seat of his new Texas Company. But he was no longer the loud, energetic, flamboyant gambler.

Visibly ailing, Gates appeared subdued to the point of shyness, in pain even as he traveled from one to another of Europe's and America's best physicians. Their prognosis was unanimous. One suspects that when John W. Gates heard their verdict he said contemptuously, "Want to bet? Ten will get you twenty . . ."

Time leavens as well as heals. In 1978 Morgan's colossus, United States Steel, for decades America's largest corporate enterprise, reported revenues of $9.61 billion. But John Gates's final endeavor, that little company he founded at Port Arthur—Texaco—showed revenues of $27.92 billions!

The Coming of Oscar

The Coming of Oscar

$\mathcal{L}$egends growing up around revered institutions often have for their origin some intriguing event, imagined phenomenon, some exceptional personality. Where such viable embryos do not exist publicists and other legend crafters find it expedient to create them. Much as triumphal arches were erected in Rome: Needing one in a hurry, enterprising Romans simply took down an old one, stripped it of its flashier adornments, plastered new ones over them, then reerected it over on the other side of town ready for the triumphant entry of a new conqueror. For years archaeologists spent fruitless hours trying to decipher the Arch of Constantine, which depicts a time, actions and characters totally alien to the career of Constantine—Parthian captives prostrate at the feet of a prince who never carried his arms beyond the Euphrates, the head of Trajan emblazoned on the trophies of Constantine. It was all rather like Harvard's statue of John Harvard, Harvard's founder, seated in Harvard yard. Except that the likeness is not at all John Harvard's, no John Harvard founded Harvard, and where he sits isn't Harvard Yard.

Americans, as people everywhere, delight in phony legends and bogus folklore. At one point in the last century no fewer than nine Buffalo Bills toured across theatrical America. At St. Augustine, Florida, where legend has Ponce de Leon wading shore in 1513 in search of a Fountain of Youth, for years there was exhibited a great canvas depicting this epic event, even ruins of the fountain itself. Nearby, lines of tourists cheerfully paid to stand and gape at an excavated Indian burial mound displaying grinning skeletons, cracked pottery, flint weapons, trinkets of coral.

Not only did the excavators exhibit the diggings as authentic, the skeletons as the remains of genuine, vintage Seminoles, they even had them neatly laid out side by side—papa, mamma, little Indians, all holding hands!

[119]

The fact is Ponce de Leon never landed at St. Augustine; men from his ship seeking fresh water rowed ashore there but were greeted by such a terrifying rain of arrows they promptly sailed away. But whether there or at some other completely apocryphal site, Bluebeard's Castle, Jesse James's Hideout, Kit Carson's Saloon, automobile parking lots fill regularly season after season, disgorging thousands of smiling tourists queuing up, waiting to be separated from their money. What visitor to Hamlet's Castle in Denmark or the Count of Monte Cristo's dungeons on Chateau d'If or Juliet's balcony at Verona has not come away delighted to find these revered precincts yet intact, indeed, just as the mad prince, the intrepid count and the tragic lovers once knew them?

Hopefully some enterprising Englishman may yet discover the hole where Alice descended behind the White Rabbit. What a delight that would be! Or the cave where Pooh Bear "lived under the name of Mr. Sanders!"

Oscar of the Waldorf is a legend, handsomely embellished, brightly illuminated, but one of real substance, of straw enough for bricks. The world has probably known no greater hotel personality. When questioned about him today those who knew him from the Opulent Era remember few other personalities with such joy, such spontaneous smiles.

His name was Oscar Tschirkey. He was born in Switzerland where during his childhood he developed a compelling love for music and yearned to become a concert pianist. Lest one lament that esthetic frustrations detoured Oscar from the lyric Muse to instead become a celebrated *maitre d'*, such was not the case. For young Oscar once also harbored ambitions to be a weightlifter in a circus. At the piano he displayed ability. He did well with barbells, too. He took up bicycling, then wrestling.

Even after starting his New York career, fatiguing labors requiring him to be constantly on his feet and on the go, Oscar would spend his leisure hours bicycle racing on Kingsbridge Road near Yonkers—on the old high wheel bicycles. In fact, he once won the Gotham Wheel Association championship. So where once we saw a strapping, young six-footer, clean-shaven, his curly hair neatly parted, his large hazel eyes wearing an intense expression that radiated friendliness, we look again and see him as Oscar of the Waldorf, one of the most celebrated figures in New York for whose 50th wedding anniversary fifteen hundred national leaders banqueted in his honor and to whom the President of the United States dispatched a personal salutation.

Oscar was born about the close of America's Civil War in the Swiss village of Le Locle where his father managed a travel booking agency and his mother a well ordered and loving family menage. His childhood passed in nearby La Chaux-de-Fonds, a clockmaking community, with his upper schooling at Fribourg. Both parents having removed from German-speaking Swiss cantons, young Oscar, growing up in a region where the French influence was greatest, early on became bi-lingual. Life at Le Locle pretty much centered around its handsome inn long favored by many French, English, and American tourists. This and the fact of Oscar's father being agent for the French Line early exposed young Oscar to the Swiss world of professional hospitality.

From his father, an accomplished church organist, Oscar inherited his love of music and seemed headed for a musician's career. Fortuitously an older brother intervened. Brutus, having migrated to New York and prospered as a chef, wrote one day urging others of the family to pack up and come to America. Oscar's mother decided, Oscar's father concurred, and before very long we see Oscar and his mother aboard a French Line steamer at Le Havre, waving tearful goodbyes to his father on the quay below.

On his very first day in the New World three eventful things happened to young Tschirkey; he got a place to live, he got a job, and he fell in love with Lillian Russell—or at least a poster likeness of her. As often is the case of fantasy, this imagined attachment would remain with Oscar for several years, in fact for as long as he worshipped the glamorous beauty from afar.

Young Tschirkey's first job harbored the lodestone of success for his entire career. After regular working hours at Edward Stokes's excellent Hoffman House, where Oscar's novitiate scaled upward from bus-boy to room service waiter, to waiter of dining-room rank, to Stokes's selection of him for weekend service aboard his yacht. Stokes's yachting companions were affluent, convivial and strenuous.

Marathon poker parties featured many cruises on which Oscar alone was in attendance, usually resulting in their earmarking half the final game's jackpot for Oscar. More importantly, Oscar's talent for serving well and making friends readily brought him influential connections that never left him. Doubtless Stokes had selected Oscar because he knew he could depend on Oscar's discretion. When tiring of poker, Stokes's guests frolicked with dancing girls. Oscar's gaze would be forever seaward, his ears hearing nothing but seagulls.

Faithful in pursuit of his Dulcinea, Oscar left Stokes's service; one day he'd actually seen Lillian Russell get out of her carriage at Delmonico's; that would be the place for him! Alas, his Delmonico's assignment was the Men's Cafe and since La Russell did not dine in the Men's Cafe other years must pass before he'd even catch a glimpse of her.

Oscar liked Delmonico's, prospered, saved his money, and as the vision of La Belle Lillian receded, another younger, fairer, took its place. She was Sophie Bertish, a striking, handsomely proportioned young German woman whose brother owned a restaurant on Third Avenue along the route young Tschirkey must traverse twice each day.

Sophie, the restaurant's cashier, was stationed near the entry in full view and here Oscar would loiter, ever longer each time, his eyes on Sophie. Soon he began breakfasting there, breakfasts that began earlier and lasted longer. Before many weeks it was the theater once a week with Sophie, then Sunday buggy rides in Central Park, "when we could afford it."

Sophie was a popular girl, interested in everything and everybody. "And in those days to be engaged five years before marriage was not out of the ordinary," Karl Schriftgiesser, Oscar's biographer, reminds us. Whether or not out of the ordinary, Oscar and Sophie did not wait five years. Oscar had found the ideal girl. Her life was soon to become forever wrapped up in his, his extraordinary success, and the raising of their two fine sons.

Some years later a shattering experience rang down the curtain on Oscar's imagined romance with Russell, sparing him a violent encounter with Diamond Jim Brady who, as all New York knew, had extravagantly staked out his claim on the glamorous Lillian. The scene, the Waldorf; Oscar, at last, privileged to serve this magnificent couple. It was his big moment.

To Oscar's astonishment, Diamond Jim, reputed to have a gargantuan appetite, ordered sparingly; this diamond-studded, gregarious celebrity who neither drank nor smoked, asked only for a dozen raw oysters, a small filet mignon and one green vegetable. But Lillian! Alas, Oscar remembers it well: raw oysters, soup, fish, roast beef, two vegetables, sherbet, game salad, ice cream and cake, along with coffee and several glasses of wine. If love laughs at locksmiths it weeps at gluttony. From the experience Oscar would have no dreams of Lillian uncloyed by stacks and stacks of soiled dishes.

Oscar's first Waldorf encounter came one sunny morning in 1890. It was Easter and he and his father, who had recently arrived, joined the throngs parading Fifth Avenue, New York's traditional rite of spring. They would attend mass at St. Patrick's cathedral, to enjoy the finest organ music in New York.

Crossing 33rd Street they paused before a boarded-up construction site and Oscar wondered aloud what new structures would occupy it. "If you read the daily papers as carefully as I do," admonished the senior Tschirkey, "you'd know that William Waldorf Astor is going to put up a new hotel here. But, come, Son. Hurry. We'll be late for church." During mass Oscar's thoughts were of the new hotel—new jobs, greater opportunity, having long since concluded that before advancing further at Delmonico's several others senior to him must either retire or die and there seemed no early prospect of either event. These thoughts continued to occupy Oscar for the remainder of that well-remembered Easter. That night he went to bed resolved to seek an interview with Mr. Astor first thing next morning.

When Oscar of Delmonico's presented himself at the 24th Street offices of John Jacob Astor's heirs, Mr. Astor was not in, said the receptionist, but Charles A. Peabody, Mr. Astor's cousin and manager of William Waldorf Astor's holdings, sent out word that he would see Oscar; luckily Peabody recalled that Oscar had often served him at Delmonico's.

Peabody was impressed with a young man having foresight and aggressiveness to put himself in line for a job at a hotel three years away from completion. Yes, he promised, when the right moment came he'd see that Oscar got a shot at it. He kept his word. When Oscar was eventually put in touch with Boldt, Boldt's manner was grimly perfunctory. Could Oscar bring some letter of recommendation? Certainly. When Oscar's letter did reach the imperturbable Boldt, it gave him a very perturbable jolt; its signatories were the leading patrons of Delmonico's and the Hoffman House, the "Who's Who" of New York, including Mackeys,

Twomblys, George Gould, Chief Justice Andrews, Samuel Rea, president of the Pennsylvania Railroad—in all there were ten pages of signatures! Oscar was hired; two hundred and fifty dollars a month.

"I signed a contract, a little piece of paper I placed in my pocket that day would became the most important single document I had ever signed in my life. I was bursting with pride. Headwaiter at the Waldorf! Mr. Boldt and I talked for more than two hours; how many waiters would we need? What plans had to be made for the kitchen, pantry, dining room? What quantities of silverware—knives, forks, spoons—napkins, tablecloths, linen closets?

" 'Fresh flowers on the table, Oscar, always!' admonished Boldt. 'Promptness, courtesy . . . All waiters must speak French.'

"He recited some statistics: There are 530 rooms in the hotel, 450 of these are bedrooms, 350 with private bathrooms!

" 'It's a big undertaking, Oscar. Four million dollars have been spent on the Waldorf! We are going to prove that it was worth the investment!

" 'Anyone who wants to know the hotel business thoroughly must start at the lower back door where the packages of food come in, where the trash and garbage go out. He must work his way up carefully from that back door through the kitchen to the dining room, from the cheapest bedroom to the finest suites.'

"Any success I have had through the years largely came from what George Boldt taught me that first summer."

Oscar recited Boldt's catechism, his five cardinal rules:

First, always have sufficient hot water on tap to supply every faucet in the hotel simultaneously. ("There are more hot water cranks than any other kind.")

Second, never speak abruptly to a woman guest nor be indifferent to her complaints. A woman's attitude about a hotel is based on two assumptions: That she is there to have things done for her without any trouble to herself; that she can leave when she wants on five minutes' notice. A woman guest must be listened to. One fine thing about women guests—if they are not pleased they will say so in a twinkling while a man will sulk or mumble to himself.

Third, the guest is always right. Be as courteous to the man in a five-dollar room as to the occupant of the royal suite. "We have entertained a prince of the royal blood whose quarters occupied the entire third floor.

The Coming of Oscar

We have entertained a prince of good fellows in a single room under the roof on the fourteenth floor. And we have earned the gratitude of each."

Fourth, see that every order is obeyed with military discipline.

Fifth, know the name of every guest; remember it when he comes the next time.

Boldt had set his eyes on the international trade. He insisted that a man arriving from Berlin or Paris could come direct from the ship and know that his wishes were clearly understood. Oscar must hire no waiter who could not speak French, German and English. Oscar was then 36. At 38 he became the maitre d' hotel of the Waldorf-Astoria.

What is a maitre d'hotel? He is not a chef. Nor even a salad chef. Nor for that matter are his responsibilities exclusively confined to the dining room. In Europe's great hotels it was recognized that the proprietor needed a chief mate, one having supervision over the entire staff's performance. In American hotels this chief officer is also responsible for special functions. He is in fact, "master of the hotel"; he makes it go, for in Europe the owner-director , a personage often of gentleman-status would no more identify himself with the hotel's menial day-to-day functioning then might William Waldorf Astor be expected to do so. The maitre d' runs the establishment.

Oscar, whose warmth and cheerfulness emblazoned each arrival's remembrance of his first view of a festive Waldorf scene, brought into existence the velvet rope, that inoffensive but unyielding barrier beyond which no one passed without his recognition. He did not stand waving one end of it in his white-gloved hand as one newspaper caricaturist displayed him. Yet it was no less a scepter in his hand; until it lifted one was not admitted. Those for whom Oscar dropped his barrier and greeted by name were socially in, solid! Important men have paid and paid for that, just that tiny, obeisant salute accompanied by Oscar's joyous recognition. For two great decades Oscar greeted the noble, the wealthy, the accomplished. It was Oscar who saw to the wants of kings, princes, viceroys, presidents. It was Oscar who made them all his and the Waldorf's friends.

Only once did Oscar journey inland from New York. Boise Penrose invited him to come out and take a look at his handsome new Broadmoor at Colorado Springs; Penrose would perhaps have liked to lure Oscar away to manage his impressive new caravansarai. On another occasion, George

Boldt summoned his faithful lieutenant and promoted him on the spot to manager. That, too, Oscar declined, for a multitude of reasons, and Boldt had to retract his announcement of it to the press.

Boldt should have been perceptive enough to know that if Oscar were remotely stashed away in some executive management capacity the hotel's umbilical cord to its patronage would have been irreparably severed. Moreover, Oscar's gratuities, his stock market tips from grateful guests, perhaps netted him more income than Boldt's. Oscar did not build a turreted chateau for his retirement. He owned no group of hotels, no impressive portfolio of blue chips. His savings went into a modest thousand acre tract in the Catskills overlooking the Walkill. Those thousand acres sold today as building sites would pay for many mansions including the island on which stands the sepulcher of Boldt's unfinished castle.

When royalty arrived at the Waldorf, customarily a great red carpet unrolled from its door to the step-plate of the guest's carriage. This, needless to say, like every Waldorf event, was carefully rehearsed, the timing precise, everyone placed in position; the carriage would arrive, its door would open and instantly out rolled the carpet. On one notable occasion this didn't come off. All was ready, Boldt and Oscar by the entrance, uniformed figures at the curb stiffening to attention. The carriage arrived. The carpet unfurled, then halfway down it appeared a little tailor crouching to mend it. "Get that man out of there," Boldt said hoarsely. Oscar looked. Sure enough it was the same man, the same little upholsterer who would appear from nowhere just seconds before the arrival of some celebrity. There he was again plumped down, pretending to mend the carpet! Oscar lurched for him. Too late. From the carriage stepped His Royal Highness, Henry, Crown Prince of Prussia. Directly in front of the royal guest the little tailor leapt to his feet and with a majestic salute, in faultless German boomed, "Welcome, Your Highness, welcome to the Waldorf!"

Oscar's favorite tale was the drama of the Panama Canal that unfolded in Waldorf suites. Students will remember that a French corporation headed by Ferdinand de Lesseps, famed digger of the Suez, first tried to breach the isthmus with a canal at Panama and failed for want of funds. The engineering and surveying had been done, nevertheless, and from those years of effort the French hoped to salvage something with America's announced intention of splicing these two great seas.

Learning from the French failure Congress had all but decided to have a go at it, but through Nicaragua. Only Senator Mark Hanna, Republican boss of Ohio, championed the French route via Panama.

Hanna earlier had fought Theodore Roosevelt's election to the White House and as matters now stood, whatever the merits of the idea, if Hanna were for it Roosevelt's congressional supporters, still battling Hanna for control in Ohio, would surely oppose. Nevertheless, Panama seemed the better route; certainly United States engineers had much to profit from France's experience. Because a large sum of site lease money was involved, a vociferous lobby in Washington demanded that the Nicaraguan route be selected.

Knight errant of the French company's hopes was Phillipe Buneau-Varilla, a personable young engineer in his early thirties who had spent years in the Panama jungles, knew the terrain, the local politics, how to cope with the malaria threat. From his Waldorf command post, Buneau-Varilla, via Hanna, despairingly would see one senator after another recruited in favor of a Nicaraguan venture. Final voting was near.

Fate would intervene. Just days earlier the whole world was stunned by news of volcanic devastation in Martinique: Mt. Pelée exploded and within minutes an entire city, 38,000 persons, lay dead beneath a red hot sea of lava.

"—and Nicaragua has earthquakes," Hanna's men warned.

"Nonsense," replied the Senate's Nicaragua advocates. "Only rarely are there earthquakes and these but minor quivers. Nicaragua has no major earthquakes."

Earthquakes or no earthquakes, knowing Hanna was behind Panama's selection the Senate simply wasn't having any of it. That earthquake fable, said they, was dreamed up by Hanna and Buneau-Varilla. Nevertheless, to spend a fortune digging a waterway which an earthquake or another Mt. Pelée could obliterate in minutes would be foolhardy in the extreme.

At noontime one day a neat-appearing stranger walked into the Waldorf and asked to see M. Buneau-Varilla. "I must see him on a matter of great importance," he confided to Oscar. Oscar frowned. M. Buneau-Varilla was at lunch, he said, and had asked that no one without an appointment disturb him. The man insisted, Oscar relented, agreeing finally to try. Up he went to the Frenchman's suite.

"This man seems to have something of interest to show you," said Oscar.

"Okay, Oscar, if you say so, I suppose I must see him," Buneau-Varilla's tone smacked of sarcasm.

The stranger was shown up to the Frenchman's suite. "I have something for you," he said, after mumbling his name. "A postage stamp." He opened his wallet.

"A postage stamp!"

"Yes, look." He laid the stamp on the white tablecloth. It was a new one, a Nicaraguan, beautifully etched. "See anything interesting?"

Buneau-Varilla looked, his frown vanished, his eyes beamed, he grinned.

"How many of these do you have?" he asked.

"Just this one. But the Nicaraguan legation and their consulates may have others."

"Let's go!" whooped the Frenchman. Darting up from the table he put in an urgent call to Oscar, "Come up quickly."

When Oscar arrived the French engineer was writing a telegram to Hanna. "Oscar, please get this off at once. It is very urgent. I must get Senator Hanna here immediately."

Later Oscar was waiting at the entrance when Senator Hanna arrived. He led him to Buneau-Varilla.

"What's all this about Nicaraguan stamps?" stormed Hanna. "I can't delay the Senate's debate because of a postage stamp. It must go ahead tomorrow. You know that."

Buneau-Varilla waited until the Republican boss had simmered down. Then he showed him the stamp. All morning he had been out buying Nicaraguan postage stamps, every stamp that he could find of this issue. Then he had sent one to every member of the Senate. Senator Hanna listened, placed the stamp in his wallet and hurried to Washington for an urgent meeting of his supporters.

When the Senate opened debate on the issue the next morning Senator Gallinger got to his feet. "Yesterday I received this Nicaraguan postage stamp in the mail." He held it up for others to see; most had received one like it in their own mail.

"Today I ask my Senate colleagues if they can in reason vote to begin this colossal work in a country which has taken as its emblem on its postage stamp a volcano in eruption!"

There it was, Mt. Monotombe spraying the heavens with fire and

The original Bull 'n' Bear, later known as the Men's Bar. (Courtesy Waldorf-Astoria Hotel)

An opulent sitting room in the Waldorf of 1893, with Persian carpets, elaborately carved mantel, crystal chandelier, and a mixture of paintings ranging from Ingres to Remington. (Courtesy Waldorf-Astoria Hotel)

A caricature of William Waldorf Astor,
by Albert Levering, from *Life*, 1905.

John Jacob Astor III.

George Boldt, the original proprietor of the Waldorf. (Courtesy Waldorf-Astoria Hotel)

Oscar Tschirsky, the famous Oscar of the Waldorf. (Courtesy Waldorf-Astoria Hotel)

John W. Gates, known as "Bet-a-Million Gates," photographed in 1908 on a steamship pier with a friend. Gates is the man with the cigar, naturally. (Museum of the City of New York)

Andrew Carnegie. (Museum of the City of New York)

"Blue Bloods Playing for Blue Chips," 1895, a lithograph by A.R. Wenzell. (Museum of the City of New York)

.P. Morgan. (Museum of the City of New York)

Lillian Russell, probably as Cleopatra, photographed by Mora, date unknown.

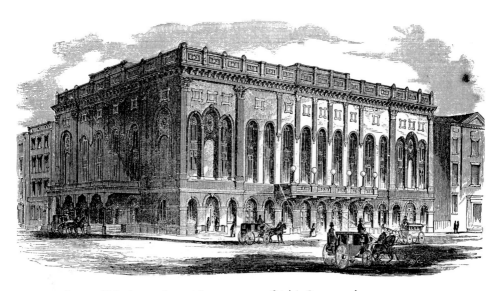

The Academy of Music, at the northeast corner of 14th Street and
Irving Place.

A charity ball at the Metropolitan
Opera House, circa 1884,
not long after the building's opening.
The seats on the orchestra were boarded
over to provide the dance floor.
(*Frank Leslie's,* January 12, 1884)

The Bradley Martin Ball, February 10, 1897. Drawing by Harry
McVickar. (Museum of the City of New York)

Room in a tenement flat, 1910. The Bradley Martin Ball, and others
like it, had done little to alleviate the plight of the poor. Photograph
by Jessie Tarbox Beals. (Museum of the City of New York)

The popular newspapers' view of the elegant goings-on at the Waldorf.
(The New York Public Library Picture Collection)

lava. Across its base the engraving depicted the canal's proposed route! Promptly the bill favoring the Panama route was called up. It passed with a whopping majority.

New York entertained such a star-studded galaxy of royalty at the Waldorf crowds constantly gathered around its impressive entrance for a glimpse at fame. A Waldorf telephone operator once answering a caller's request to be put through to the king asked, "What king, sir. We have two with us today." Not only had the monarchs of Europe become its faithful patrons, early in this century the Waldorf-Astoria became the New York address of most Latin American presidents and dictators. A resourceful State Department protocol officer named Nye seemed ever waiting in Washington, ready to descend on Boldt as quickly as confirmation of any state visit was official. The arrival of a dignitary to be feted in state would be first announced to the hotel by a simple five-word telegram from the State Department: "Mr. Nye will arrive tomorrow." That said it all. The Waldorf-Astoria measured up; it knew how to make any potentate's stay a memorable one, it also knew what security precautions had to be taken to protect its guests—royal or plebeian—from assassins, cranks, swindlers or scheming females.

For instance, with two thousand guests seated in the Empire Room, a battalion of waiters ready to go into action at the touch of Oscar's electric buzzer, there might have developed any manner of untoward happenings should the banquet's guest of honor have to thread his way through half an acre of humanity to gain the dais. This was cleverly avoided. Should a guest glance up at the head table, there, as though he'd suddenly dropped from the sky, sat the guest of honor, and no one had seen him enter. The wall immediately behind the head table, often draped with flags, hid a secret passage, a narrow door. Escorted by Oscar, the great of the world were led down a labyrinthine passageway to this door, which only Oscar's special key could open.

Today on state occasions if waiters serving the head table or those immediately in front of it seem distracted or inexpert, it is likely because most are not really waiters but detectives or Secret Service agents. However necessary all this, America may sigh for its halcyon youth, for untroubled days when President Grant would travel alone on the train up from Washington and would be seen greeting admirers in the old Astor House lobby, or those calmer days when President Cleveland cleared his White House calendar "for anyone wishing to drop in for a chat."

Whatever his reputation in food circles, Oscar was never a cook. His wife, he said, would never allow him in the kitchen! Yet several cookbooks have appeared with his imprimatur; in fact, once in a federal court lawsuit to determine whether a product was properly named "French ice cream" the verdict was reached entirely by the weight of Oscar's "expert" testimony. Such qualifications granted him by the public and the law courts Oscar never pretended to. As the dining room major domo, an expert at tossing salads, his critical eye on every dish insuring that it satisfied the most fastidious tastes, everyone supposed that Oscar had experienced a long career in the kitchen. What he did have was an assiduously pursued career of meeting important, often eccentric people and knowing how to please them, a talent that produces profits in the luxury hotel field.

An organizer? Schriftgeisser tells us how the play was run. Let's look in one evening on the Empire Room, or the Sert Room, or the Grand Ballroom. It is approaching zero hour, minutes before their doors will open, to several hundred—or several thousand—dinner guests.

Advance preparations for this moment mean the decorators will have already taken over, performed their magic, then made way for the florists who must not appear before five so that their blooms remain dewy fresh. Oscar's table by table inspection finds every teacup, every fork in place, every waiter clean, properly uniformed and in place. In the kitchens the chef's squadron awaits his signal. Right on the minute the doors swing open and Oscar's signal is flashed to the chef.

Food servers spring into action. In two minutes oysters are carried to the banquet tables by a column of waiters who file to their separate posts and stand quietly. Once the guests are seated to the first course, the "wine men," one for every two tables, march in to pour the beverage prescribed for this stage of the banquet, filling each wine glass before the guest has even unfolded his napkin. When it seems to Oscar that the majority of the guests have finished their oysters he touches another button. The bell is muffled; diners never hear it but every waiter on the floor does and instantly, as one man, they move out to take up the oyster plates. Less then four minutes elapse and these same waiters return with the soup. Meanwhile the wine men are pouring sherry.

"Guests might wonder how more than 1,000 plates of soup can be brought to the table steaming hot," said Oscar. "The mystery is easily explained. Just before we remove the oysters I call the kitchen. The soup cauldrons come up and the soup goes into the heaters on the carving table and there it stays until it is very hot. While the oyster plates are coming out the soup is being poured into plates. The waiters file by, picking up soup plates and the oyster dishes are hustled onto conveyors to the kitchen dishwashers. It is as simple as that."

In this way the dinner proceeds, each course trolleyed on hot wagons from the kitchen just before serving. There is no colliding of waiters. They march in regular columns. Each man knows his place in the column. He simply follows the leader.

"Of course, the normal routine may vary with some banquets," Oscar added. "A highlight of the Prince Henry affair was an elaborate procession of ices. I lined the waiters up in the hallway first, emphasized the solemnity of the occasion and rearranged the ices according to color, size and shape. When all was well I poked my head inside the door and nodded to the orchestra leader on the balcony.

"The musicians struck up a military air, the lighting changed, spotlights came on, and I gave the waiters their command to march. They filed into the ballroom and were greeted by a storm of applause for the beautiful creations they were carrying. Most acted with such dignity and gravity you would think they were carrying the head of John the Baptist on their trays."

In 1924 Oscar and his wife traveled across Western Europe. In Paris they shopped, admired the shops, strolled the boulevards, toured the galleries, parks and handsome monuments. Oscar also visited the Crillon's kitchens (noting that this hotel employed thirty-four cooks whereas the Waldorf-Astoria employed eighty-two), then they took the night sleeper to Switzerland.

"There is excitement in revisiting the scenes of one's boyhood," Oscar said, "whether it be in Michigan or Kansas or Switzerland and I was not lacking in sentiment that morning. Nature herself seemed to welcome us. The sky was clear and blue overhead and time had not dimmed the majesty of the Alps.

"There were old friends in Chaux-de-Fonds and in Fribourg, though my old teacher, the organist, had passed on. I walked down to the river to compare first hand the bridge of my boyhood with Brooklyn Bridge and the other bridges radiating from the island of Manhattan. I fancied I could hear the soldiers and their fascinating change of step as they marched across that bridge. My friends pressed me to remain longer in Switzerland. My roots of affection for that country were very deep. But I could not stay. I discovered that I was no longer a Swiss."

Seven

Their All for a Hyphen

$\mathcal{N}$ormally, the extravagant antics of America's society darlings make few waves, leave fewer watermarks. Says the average American, "It's their money. If they wish to blow it in some absurd, profligate display, that's their business."

Normally.

Two unreckoned factors conspired to make the Bradley Martin Ball an exception, one that produced turbulent waves and left ugly watermarks: First, its deplorably bad timing. When it came off, February 10, 1897, New York was in the throes of economic "panic." Thousands were out of work. Long breadlines, a depressing spectacle of good men and true reduced to beggary, snaked down Manhattan's back streets. America of that day had no government welfare programs, no old age pensions, no unemployment insurance. When hard times hit the misery of its destitute urban families was ineffable.

Another force ballooning the Bradley Martin Ball to dimensions of a *cause célèbre* was the press. "This appears the greatest Society news story in American history, the Bradley Martin Ball," historian Dixon Wecter reports. "It was an expensive and uncommonly vulgar display of wealth but there was no cogent reason for its becoming, from Seattle to London, the wonder of the English-speaking world. That was the caprice of the newspapers languishing in the doldrums between the Vanderbilt-Marlborough wedding and the Spanish-American War. It happened also to fall in an era of journalistic minutiae when every loop in a festoon, every bit of passementerie, and every restored feather of pheasant served á la mode, was tallied in loving memory." From London expatriate Henry James chortled agreement. Dismayed at the childish character of American society he too blamed "the newspapers alone for doing so much to feed it from day to day, with their huge, playfully brandished, wooden spoon."

[135]

The Bradley Martins came from Troy, New York, an obscure fact which they seemed pleased to leave omissible. Mr. Martin, with the slow growth of an invisible hyphen, "Mr. Bradley-Martin," was the son of a successful lawyer with a perceptive instinct for what went on in that perilous canyon of bulls and bears between Old Trinity and the East River.

Mrs. Martin was born Cornelia Sherman and shared that family's predilection for *la dolce vita*. The Martins, who'd budded in Newport and New York as favorites of Society arbiters Ward McAllister and Mrs. Paran Stevens, burst into full bloom in the salons of Europe with such èclat they wound up having a townhouse in London, a shooting box in Scotland, and their sixteen-year-old daughter married to Lord Craven.

At breakfast one morning during the winter of 1896 Mrs. Martin, distressed by what she was reading in the newspaper of the jobless poor, had a sudden inspiration. She would give a ball! "It would give such impetus to trade!" she exclaimed. And in less time than it took J.P.Morgan to accept Andrew Carnegie's offer, Mrs. Martin's project became grandiose and grandioser. In short order she did indeed manage to stimulate trade, to the extent of an estimated $369,200, which computes to about two and a half million of 1980's pre-shrunk dollars. Couturières in New York, Philadelphia, Boston, even faraway Paris and London, were soon busy creating Renaissance, Elizabethan, Van Dyke and Pompadour costumes lavishly adorned with seed pearls or spun with cloth of tissue gold and the shimmering lace traceries of Malines. The theme of the affair, the hostess decreed, would be the court of Louis XIV.

In due time a corps of messengers was dispatched bearing twelve hundred invitations to which only five hundred regretted. These do not seem to have been missed; the Martins were playing their averages; it's not how many but *who* comes. Unkind wags had it that Cornelia Martin had known for months that the Metropolitan Opera that night would premier d'Albert's *Martha* and peevishly wanted to show how effectively she could guarantee it a quiet reception.

Until the Waldorf appeared, providing New Yorkers an entire new dimension in luxury, society balls were not held in hotels. Fashionable Fifth Avenue and Murray Hill mansions had their own ballrooms, sumptuous precincts of gold and crystal, usually at ground level, that opened onto a formal garden or, come winter, a verdant palm-rimmed solarium. When affluent San Franciscans and Chicagoans built their turreted castles, ballrooms moved up and under the roof. "Here in the East," scorned snobbish Ward McAllister, "we don't go to balls by climbing up a ladder or going up in an elevator."

One day in late January, 1897, even as carpenters and painters were putting finishing touches on the stunning new Astoria, hyphened now onto the fabulous Waldorf, new platoons of professionals trooped in. It was their job to transform the Grand Ballroom into Versailles's Great Hall of Mirrors. Garlands of velvety orchids intertwined with smilax were strung the length of the room's golden cyma recta moldings. Walls became masses of clustered pink roses all but obscuring the forty-foot Ionic columns that separated the splendid chamber's six massive mirrors. Billowing from the ceiling were canopies of blue satin lavishly appliquéd with clusters of roses and clouds of asparagus vines. "Garlands of orchids streamed to the floor like the untied bonnet strings of a thoughtless child," a *Times* man wrote. Draped with pink roses and clematis freshly fetched up from Virginia were the great chamber's two large musicians' galleries. Beneath these several beguiling little trysting places were fashioned by artful arrangements of potted palms and heavy foliaged tropicana, their entrances half-hidden behind great jardinières of roses. The smaller ballroom adjoining was destined to become a throne room. On a gilded dais, a blanket of roses for its backdrop, a regal hostess and her splendidly starched, ruffled and bewigged husband would receive their guests.

At the Vanderbilt ball of 1893, Mrs. Bradley Martin had appeared as Mary Queen of Scots wearing a white bodice and a headdress of ruby velvet. That proving a great success, she now determined to do another Mary Queen of Scots but in a bodice of black velvet lined with cerise satin, an overdress opening over a white satin petticoat, a richly jewelled stomacher and a pointed cap of silver, plus a sparkling ruby necklace. Her *pièce de resistance* was a fabulous cluster of diamond grapes which once had belonged to Louis XIV. The Martins' fastidiousness was, alas, totally lost on the *Times* man who thought she was Queen Elizabeth and her husband some courtier, not the elegant Louis XIV he'd costumed himself. "There were several Louis XIV's including Bradley Martin," was another journal's put down. Outdistancing these was August Belmont in a full suit of Sheffield armor inlaid with gold which had cost him $10,000 ("Were the price tags showing on all costumes!" sniped the *London Chronicle*).

Anne Morgan, youngest daughter of J. P., appeared as Pocahontas in a beaded dress "made by Indians," though at no time would she display the original Pocahontas's delight in doing cartwheels in the nude. Honors in Indian attire went to her escort, R. W. G. Welling, impersonating Miantonomoch, an Algonquin chief, whose costume was "made under the eyes of Professor Putnam at Harvard." Chief Welling's great moment was his triumphal Waldorf arrival, standing upright in an open carriage, his face defiantly into the icy wind so as not to ruffle his magnificent headdress.

Mrs. Stuyvesant Fish came as Dolly Madison, Robert van Cortlandt was Charles II, and there were at least three George Washingtons. The Mrs. Astor, with $250,000 worth of gems aboard, wore a Venetian black velvet gown with contrasting white collar and cuffs. "The costume," smirked one reporter, "said to duplicate a Van Dyke painting, only made her look more like Mrs. Astor."

For two weeks before the ball neither those invited nor the newspapers could talk of aught else. Hairdressers charging $15.00 per hour had solid bookings starting as early as six a.m. One effulgent scribe reported, "family jewels were borrowed from decayed aristocrats in the South: The Oglethorpe gems arrived from Georgia and the Fairfax diamonds from Virginia," which seems unlikely, since the last Oglethorpe left Georgia in 1743 and the South's "decayed aristocrats" after Appomattox found themselves without jewelery or much of anything else.

The great ball story caught fire. Weeks ahead, London and Paris newspapers requested thousands of words to be dispatched by cable. Times readers were told in detail how carloads of orchids, roses and galax leaves arrived to transform the Waldorf. Town Topics gratuitously counselled prospective guests to polish up on their historical characters and to avoid solecisms. Hearst's New York Journal devoted most of its first five pages to the ball with sketches of the elegant costumes juxtaposed against some very plain Janes captioned "Some of the Four Thousand Who Were Not in the Cotillion."

Under a five column scare-head, "James van Alen Cannot Go!" the Times tearfully reported that this popular beau after much soul searching had decided that the recent death of a relative would not decorously permit his attending. Van Alen had been paired in the Quadrille d'Honneur which for several days he had been rehearsing at Mrs. Astor's under the critical eye of Professor Karl Marwig. But never mind. The very next day up from the dugout popped Fernando Yznaga, a competent van Alen substitute, and *Times* readers could breathe easier. Preliminary to the ball were a score or more private dinners, table settings variously numbering from sixteen to forty.

In joyous expectation candelabrum glowed and crystal sparkled in the great dining rooms of Mesdames Astor, Schermerhorn, Ogden Mills, Philip Rhinelander, Henry Sloane, Frederick Bronson, James Garland, Herman Oerlichs, H. Mortimer Brooks, William Pollock, Henry Parrish, Jr., and H. Livingston Ludlow.

Guests arriving at the Waldorf in their frigid, drafty carriages were quickly ushered into cozy dressing rooms where professional costumers and make-up artists stood ready to mend the rigors of weather and transport. Soon all was ready for the grand entrance!

The atmosphere was charged with excitement. Their passage flanked by approving smiles and admiring glances, as each guest approached the throne room dais a liveried page, summoned from Seventeenth-Century France, cried out the guest's name and particular character he represented, careful to specify whether the costume be from the Seventeenth or the Eighteenth Century of the Sunshine King's seventy-two year reign. Punctuating this scene were frequent, sulphurous explosions, for stationed here was Gilbert, Society's photographer, with twenty-six assistants to get it all on film. Background music for this regal scene was provided by the Eden Musée Orchestra.

In the Grand Ballroom two large orchestras faced each other from the room's opposite ends. One was under the baton of a young Irishman named Victor Herbert, whose musical career, begun as a cellist in Stuttgart, was destined to win the hearts of all America with "Babes in Toyland," the first of ten great Victor Herbert musicals.

In the prescribed manner of all formal balls, dancing began with the quadrilles, a folk dance first seen in a Paris ballet. That *Quadrille d'Honneur* which Mrs. Astor had organized was appropriately led by Mrs. Bradley Martin whose equally appropriate partner was John Jacob Astor III, he on whose boards the dance was trod. Flanking these two in the double figure were Wilsons and Tailers and Wadsworths and Mortons and Hitchcocks and Warrens and Stewarts and Fishes and van Cortlandts and, as previously bulletined, Yznaga batting for van Alen. Forget anyone? Sorry.

Bringing up the rear came that irrepressible Harry Lehr, the erstwhile champagne salesman whose meteoric social climb was launched when he frolicked under the stars in Baltimore's Mount Vernon Place fountain with the beauteous Louise Morris.

Successive quadrilles gracefully complimented the organizing talents of Mrs. Edmund Baylies and Mrs. Frederick Bronson, the first enlisting Ogden Mills, Mrs. John Jacob Astor, Mrs. Cornelius Vanderbilt, Mrs. Henry Sloane, Miss Edith Morton, and Miss van Rensselear, respectively, with Messrs. H. D. Robbins, Worthington Whitehouse and Alfonso de Navarro. An arresting number, led by Mrs. Bronson, wife of Westchester County's pioneer poloist, would introduce the season's debutantes: Miss Josephine Brooks, Miss Evelyn Sloane, Miss Alice Babcock, and Miss May van Alen whose partners included a Cutting, a Sloane, a Livingston and a Hoppin.

As expected these exhaustions would soon dispatch the celebrants to the punch bowls. But only briefly, for already trumpets sounded summoning dancers for the cotillions. In the first of these Mrs. Bradley Martin's partner was that durable Society favorite Elisha Dyer, Jr., who four years earlier had commanded the corps of ushers for the Waldorf's grand opening; whether New York or Newport, Bar Harbor or Bermuda, any Society ball without Elisha Dyer, Jr., in a starring role was as unlikely as a Wall Street syndicate without the House of Morgan.

It was now midnight. Liveried footmen passing among the guests distributed jeweled favors, a gracious American custom to prevail years after quadrilles and cotillions had given way to fox trots and tangos. For supper guests would file into the Palm Garden, its great fireplace a blaze of roses and acacias, with centerpiece for each of the hundred and twenty-five individual tables a massive bouquet of American Beauties.

"Square dances having been laid upon lavender-scented memories, now the round dances," wafts one whiff of journalistic scent. The pace quickened. First the polka, that joyous romp whose arrival on the banks of the Seine from Bohemia had brought all Paris into the streets for three days and nights of ceaseless revels. Now the schottische, a sort of wound-down polka. Then a mazurka, another Polish import, and finally the waltz. Albeit in tempo as langorous as the calm flow of the Danube, the waltz being the first ballroom figure two persons of the opposite sex would dance exclusively together, Victorian England had outlawed it, a proscription which remained until the Czar Alexander I gave it St. Petersburg's official cachet.

Native American contributions to these cherished treasures of Terpsichore include something called *The Washington Post,* more familiar as newsprint or a John Philip Sousa march than a ballroom dance selection, and the Two Step, neither of which today's dance masters can describe. Not for yet another decade would appear the sentimentally dreamy American waltz which every young lady would reserve on her prom program for her best beau.

Even farther in the future waited the dependable Fox Trot, a "slow gait followed by quick, short steps, much as a horse does when passing from a walk to a trot"; explanation enough for that America whose horse population equalled that of its biped.

All in all the Bradley Martin Ball proved innocent enough—a decorous, ritualistic affair, one to evoke nostalgic sighs that events of such social grace and splendor have all but disappeared from the American scene. Some among those Waldorf celebrants did note a few contretemps. One guest too frequently at the generous wassail, a robust reveller costumed as a Scot replete with kilts and sporran, who'd gallantly whirled through polkas and mazurkas, passed out cold on a couch snoring like a leaky bagpipe. Snickering merrymakers would now observe that this somnolent Scot's outfitter had neglected to include his breeks! Other cavorting cavaliers tripped over their swords, and poor Katie Brice, lavishly costumed as the Spanish Infanta in yards of starched crinoline, to her great distress discovered that she couldn't sit down! Reporters also noted that James Lawrence Breeze, recently in the news for his dinner party at Sherry's where an underage female "covered only by the ceiling" popped up out of a pie, strode in tonight as Henry VIII, "wearing white satin seed pearls and a fascinating leer."

At Mrs. Astor's costume the *World* marvelled: "It was perfectly astonishing how Mrs. Astor managed to find a place for so many jewels. Rather than the logical spot her jeweled stomacher was worn on the bosom and covered her like a cuirass."

Generally, as a night of fun and frolic, most participants rated the Bradley Martin Ball as anything but. Dullsville. Complained one, "It was decorous to the point of ennui. Its guests acted like children afraid of mussing their clothes."

[141]

Not so all. With supper still being served by Oscar's hand-picked two hundred and fifty servitors, long after five a.m., New York's workaday world would smile at the antics of costumed young blades manfully conveying one indefatigable old Bacchus those few yards up Fifth Avenue to liven things up at the Knickerbocker Club. Four hundred carriages having been hired by the Bradley Martins that their guests need not keep their own coachmen up all night, were to be seen threading through uptown traffic far into the next day exhibiting strangely outfitted, jaded but gleeful remnant revellers.

As an extravaganza the Bradley Martin Ball was not exceptional. By no means was it the most lavish of New York Society balls. Compared to the great spectacle honoring the Prince of Wales at the Academy of Music in 1860 (when the sagging floor almost caved in), or to Mrs. Schermerhorn's fabulous Louis IV production, or the Grand Ball in Behalf of the Sufferers of the Russo-Turkish War given by Ladies of the Society of the Cross and Crescent, or Ward McAllister's *chef d'oeuvre,* the New Year's Ball at the Metropolitan Opera House in 1890, or Mrs. Astor's great ball of February 1, 1892, when only four hundred guests could be invited because of her ballroom's modest dimensions (which incidentally, apotheosized that number Four Hundred as the parameter of New York Society).

Compared to these the Bradley Martin spectacle was no great shakes. Nor for all its arboreal splendor did it rival other feats of decoration at the Waldorf. Compare it, for example, to Randolph Guggenheim's dinner for eighty costing $250 per plate, when real nightingales, blackbirds and canaries sang in a grove of transplanted rose trees, where hyacinths and tulips bloomed, where arbors, bounded by hedges of fir, were hung with clusters of hothouse grapes, where rubies adorned golden matchboxes and vinaigrettes were distributed as favors, where the dinner service was gold, where real Neapolitans in native costumes strummed guitars and filled the night with songs of Sorrento. Or Henry Lukemeyer's seventy-two guests dinner, costing $10,000, with participants seated around a great table billowing with blossoms, its center an oval pond thirty feet long where four swans, drugged to render them tractable, brought from Prospect Park, serenely swam until they began fighting wildly and had to be chased off the premises. Frederick Townsend Martin (unhyphenated brother of Bradley) remembers another Waldorf dinner where each cigarette was rolled in a one hundred dollar bill on which the initials of the host were engraved with gold letters. At another each guest discovered in one of his oysters a magnificent black pearl.

In *Seventy Summers* Poultney Bigelow recalls an occasion when flunkies in knee britches and powdered wigs passed around jeweled cotillion favors from Tiffany "as though these were bonbons or glasses of lemonade."

The Bradley Martins' mistake was bad timing. If all seemed harmonious and well-ordered in the Waldorf Grand Ballroom, elsewhere that night numerous volcanoes of righteous wrath were ready to erupt. Indeed, several already had. Just days before hadn't Henry Clay Frick narrowly escaped death at the hands of a murderous assassin? And hadn't Mrs. Martin received threatening mail? Though reports of a bomb at the Bradley Martin home that morning had proved groundless, all the downstairs windows of the Waldorf were ordered boarded up, and under the personal supervision of Police Commissioner Theodore Roosevelt—an up-and-coming politician whose good political sense told him where his station should be—a cordon of New York's Finest ringed the hotel. Costumed Pinkerton men mingled among the guests; no one was admitted without first passing the scrutiny of Ward McAllister's Cerberus, an almost faceless individual known only as Johnson, an experienced arbiter of Society credentials, and Police Captain Chapman, ever vigilant lest some armor-suited Henri de Navarre turn out to be Danny the Dip.

During the preceding weeks, while the naive Bradley Martins dished out tidbits to the press, never for an instant did they suspect that several publishers, puckish James Gordon Bennett for one, had discovered vast reader interest in the prodigalities of the upper crust. Of this Bennett senior had long since been aware. Once, at Newport, with the connivance of a reluctant host whom he had threatened with blackmail, Bennett smuggled a reporter into a fashionable party and came off with some very spicy copy. Such transgressions then mattered much, especially to Philip Hone. Bennett, warned Hone, was out to ridicule wealth and fashion, to release the social revolution that was ever boiling beneath capitalist society's bouncing lid. Hone predicted that journalism would destroy the exclusiveness of a clique which regarded its dinners and balls as no more the public's business than its bankruptcies and adulteries." What Hone did not foresee was that Society would peaceably pass from anger to tolerance, thence be pleasantly seduced at seeing itself regularly written up. In a show of fairness Bennett junior had now agreed to meet Society half way; subordinating mockery to extravagant descriptions of pomp and grandeur. Tongue in cheek, perhaps, Bennett faithfully printed Society's reports just as he was handed them. The result was hilariously devastating.

In their discovery that little so agitates mass circulation as stories of prodigality and high living, the Bennetts were not alone. William Randolph Hearst, arriving in New York with his *Journal,* decreed that his staff would depart from old formalities and henceforth call Mrs. Fish "Mamie," and Mrs. Oerlich "Tessie." Hearst's frontier familiarity was at first indignantly resented. "But," noted Wecter, "the dignity of Society like that of its new collapsible opera hat proved surprisingly adaptable."

Would the ball cause riots? Were anarchists threatening, or was it all a false alarm? Had the police overreacted? Certainly the mood of those hardy spectators who shivered in the cold outside the Waldorf vigorously applauding these magnificently gowned ladies and their plumed, monocled, bemedalled and bewigged escorts was far from anarchist. When noble Chieftain Welling arrived with his feathers intact they actually cheered. Only one protest rally was taking place. The Nineteenth Century Club convening at Sherry's met to discuss "Culpable Luxury." Its president, John A. Taylor, quickly put matters into perspective: "Inasmuch as two of your lecture committee were not invited to the Bradley Martin Ball they thought it might be well to hold an overflow meeting here tonight and make it the subject of discussion. . . . Luxury is that which somebody else has and we ourselves cannot afford. But that is a matter which will be left to the gentlemen who will discuss it for us." Speakers were Professor Franklin H. Giddings of Columbia University and John Graham Brooks of Boston. The debate, a remarkably scholarly one, expressed alarm at the threat to Republican institutions this extravagant bacchanalia, now in full swing at the Waldorf, might become.

"The warning seems not to have penetrated its walls," quipped Henry Collins Brown. "At least none of the night's gay cavorters appeared on Fifth Avenue in sackcloth and ashes."

Smug? Premature? Isn't it always disarmingly calm in the eye of the hurricane? For if no bombs exploded in New York that night, no thousands of voices chorused throaty street chants, no bare-bosomed *citoyenne* mounted the barricades, it was because the furor the press and the pulpit had ignited earlier was slow-fused. It went off ten days later, exploding like a blockbuster, causing sympathetic detonations across the continent.

First outcries were shouted from the pulpit. "The idea of spending a fortune on a single dance where gluttony and drink were the main pursuits while thousands nearby were starving!" raged one. Carefully noting the public sensitivity to this theme, other rabble-rousers were prompt to pick it up.

Hoping to lay it all to rest, the Reverend W. S. Rainsford, rector of fashionable St. George's Episcopal Church and a tireless advocate of moderation, warned, "This affair only draws attention to the deepening gulf which separates the rich from the poor. It is hardly to the point to talk of getting money into circulation."

Only Bradley Martin's brother, Frederick Townsend Martin, would counterattack. He praised his brother's prodigality "which dazed the entire western world." Eventually, he too, recanted. In *Things I Remember,* some years later, he condemned the spectacle as manifesting "the power of wealth with its refinements and vulgarity everywhere."

At the outset the furor was localized to New York. Now came *Collier's* rebuke. A drawing by William Balfour-Ker graphically depicted the ballroom revellers shrinking in horror at the sight of an angry fist thrusting upward through the dance floor which rested on the bare bleeding backs of the downtrodden. Quickly the *Collier's* caricature was syndicated.

In the San Francisco *Examiner* Edwin Markham's epic poem *The Man with the Hoe* fortuitously made its first appearance. Markham's intent was simply to give life to Millet's famous painting of the toiler brutalized by wealthy oppressors. Markham's verse swept across the nation, inevitably appearing on the same page with the *Collier's* cartoon and editorials condemning the Bradley Martin extravaganza.

Hitherto unknown, or at least, unheard from, college debating societies emerged in print to argue whether this latest Society bash might be symptomatic of an America with perverted social values. In the quiet, detached manner of politicians (once they're elected) New York City Fathers met and doubled the Bradley Martins' property taxes.

Nor would the furor cease until the Bradley Martins forever quit these shores. On the frivolous side, Oscar Hammerstein I produced a rollicking satire, "Bradley Radley Ball," in burlesque at the Olympia which audiences found far more fun than the ball itself. The Brahmans were reassured by the *London Chronicle's* applause: "We congratulate New York Society on its triumph! It has cut out Belshazzar's feast and Wardour Street and Madama Tussaud's and the Bank of England. There is no doubt about that!"

Popular dissatisfaction and their taxes both on the upsurge, the embittered Bradley Martins, as ingenuously isolated from popular moods and humors, were soon to follow William Waldorf Astor into permanent exile. Defiant even as they bounced in the tumbril, Bourbons to the end, before taking ship the Bradley Martins gave a farewell dinner for eighty-six persons costing $116.28 a plate, prompting Pulitzer's *World* to fire a *coup de grace:* "A dozen men were present at that dinner worth upwards of ten million, twice as many with five million, and among the grand total of forty men only a bare half dozen were not at least millionaires. . . ."

Here a provocative corollary inserts itself. New York's first *Social List* published slightly more than a hundred years earlier was a roster of educators, writers, clergymen, military leaders, world traders and statesmen. Not a single millionaire was included.

The Bradley Martins' flight into exile would not be Society's last. Other extravagant socialites on whom friendly, fickle Fun City would vent displeasure were destined to seek the solace of a more understanding, or at least more indifferent, Europe. James Hazen Hyde's $200,000 ball at Sherry's in 1905 all but wrecked his father's highly profitable Equitable Life Assurance Society to which young Hyde had succeeded as principal stockholder, and Hyde, too, went forever into exile.

Did Society learn anything from the Bradley Martin fiasco? Interpreting "Society" as a simple euphemism for gregarious folks with money, there has been little evidence that it did. Persons with wealth seldom behave any more sensibly than those without it. Often bored with itself much of the time, doomed by idleness to suffer ennui in larger doses than their fellow money grubbing mortals, Society, having both the money and the desire to indulge excesses, is the sooner tempted. At times it exhibits an insouciance amounting to contempt for public favor. For example, Harry Lehr's Canine Dinner at which socially-elect dogs, including one wearing a $15,000 diamond-studded collar, dined on imported *paté de foie gras.* Another to tower in the annals of low comedy was Mrs. Stuyvesant Fish's formal dinner honoring "Prince del Drago, a visiting dignitary," where guests solemnly trooped in to find in the place of honor a monkey attired in full dress. Similar honors go to addlepated, bon vivant C. K. G. Billings for his horseback dinner at Sherry's. On this occasion the restaurant's big fourth-floor ballroom had been expensively converted into a woodland glade replete with trees, shrubs and sodded turf. As Billings's guests arrived, booted and spurred, waiters liveried as groomsmen escorted them to a great circular manger of sweet hay around which were tethered saddled mounts. On the pommel of each saddle a small dining table was affixed, and solemnly seated in their saddles the stalwarts of New York Society, or some of it, dined in an environment which, despite hurried shovelings, soon looked and smelled more barnyard than banquet hall.

Whether from the chilling influence of a vigilant Internal Revenue Service or by virtue of its reaching maturity, America's wealthy seem less disposed to lavish display. Occasionally the prodigality of some reveller will break into print. Take Palm Beach's George Munn. Suffering one day in Paris an acute attack of homesickness, Munn hopped aboard a Boeing 747, bought up all the seats and commanded "Home, James, and no stops." Munn's ticket cost him $177,000.

And today many doting fathers go all out for debutante parties, launchings often planned as much for their news splash as for ferreting out a suitable son-in-law. The Misses Charlotte Dorrance, Eleanor Post Close, Gloria Gould, Barbara Hutton, among others, were sent skimming down the ways at monumental expense. Another riot-provoking affair was the début ball of Miss Helen Lee Eames Doherty, coming as it did during the Great Depression of the Thirties. The setting was Washington's Mayflower Hotel; the cost topped $100,000. Warm-up for the big event was Miss Doherty's intimate little dinner for a dozen friends, to each of whom she gave a custom-built Ford cabriolet whose sides were painted with hunting scenes, reserving one for an absent admirer, Alphonse XIII, sometime King of Spain.

Reading accounts of the Bradley Martin brouhaha, William Waldorf Astor would have indulged a wry smile. He had learned. Left to the press, popular moods could be as readily stimulated towards contempt as envy.

"You have broken my confidence!" he once stormed at his friend to whom he had leased the Belvedere. "You have given an interview to the newspapers!"

In three-score years of spectacular galas, the Waldorf-Astoria has been providentially spared other major social aberrations. Unscathed, it rode out the Bradley Martin storm. With admirable aplomb, its management elected to bite the bullet, not the hand that fed it. Ceremoniously it named their little throne room the Bradley-Martin Room, thus formally conferring on the Bradley-Martins their longed-for hyphen.

Eight

The House Dick

$\mathcal{S}$he was about thirty, stylishly dressed and spoke with a trace of a French accent. Costly jewelry she wore tastefully without flaunting it. Her poise and manner bespoke education and refinement. She registered simply as "Mrs. Maignen, Philadelphia" and selected an expensive suite.

From the moment of her Waldorf arrival she became the object of much quiet admiration. One day she went shopping among the Fifth Avenue jewelers and with expert discernment selected $40,000 worth of diamonds at Tiffany's and $60,000 worth of gems at another well-known jeweler's. In both cases she directed that her purchases be sent to her hotel, saying that if she were not in her suite when they were delivered, her purchases would be paid for at the desk. The jewelers saw nothing strange in this; she had an aura of wealth, the stones she selected were proof of the real connoisseur.

The jewels were delivered promptly, but Mrs. Maignen was out. Neither had there been money left at the desk to pay for them. After recovering from his surprise the cashier professed ignorance of the entire affair; paying out $100,000 and charging it to the room of a guest unknown to the management is not the practice of any well-regulated hotel. Soon the jewelers were on the phone to the hotel. Politely they explained their wish to complete delivery of the gems brought back by their messengers. They wanted their money. The whole transaction seemed extraordinary enough to invite looking into. When Mrs. Maignen returned to the hotel, Captain Joe Smith, Chief Security Officer, went to her suite.

It was as though she expected him. She opened the door promptly and politely invited him in. As Smith stepped inside, she slammed the door, locked it, and put the key in a pocket in her dress. Then stepping back out of reach but close enough to be sure of her aim, she swung around facing him, a revolver in each hand.

[151]

"You wretch," she hissed, teeth clenched, "why do you insist on pursuing me?"

Smith stared, speechless. He had never seen the woman before. Before he could stutter a reply, "You've persecuted me long enough," she muttered. "I am going to put a stop to it. When I count three I will kill you!"

Her expression was wild, terrifying; Smith knew he was dealing with a maniac.

"One!" she counted, her eyes coldly searching for some sign of fear in him.

Smith watched her closely, looking for some sign of nervousness, some false move to give him the chance to grab those guns.

Quietly Smith tried to talk her out of it. She was confused, he said; he had never spoken to her before. He had only seen her this once since her arrival. So, it could not have been him; perhaps another man who looked very much like him had been pursuing her. He had seen this double of his just a few minutes earlier; in fact he might right now be down in the lobby.

"Why don't we go downstairs together and get him?"

"*Two!*"

Joe Smith felt beads of sweat popping out on his forehead. He prayed that something miraculous would intervene.

Just as she formed her lips to count "Three!" the catch on a window-shade roller behind her worked loose. Up flew the shade, clattering like a machinegun as it spun against the molding. For a split second the woman took her crazed eyes from Smith. With a leap Joe seized her wrists, wrung the guns free and shoved her rudely into a chair.

Without pistols the woman became suprisingly quiescent. Now, wondered Smith, how to get her quietly out of the hotel and into the psycho ward at Bellevue.

Soothingly he suggested she accompany him into the lobby. Together they would find that man she'd mistaken him for, the man who had been pursuing her.

She agreed. Taking her firmly by the arm Joe steered her downstairs.

"If you will wait quietly in my office," Joe said, "I'll bring this man to you."

She nodded. Joe signalled a bellman. From his office a door opened directly onto the street. Quickly they hustled the woman into a cab and headed for Bellevue.

Before leaving her room Joe had seen the woman pick up her handbag. As the taxi sped along Joe noticed her fussing with it. When she opened it he snatched it away. Inside was a third revolver, fully loaded.

"I intended to kill you with that," she said evenly. Joe's answering smile was a mixture of relief and indulgence. Not so the bellman. Seeing that gun, realizing how close had come his possible demise, this worthy almost went into cardiac arrest. He was shaking when they reached Bellevue.

In the admissions office the woman suddenly went berserk; grabbing up a letter opener she made a dive for Smith. Two powerful matrons were needed to secure her in the psycho ward.

Policewomen searching her found a dozen little pockets on the inside of her skirt filled with bits of colored glass. Mixed with these were real jewels. Hurried inquiry revealed that she belonged to a reputable, wealthy Philadelphia family. As promptly as they were apprised by phone of her predicament they dispatched someone to take her in hand.

"I was more than a bit nervous after it was all over," remembered Captain Smith. "I'd the unreal feeling that this wasn't happening. But those two guns loomed very large. I'd no doubt she would start them going if I moved. At such close range she couldn't miss!"

* * *

An important catalyst in the rapidly crystalizing Waldorf tradition was Captain Joe Smith, for thirty-one years the guardian of the hotel's most precious possession, its reputation. Years of labor and great sums of money will go quickly down the drain once a hotel, wittingly or no, becomes the scene of crimes or scandals. Owners of a downtown Cleveland hotel, once highly respectable, date its decline from the day its name was bandied about on a local vaudeville stage. In New York, "The Girl From Rectors" was title of a song inspired when its composer, Paul Potter, alighting from a cab saw a smashing young beauty emerging from that famous restaurant-hotel. The song became a hit nationwide. It made huge profits. But it dealt a mortal blow to the reputation of Rectors; respectable traveling men dared no longer stop there.

One day a well-dressed man strode into the lobby of the old Grosvenor Hotel on lower Fifth Avenue and made dinner reservations for himself and eight friends. They would arrive, said he, after a coaching party. The hotel noted the reservation and prepared a prominent table in its highly fashionable dining room.

When the group arrived it was at once evident to the management and other guests that the women were streetwalkers; not the smartly dressed, stylishly coiffed, innocent-looking prostitutes that today parade certain parts of the city. These were harpies, garish in their make-up, tasteless in their dress, bawdy in their behavior.

If their appearance did not betray them their raucous manner, toothy laughter and embarrassing little inter-table flirtations soon would. There were no loud obscenities, no vulgarities, no provocations to cause the management to evict them, but before long the whole dining room tensed with embarrassment and rising indignation. One-by-one the other guests summoned their waiters, paid their checks, and left.

Had the man fetched in those bawds maliciously? Had he some grievance against the hotel? Or had he staged the display for effect? Insofar as the Grosvenor was concerned the net result was the same. By that single contretemps the hotel's reputation was mortally struck. Nor did it ever fully recover. In any hotel's patronage a sort of Gresham's law is at work.

Legally a hotel is required to protect its guests. Both in America and Europe this has meant little more than to require that the hotel not expose its guests to thieves and intruders. Several early New York hotels operating bars regularly hired off-duty policemen or ex-prize fighters to bounce troublesome drunks out into the road.

Other than this few innkeepers ever concerned themselves with manned protective services. Because the law required it, guests were advised to deposit valuables in the hotel safe and lock their doors at night. When robberies or other crimes would occur the police were called in and the matter placed in their hands. Legally this absolved the hotel of responsibility, but morally, at least in the Waldorf-Astoria's view, the inn's responsibility went much further. Too many of its carefree, unsophisticated guests coming from the great American hinterland on holiday were ignorant of the big city's wicked ways. Hence it develops that the Waldorf, under the direction of Captain Joe Smith, pioneered the establishment of a hotel security staff comprising both plainclothes house detectives and uniformed watchmen, another innovation destined to establish a practice for great hotels worldwide.

Joe Smith was a young Londoner with brief Scotland Yard experience, his captain's title earned in America's army during World War I. He came to the Waldorf when George Boldt discovered that the hotel's subterranean treasures of wine and expensive cigars were disappearing in large amounts. Hotels, like department stores, learn to cope with petty pilferage, but the expensive cigar and fine wine losses went beyond acceptable limits, up into thousands of dollars. In jig time our man Smith determined that the thefts seemed to follow a timetable which coincided with removals of laundry and kitchen refuse. The rest was easy. Smith promptly tracked down the felons and stopped the loss. From that success he became a permanent fixture, and across the next three decades crime at the Waldorf, if not prevented, assumed such insignificant proportions in terms of other growing pains to render it inconsequential. Captain Smith's Waldorf never had to defend a single suit for negligence and its reputation was as unblemished at its end as when it first opened its doors. "Goodwill," a judge once defined, "is the desire of the customer to return to that place where he has been well treated." Based on its wealth of regular customers, if an accurate cash value could be placed upon it the goodwill assets of the Waldorf-Astoria might easily have equalled the value of its realty.

How the Waldorf protected itself against criminals comes under what is sometimes called preventive maintenance. Smith's regular staff of detectives—beefed up during daylight and evening hours of heavy traffic, greatly enlarged when important state guests were present—included a corps of uniformed security guards, men who constantly patrolled halls and entries day and night, their eyes and ears opened for any untoward sight or sound. Additionally, several hundred housekeepers and their assistants, elevator men, bellboys, chambermaids, scrubwomen, all formed a well-trained police network, each one instructed to report at once anything or anyone of a suspicious nature.

Women receptionists in charge of room keys on each floor were taught to be alert and watchful. Should the detective force get a tip that some suspect was about to show up at the hotel, a machine-processed description was quickly distributed to every member of this organization. Hundreds of pairs of eyes scanned each arrival, every guest thus quietly appraised

[155]

as he signed the hotel register, his manner and his baggage being carefully noted. If he were a stranger, once he had been shown to his room his registration card was checked to see who he was, where he came from, whether his be a name, or an alias, that had appeared on the lists of hotel swindlers each detective carried and always kept current. If the new arrival conducted himself properly, no further attention was paid him. If on the other hand he seemed to fit the description of some known hotel crook, or if there be anything suspicious in his looks or behavior, a silent but efficient surveillance system came quickly into play.

Suppose the valise of the new arrival were light enough to seem empty. The bellhop showing him to his room promptly reported "light luggage," a signal for the detective force to get busy; an empty bag being the surest indication of a "skipper," a guest who plans to jump his bill, or a thief planning to steal something and make a fast getaway. First a chambermaid would be sent to the suspect's room, pretending to see whether it be in order but actually to open the baggage and see what it contained. If it were locked and shaking it revealed no substantial contents, or if found empty, the owner was at once subjected to closer observation. A similar procedure was followed if a stranger were detected loafing in the lobby during business hours and seeking to engage guests in conversation, especially if he tried to strike up conversations with women, or if he had women visitors from outside the hotel whose manner seemed at all furtive.

Once a guest had aroused suspicion, surveillance of him continued on a twenty-four hour basis until his standing and character were found to be satisfactory. When they were found not to be, a detective, posing as another guest with time on his hands, was assigned to draw the suspect into conversation and question him discreetly. Any statements he made about himself were then checked. If they were substantiated, the matter was dropped. Where grounds for suspicion remained, the suspect's telephone calls might be traced. Every person he communicated with either by telephone or personally in the hotel was noted. In cases of extremely suspicious activities a detective might even monitor the suspect's phone conversations. Once suspicions positively indicated that a crime was in the making, detectives were assigned the room opposite to observe the individual's comings and goings and get a look at persons who visited him. If a suspect had a tower room on the inside, a detective might be placed in the room opposite, from which his movements would be watched. Extra men from the outside—former New York police, F.B.I., or Secret Service mostly—were employed for this.

Generally, by the time an investigation had reached the point where a suspect was kept under continued surveillance, the moment had arrived for decisive action. One of three consequences followed: the man discovered he was being watched, paid his bill and left; or he skipped leaving the hotel in the lurch; or he was caught in the act of his intended crime. If a persistent-type room thief, he was permitted to force his way into the targeted room, and was then arrested before he had time to do any damage. The hotel believed that it was better to have these types in prison than left at large.

Speaking one day of professional hotel thieves Smith theorized that the oldtimers possessed more physical courage than modern crooks. "But they were not so dangerous as far as physical violence is concerned. Only a few of them were on drugs; most were specialists and each stuck pretty close to his line. For example, there was one type who never entered a hotel except through a window, up a fire escape or across a neighboring window ledge. He would never be seen in the lobby. He could ransack a room as fast as a blast furnace can consume a lace handkerchief. But each had his own little tricks, his special identifying *modus operandi,* and these leave a pretty clear trail. At one time it was possible to look at a room that had just been burglarized and, nine times out of ten, tell who had robbed it.

"The cleverest of them all," Smith recalls, "the one with the most individualistic touch in his work, was a crook named Moran. He operated with the neatness of a Dutch housewife. He seldom overlooked anything of value but he was scrupulously careful about putting everything back exactly as he found it. This, of course, worked to his advantage. In many cases there would be a delay of hours, often a day or more, before the guest would discover his loss. Moran had time to make a getaway, even build a solid alibi, since it was difficult to fix the exact time of the robbery."

Others, Smith recalls, took a fiendish delight in maliciously destroying clothing, expensive underwear, even luggage when they found nothing much of value. Some crooks owning an odd sense of humor would leave a jewel case which had been hidden carefully away clearly exposed on the dresser with the cover removed. These in reality were leaving their card. Veteran crooks had their own way of adding a personal touch to their operations which made it easy to fix the responsibility and make the arrest. "We knew their haunts and how to find them, but it was quite another matter to convict them without learning where they had pawned or sold the stolen stuff.

"Then there was the gentlemanly-appearing fellow who would hang around the lobby close to the desk as though waiting for someone. A guest would come down, toss the key to his room on the desk and go out. If the clerk was engaged at the moment this character would step up to the counter, take his hat off and place it carefully over the key, and ask the clerk if there was any mail in such-and-such a box, which he had previously noted was empty. When the clerk turned to look into the box the man would pick up the key and conceal it in his hat until he could slip it unnoticed into his pocket. Now he would go up to the room and go through it.

"Another variation of that type worked along similar lines. He would sit in the lobby until he saw a prosperous-looking guest register. On the pretense of expecting the arrival of a friend he would look over the register, note the number of the room to which his intended victim had been assigned. Then he would sit around until the new arrival came down, had deposited his key in its box and departed. As a rule he would not have long to wait, for most men stay in their rooms only a short while when they first reach a hotel. The thief would follow the man out, walking close beside him, often making some casual remark to him as they headed toward the entrance, to create the impression, in case they were being observed by any of the security force, that the new arrival was the friend for whom he had been waiting.

"Pretty soon the thief would come hurrying back, step briskly up to the desk and call for the key to the room whose number he had fixed in his mind. In most cases his self-assurance enabled him to get away with it, the crook having made sure when the man registered that he was a stranger to the clerk, a newcomer to the hotel, there having been no sign of recognition from either. If the clerk asked any questions he would say without glancing at the register that he was Mr. Blank from Podunk, giving the name and address of the guest. A particularly observant clerk might tell him bluntly that he was not the man whose name he gave.

The thief was prepared for that. His glib explanation being that he was a friend of Mr. Blank for whom he had been waiting and that Mr. Blank was tied up in a meeting downtown and had asked him to return to his room for papers he had neglected to take with him.

"In such cases the crook would not get the key and would leave in a pretended huff, but there was nothing for which we could arrest him. In the majority of instances of this kind the thief was handed the key and went through the room at his leisure. Even when we trailed them and caught them in the very act of robbing the baggage of a guest these seldom lost their cool. They accepted arrest with the same smiling indifference with which they had bluffed the clerk. They had played the game and lost—that was all."

For a long time these won oftener than they lost, which caused the Waldorf a lot of concern. Hotel thieves are sometimes known as "prowlers." They rent a room and prowl through the halls late at night seeking access to rooms through unlocked doors or with the aid of skeleton keys. The number of guests who will go to bed leaving their doors unlocked, even leaving the keys dangling outside, is appalling. Smith remembers when he could walk through the Waldorf at midnight and fill a basket with keys projecting from unlocked doors. "It isn't as bad today as it used to be thanks to frequent reminders. But still bad enough. Equally strange is the fact that many guests resent having hotel watchmen call their attention to their unlocked doors, even those who leave the key sticking out in the hall as an invitation to robbery. Some even become angry over what they consider an intrusion into their private affairs!

"The modern hotel thief is generally on drugs," said Captain Smith. "When high on drugs is about the only time he has nerve enough to attempt a robbery. And he is likely to shoot anyone who interferes with him," Smith warns. "The old-time thief seldom went armed; most of the prowlers today carry guns. This breed keeps us on our toes all of the time. They require constant watchfulness but in fact do little damage.

"The really smart crooks are not all dead yet nor are they all in prison. These are the boys for whom we are always on the lookout. They are forever devising new ways to beat a hotel.

"Sometime back these worked a racket on a large New York hotel which shows with what skill and thoroughness they arrange their swindling schemes, to what lengths they will go.

[159]

"The hotel received a letter from a Chicago firm saying that Mr. Brown, we will call him, their vice-president, would arrive in a few days and would be a guest for some time, the purpose of his visit being to open up an eastern branch. As he was unacquainted with New York and had no financial connections here it was requested that he be extended any financial courtesies that he might require. A list of references was enclosed which included the Chicago River National Bank.

"The hotel promptly wrote the bank and several of the references inquiring about Mr. Brown. A reply came back from the bank stating that Mr. Brown was one of their most valued customers, that he had carried a balance running well into five figures with them for years; that he always kept his commitments, that they had loaned him large sums of money from time to time on his unsecured note. Replies from the other references were equally satisfying. Everything seemed in order. The hotel forwarded its own credit card to Mr. Brown.

"In due course Mr. Brown arrived at the hotel. His manner and personality were consonant with the reports that had been received about him. He appeared to be the prototype conservative, successful American businessman. It was late in the day, after banking hours, when he reached the hotel. After registering, he identified himself by presenting his credit card to the cashier and gave him a check for $1,000 on the Chicago River National Bank, which amount was to be credited to his account. The next morning, when a different cashier was on duty, he presented a check for $500, drawn on the same bank. This time he was given the cash. Later in the day, after another personnel shift in the cashier's cage, he displayed a telegram from his office in Chicago asking him to go to Boston immediately on an important matter and requested his bill. After the amount of his bill had been deducted he was handed cash for the balance remaining to his credit from his first check for $1,000. Then Mr. Brown departed and got lost. Both checks came back with the notation that the Chicago River National Bank was unknown in Chicago. The other references whose letters had been written on expensive and impressive stationery also proved non-existent."

The swindler worked the same scheme in Boston and in other cities. Accordingly, Smith organized all New York hotel detectives to keep each other advised of security devices, new tricks, or new crooks.

Today, hotel residents have more confidence in house detectives and security generally than in other years. The selection, training and skills of house detectives, Smith believes, have notably improved. In selecting his regular officers as well as the extra men whom the Waldorf hired from time to time, Smith sought men of character and refinement, men who could meet the guests on equal footing. When the hotel is entertaining royalty or other celebrities whom the public clamors to see, or when there is a large convention or banquet, there are always from a half-dozen to a score or more auxiliary officers added to his regular force.

"It may seem strange but it is a fact that the men with no police training make the best hotel detectives." Smith said. "Men who have police experience have a very different point of view from that required of a hotel detective. They have been mostly ensconced in a criminal environment while we associate mostly with respectable people. Regular police officers find it difficult, impossible in most cases, to adjust themselves to these changed circumstances. Unfailing courtesy is our first rule. The ordinary city detective's brusque manner would be resented by our guests and cause endless trouble. Green men who are naturally bright, intelligent and gentlemanly in their manner can be quickly trained in the right way because they have nothing to unlearn, no fixed ideas of how to deal with situations. Not long ago a man applied to me for a position with the statement that he knew every crook in the country. I told him he might be invaluable to the police department but he would be of no use to me. We have a collection of photographs and descriptions of hotel thieves which is said to be the largest, the most complete in the world. Perhaps it is. But we preserve it only as a curiosity. It has very little if any value; we know all the old crooks. It is the new ones with whom we are concerned; the ones with whom we haven't yet struck up an acquaintance. And there are enough of them running all the time with enough new tricks to keep us busy.

"The American crook is the smartest in the world," concluded Captain Smith, the faraway look in his eyes suggesting many encounters to substantiate this dubious compliment. "But the American woman crook is the smartest of them all."

Women hotel crooks? More troublesome than men!

"Yes," said Smith. "During the course of a year the hotel detective is compelled to give more of his attention to men, both guests and crooks, than he does to women, principally because the latter are less numerous. But women crooks make up in quality for what they lack in numbers. The woman guest is more careless of her valuables than men and the female rogue is far ahead of the male in shrewdness. She will outsmart any man in nine cases out of ten unless he is on to some of her tricks.

"As I mentioned, chief annoyance among hotel criminals is the prowler who registers as a guest and goes sneaking through the halls at night hunting for unlocked doors or ones that can be opened with skeleton keys. Here again 'the female of the species!' et cetera, et cetera! She is the cleverest of all prowlers. While she does not prowl, literally, she belongs in that category. She is open and brazen about it. Men are furtive and sneaky, but her bravado so often disarms suspicion she can get away with a robbery that a man wouldn't have nerve enough to attempt.

"The female prowler is always smartly dressed but never conspicuously so. She is prepossessing in appearance and pleasant in manner. She is an accomplished actress, particularly in her feigned use of injured innocence—that 'baby stare,' that demure disarming expression always ready in response to any challenging look or question.

"This lady generally arrives with two bags. These give her a more substantial appearance and discourage her being sized up as a 'fly-by-nighter.' She registers at the hotel and is shown to a room. The first day she usually spends much time in her room with the door open, apparently reading or busy with her things. Actually she is watching the other guests on her floor, picking out the most promising looking ones, locating their rooms. Most hotel guests go out soon after breakfast; men go about their business and their wives go shopping. This gives the female prowler her opportunity while the maids are busy putting the rooms in order.

"She will walk through the hall with her key in her hand as though she has just come up from breakfast and is on her way to her room. She saunters along slowly with an unconcerned air, but she is observing things very carefully. When she comes to a room in which the maid is at work, its door open, if it happens to be one she has previously spotted as occupied by promising victims, she will enter it as if it were her own room. She apologizes pleasantly to the maid for interfering with her duties and asks if she may have the room to herself for just a few minutes while she changes her clothes. Her easy assurance and display of her key satisfy the maid that the lady is the occupant of the room so she promptly obliges and steps out. Then Miss Prowler deftly rifles all the baggage she can get into, being careful to leave everything just as the owner left it. If she finds nothing of value she leaves and quickly tries a room on another floor, leaving an unsuspecting maid behind and no trace of her visit. If she makes a good haul she will pay her bill and leave the hotel at once. But if the results of her first robbery are not rewarding she is likely to try her luck in two or three more rooms on different floors before making her getaway.

"The Waldorf system, having a clerk on every floor, makes it more difficult for these thieves to operate. There is always fear in their minds that a suspicious maid will ask the clerk if the occupant of room so and so corresponds to the description of the woman who asked her to vacate it for a few minutes. Their haul rarely runs into large amounts, but in the aggregate these prowlers are the most costly crooks with whom we have to deal.

"For our guests, or at least our male guests, the woman blackmailer is the most dangerous. Fortunately, women of this type have never had any luck around here. We know them all, know their confederates, know how they work. When one of these gets a man in her clutches there is seldom any way out except by paying through the nose. And once he starts to pay he is lost.

"The Waldorf has always been a great meeting place. Almost anybody of respectable appearance can meet anyone in our lobbies without being looked at twice or questioned once." Smith smiled, adding, "Anybody except crooks, swindlers and blackmailers. Those are chased away the minute they appear, with even less ceremony than when thieves are concerned. If a guest is picked up by a blackmailer outside the hotel and goes willingly to her place, that's not our business. Whenever we see a guest in the company of one of these we warn him. After that he is on his own."

If the Female Prowler is the constant source of worry for the house detective, no less troublesome is the Careless Woman. Hardly a day passes when one has not left her bag in a taxi or has walked away leaving her pocketbook or fur coat in a chair next to where she'd been sitting. The Waldorf's security force has standing orders to keep its eyes open for such articles and most of them are recovered and waiting for their owners by the time they discover their loss. In some cases, however, they are picked up by dishonest women waiting for just such opportunities. Invariably it is the ladies' restrooms where most valuables are lost or stolen.

One woman out of three, Captain Smith estimates, removes her rings when washing her hands, and at least one in twenty goes away forgetting them. In many cases these too are recovered by an attendant or picked up by an honest woman who turns them in at the desk. But not always. Clever female thieves are forever hanging around to exploit the carelessness of others.

These crooks always work in pairs. They are expensively dressed and convey an air of good breeding to the casual observer. They sit in the adjacent lounging room, perhaps to smoke a cigarette, and when some promising-looking woman enters the restroom they follow her. If the woman removes her rings and places them on the stand while washing her hands and if the rings look valuable one of the two thieves will jostle her apparently by accident. In the following confusion, while the offender is apologizing, her confederate will snatch up the jewels and, screened by her partner, disappear. By the time the jostler has finished her apology and the lady has discovered that her rings are missing the thief is out of the hotel and safely away. Her confederate, remaining behind, will promptly offer herself to be searched, if under suspicion, or even if she is not. Naturally nothing will be found, nor is there any proof that she and her pal were working together, though the house detective may be sure of it. Strange women idling near the ladies' rooms in hotels are constantly under watchful eyes."

Not all dishonest women are professional thieves. The hotel knows most professionals or can identify them from descriptions circulated among hotel detectives. Amateurs, individuals overcome by sudden temptation, present a real problem.

One morning a woman guest went down to breakfast carrying her most valuable jewels in a chamois bag around which she had wrapped her handkerchief. After breakfast she visited the ladies' room, laid her little package on the stand while washing her hands, and walked out without it. In a few minutes she was back again, but her handkerchief and its contents had disappeared. Hurriedly the loss was reported to Captain Smith. "Walk through the corridors with me," he told her, "see if you recognize any woman who was in the ladies' room at the time you were."

In the lobby on the south side she pointed out a woman who had stood beside while she was washing her hands. This woman was looking in another direction. She did not see the detective and his companion. "Okay," said Joe Smith to the guest. "You run along and keep out of sight."

Sending a bellboy for his hat, cane and newspaper, Captain Smith found a seat near the suspected woman. In a short time she was joined by a man for whom she had apparently been waiting. The two started toward an exit with Joe Smith close behind. Just before they reached the exit Smith heard her say to her companion, "I don't know what's in it, but I've got it in my bag."

"Pardon me," said Joe, stepping around in front of them, "did I understand you to say that you had found something? I am connected with the hotel."

Blushing, obviously nervous, "Oh, yes," she said, opening her bag, "here is a little package that I found in the ladies room. I was just going to return it."

Joe might have suggested that she was walking directly away from the office, not towards it, but he was pleased enough to recover the chamois bag. In it were $15,000 worth of diamonds. Once the owner verified that her jewels were intact, their greatly agitated finder and her boyfriend were allowed to leave; no runs, one hit and one error.

"The most troublesome," Captain Smith avers, "is the woman who comes in and sits around in the lobby waiting to be picked up by some flirtatious but innocent and confiding guest who will take her out to dinner and give her a chance to rob him. She is looking for a good dinner but prefers one with cocktails and wine. Of course she knows a 'really cute place.' What she usually ends up with are the money and jewelry of the guest who picks her up.

"How are we to know a woman belongs to that class? A few years back that type carried her profession on her face, but the way women dress now it is impossible to tell a good woman from a dangerous one. You can't see their real faces. All you can see is legs, and legs, unfortunately, are not an indication of character.

"We can only tell them by looking them over carefully, and frequently we have to watch them for a very long while. They usually come in late in the afternoon through one of the side entrances. The smartest of them takes a mezzanine elevator to one of the upper floors, then comes right down the lobby to create the impression that she is a guest of the hotel.

"They sit down in one of the corridors or cocktail lounges after a look at the clock or their watch, as if they were keeping an appointment. That gives them a reason for looking at all the men who pass and sizing them up, assaying their value in ready money. These women are expensively and tastefully dressed wearing a discreet display of jewels that is never out of style. Their whole get-up suggests luxury and breeding; there is nothing about their attire or manner to set them apart from other women seated around them. In face and figure they are as attractive. Most importantly, they are shrewd judges of men and are as discreet as they are discriminating.

"The man who draws the first fleeting smile or a quick sidelong glance must be a likely catch in their judgment. That means he looks prosperous and has the open, kindly face that suggests a generous nature. Mere physical attraction or sex appeal counts for nothing. Ordinarily the first advance must be made by the man, which is further evidence of their smartness. If he looks like a man who could be victimized without great exertion he gets a demure response and the game is on. But if his eyes are keen and alert and he seems wordly wise, capable of finding his way in the dark, he gets only an icy stare or an unconcerned look. These women have no time to waste on the street-wise. If the right type victim doesn't show up they finally call it a day and go home to come back the next day.

"It is through their persistence in coming back that we land them. When we see the same women sitting around in the lobby day after day we know they are there for no good purpose. We keep an eye on them until we are sure we are right. Then we politely invite them into my office and ask them their business. They are always 'waiting for a friend'— the old gag. We advise them that we do not care to have our corridors used by ladies who have so many friends and tell them to go away. To make their prompt departure certain we escort them to the door. If they come back again, which they rarely do, they won't even get a chance to sit down if we see them first.

"We have never yet made a mistake," Smith touched wood, "and I pray we never will. I'd rather have a dozen of these women sitting around for weeks than insult one respectable woman. There is nothing really objectionable about them, their appearances or actions. But we will not have the Waldorf used for these purposes. It isn't good business to have men traveling about the country telling how they were robbed by a female pickup in the Waldorf lobby. That kind of advertising, that reputation, we do not want.

"There are gigolo types, too. They are more easily handled. These are altogether obnoxious, much more offensive, for their whole aim in life is to prey on women. It may be as the feminists say that their sex has become as strong as the male and they are as able to support men as once men supported them. But there are still some of us old-fashioned enough to regard women as the weaker sex. In any case I hate to see them bled by human leeches.

"Those types were once known as 'lounge lizards'; later they were 'sheiks.' My name for them shouldn't be printed. They are always perfectly dressed, well-groomed, and they spend their afternoons—their evenings, too, if they've had no success during the day—looking for some woman who will spend money on them. If they find one who is rich enough to maintain them in luxurious idleness in return for their company at such moments as she requires it, they have attained their goal in life. They think the Waldorf a good place to look for wealthy women.

"Most show plainly what they are and are given short shrift. They are shown the door with none of the outward courtesies that are extended their female prototypes. Sometimes they are kicked out, literally; in aggravated cases there is an irresistible temptation to place a boot where it will do the most good. That man never comes back; he is too cowardly to take another chance.

"Some are better actors. To make certain we have not overlooked these we periodically have what we call our 'cleanup!' Now is where our female detectives come in, if you want to call them that—their only appearance on our stage. Strictly speaking, they are not detectives at all, only decoys. About once a year, oftener if there is need for it, without any warning or announcement we employ eight or ten attractive young ladies to sit around the lobby as traps for male adventurers. We try to get young women from the stage who know something about acting, how to dress and who are cultivated in their speech.

"The women we select enter right into the spirit of the thing. It gives them some extra money and they look on it as a good cause. They take their work seriously; they are, after all, preventing another woman's exploitation. They are expensively gowned and wear costly jewels, both rented for the occasion. They surround themselves with an aura of luxury and leisure. Their instructions are to make no advances of any kind and they always play the game fairly. All they have to do is sit around and wait for some man to approach them and try to strike up an acquaintance. As a rule they haven't long to sit.

"Our decoys are wise enough to know whether the man who smiled so nicely and tipped his hat is a guest of the house or some other decent man who is simply out for a flirtation with a beautiful woman or whether he is one of the rogues we are after. If he is a house guest she gives a signal to one of the house officers who is observing the operations, and the man is called quietly aside and politely told that we will not have our guests annoyed in that manner, so kindly do his flirting elsewhere. From the way he accepts this warning we can tell whether the decoy has been correct in her appraisal.

"But if the man who makes the advance shows himself to be one of the leeches, or even on suspicion that he may be, the procedure is different. In that case, after he has shown his hand sufficiently, or enough to make her suspect him, the young lady engages him in friendly conversation and, on the pretense of looking for a friend, parades him through the corridors and lounges so that he may be seen by all the house detectives— the whole force is on duty while the decoys are at work—and seen as well by all the office and floor employees on duty at that time. This is to make certain that he will be recognized by someone if he ever comes around again. Now, after everyone has had a good look at him, if he is unable to give a good account of himself he is shown out and told if he ever comes back he will be thrown out. Meanwhile, our young lady who's been powdering her nose proceeds to set another trap. When we reach the point where we are making no more catches, the game is closed, the decoys retired.

"In this way we manage to keep the place pretty free from both male and female parasites. These move on to another hotel, or to another city, if they have worked all the big New York hotels, for they seldom change their ways except for worse. Of course, some new faces are showing up all the time, but they are soon turned to the wall.

The House Dick

"The Police Commissioner once asked me how we kept the hotel so clean without a lot of lawsuits from people we threw out. I told him it was by keeping our eyes open and knowing who we are dealing with."

Captain Smith sighed, "Not that we haven't made mistakes."

In a darkened bedroom of an unprepossessing frame house in Queens, on Saturday, March 19, 1927, lurked Judd Gray, waiting to kill a man. His intended victim, Albert Snyder, had gone out with his wife for the evening. Judd Gray did not know Snyder but Snyder's voluptuous wife, Ruth, he knew intimately. For two years they had been lovers. The mounting passion of their affair had now determined them to murder her husband.

Waiting nervously in the darkness Judd Gray took a drink from his pocket flask. One by one he examined the instruments Ruth had selected for doing her husband in: rubber gloves, chloroform, a heavy sashweight. Suddenly a noise downstairs announced the Snyders' return. Judd could hear their steps on the stairs. He heard their bedroom door close. His pulse quickened. He took another stiff drink from his flask. After what seemed a very long time he heard a door open. "Are you there, Bud?" whispered Ruth.

"I'm here," said Judd.

Ruth was dressed only in her slip. For the next hour the lovers tumbled about in frantic copulation. Another drink and they were ready; Albert Snyder by now should be fast asleep.

Quietly the two tiptoed to his bedside. It would all be so easy, decided Judd Gray. Why bother with rubber gloves? Or chloroform? With both hands he raised the sashweight and brought it crashing down on the skull of Albert Snyder. It was a glancing blow. Roaring with pain, Snyder sat up. He grabbed at Gray. Gray panicked. "Momsie! Momsie!" he yelled at Ruth, "for God's sake help!"

Ruth raced around from the other side of the bed. Snatching the weapon from Judd with both hands she brought it down onto her husband's skull. He was dead; his head split open. Breathing heavily, the two murderers for a moment stood silent. Fearing they may have awakened Ruth's nine-year-old daughter, cautiously they crept down the stairs, waited and listened again. Relaxed, they poured another drink then methodically set about upsetting lamps and chairs and tables. Judd now bound and gagged Ruth to make it appear that intruders were guilty of the murder. The set ready, Judd left. Waiting a few minutes, Ruth pulled out the gag and screamed.

The murderers' plans for its cover-up proved as inept as the crime itself. In record time police had them both in jail and had extracted detailed confessions. Months later America would be treated to one of the most hyped-up trials on record—lurid, sordid, meretricious and vulgar—just about as reprehensible as "yellow" journalism of that day could achieve. Celebrities by the droves crowded that courtroom: Mary Roberts Rinehart, the novelist; Hollywood producer D. W. Griffith and Broadway producer David Belasco; savant Will Durant; seven-times-wedded Peggy Hopkins Joyce; evangelists Billy Sunday and Sister Aimee Semple McPherson— the latter as sob sister for the New York *Evening Graphic;* all were in regular attendance, most armed with newspaper assignments. If not due process at least mass media would be served by this spectacle. For weeks across America, pictures, interviews, every item of testimony from the trial dominated the news. That both Ruth and Judd would blame each other for the crime comes as no surprise to anyone familiar with the desperate maneuvers of frustrated defense attorneys. That both were found guilty and died in the electric chair hardly surprised anyone either.

It seems that following their first meeting, when Judd, a corset salesman, obligingly massaged Ruth's sunburned back with lotion, the lovers kept regular hotel room trysts. To these assignations Ruth would bring her small daughter, leaving her to play in the care of attendants in the lobby. Where? Where indeed!

"Those people fooled us completely," sighed Smith.

A different kind of hanky-panky to thrive in the Waldorf environment fortunately was not the concern of Captain Smith and his eagle-eyed sleuths. Back in 1888, five years before the Elegant Inn's opening, New York Society was becoming increasingly discomfited by one Colonel William D'Alton Mann, those most painfully so being the ones forced to pay through the nose lest Mann's *Town Topics* open darkened closets and rattle tale-telling skeletons. This particular rogue—an impressive figure with scented white moustache, red bow tie and clerical frock coat—most anyone would mistake for some kindly old gentleman who always carried lumps of sugar in his pockets for horses. But stashed away in Mann's memory or allegedly in his office safe were proofs of enough peccadilloes to provide Mann a handsome living. On *Town Topics'* generous payroll were housemaids, butlers, barmaids, waitresses, keepers of bawdy houses, a few notorious gossips such as Harry Lehr, and a corps of scandal sniffers.

Colonel Mann, a native of Sandusky, Ohio, had earned his military title by organizing the Seventh Michigan Cavalry in the Civil War. After Appomattox he journeyed deep into the shattered heart of Dixie to settle in Alabama where he built a mill to extract cottonseed oil, made a brief try at journalism, and otherwise distinguished himself from most Carpetbaggers by joining the Ku Klux Klan. In 1872 he patented the Mann Boudoir Car, a deluxe railway carriage which he sold to George Pullman's Palace Sleeping Car Company. A second such venture was the luxurious railway car he designed and built for Belgium's Leopold II, an achievement which for years prompted him to badger that monarch for a royal decoration. Mann also invented a cannon, wrote military treatises, and indulged in several scholarly if less lucrative tasks before finally deciding that an easier way to jolt people loose from their money was to salve their vanity. Or, even better, dig up a little dirt about them and shake them down for suppressing it—blackmail.

In 1891, Mann's brother, convicted of sending obscene matter through the mails and urgently needing cash, sold the colonel a New York Society journal called *Town Topics*. Mann now had the single weapon he needed to become a front-rank racketeer.

Originally established in 1879 as Andrews' *The American Queen,* a "Magazine of Art, Music, Literature and Society," the publication was showing promise, numbering among its highly respectable sponsors T. J. Oakley Rhinelander, James B. Townsend and Louis Keller, this last founder of the *Social Register*. When one day Andrews, its editor, mysteriously vanished leaving the publication's affairs in a mess, Keller took over and held it together for three years as *The American Queen*. Soon E. D. Mann, Colonel Mann's brother, would buy it, rename it *Town Topics* and launch it on its career of keyhole journalism. It printed hints of forthcoming divorce suits; it scooped the daily newspapers with news of Wall Street bankruptcies; it gossiped about doweries; it advised certain debutantes to use mascara more sparingly; and regularly published scornful bulletins from Chicago under the dateline "Skunkville." For example, a January 13, 1887, item: "Nobody in the Union Club was astonished to learn that Bob Townsend had married his cook. Unless he has reformed of late years it is generally held among those honored with his acquaintanceship that the sympathies of the public belong to the cook." Nastier gossip of higher legal risk took refuge in anonymities: "A Philadelphia clubman married to a wife whose social freedom with certain society youths in and about the Bryn Mawr Hotel a couple of summers ago would lead to the belief that her husband is mistaken when he says she is as cold as she is fair."

Such spicy editorial tidbits, malicious and often spiteful, were not the colonel's moneymaker. Mann thrived in the dark menace of scandal. What he would offer not to print would yield far greater revenues; the knowing wink, the sly smile, the veiled innuendo, elephant-hoofed hints of secrets locked in his safe, Mann's alleged repository of "the reputations of New York's Four Hundred." As a musician or a butler, Mann's shadowy Newport correspondent may well have entered the homes of wealthy; in any case, Mann's agents spread offers of ready cash to tattle-tale Fifth Avenue and Palm Beach backstairs help. Erstwhile champagne huckster, Harry Lehr, an irrepressible gossip whom Society found amusing because he could wiggle his nose from side to side, play the piano and sing falsetto, was one dependable *Town Topics* conduit. Other of Mann's spies were the hangers-on, those never quite accepted in Society's inner circle who nourished spiteful grievances.

Mann's editorial strategy followed a pattern; first, the tiniest morsel of gossip, a hint in *Town Topics,* just the tip of his rapier, never thrust enough to kill, but threat enough that more might follow unless . . . Then Mann simply sat and waited. He avoided lawsuits for libel by printing a paragraph, for example, describing the indiscretions of an anonymous lady and her gentleman friends, then following it with a harmless "key" paragraph in which all the missing names would appear. This provided the reader an intriguing little conundrum to solve.

To actually publish spicy scandal was not for Mann; he preferred cash for suppressing it. Nor was he selfish; everybody on the staff got a share of the take—or so Mann's assistant, Ahle, confided one day to Edwin

Main Post, husband of the celebrated Emily, arbiter designate of social etiquette. Post was being shaken down for $500, but had the foresight to have a representative of the district attorney's office present during Ahle's interview.

Once while launching his masterwork "puff sheet," a book titled *Fads and Fancies of Representative Americans,* Mann dispatched to his field command this directive:

Dear Wooster:

I believe you can get J. Edward Addicks if you go right after him. Did you try Arbuckle, the sugar man? You must go over and pin Governor Murphy. If you were to go over to the West End, Long Branch, and stop there a day or two so as to have time to catch John A. McCall, you can interest him; his vanity will lead him to have that half-million dollar house handed down to posterity, and he would certainly go into the book when he finds that such men as Woodward, Whitney, Morton, Astor, Vanderbilt, Aldrich, Dryden appear. . . .

Sums being solicited were for inclusion in this posh Society Who's Who. The shocking cost, Mann's unsmiling solicitors explained, was because "each volume required an entire hide for its binding"!

For several years Mann's henchmen sold editorial space to prospective interviewees collecting advance subscriptions at $1500 per copy, some higher, depending upon the weight of Mann's subtleties about the contents of his safe. The vulnerable paid and won flattering biographies; others paid and avoided exposure. Justice Joseph M. Deuel of New York City's Court of Special Sessions, a stockholder in *Town Topics,* was its legal adviser as well. From him was dispatched a somewhat more metaphorical reminder to that same Wooster: "You are seeding the garden, and I trust, with the gentle cultivation of which you are capable, we will yet fill our basket quite full of either flowers or fruit." The judge's delicate hyperbole, said the *New York Evening Telegram,* "Sounds better than proposing to go out and violently shake a plum tree."

Town Topics had its favorites and true to its code protected them. One was James Hazen Hyde, whose Equitable Life Assurance Society had made Mann a loan of $165,000. Another was Perry Belmont, from whom

Mann "borrowed" $4,000, a good hit in light of the fact that Perry's brother, O. H. P. Belmont, had just turned Mann down cold for a paltry $2,000. On June 30, 1905, Mann dispatched a letter to his editor:

> Dear Wayne—Use the enclosed notes. I have especial reason to be nice to McCormick and Mrs. McC, and I also wish to show that Perry and Mrs. Belmont go to the best affairs here. All well. Kindest regards. W.D.M.

What editor could sound more gracious? Just weeks earlier Mann had granted special clemency, saying, "Let up on Henry T. Sloane." He also ruled, "*T. T.* will be careful of anything said about Mrs. Inman of Atlanta. Nothing unpleasant," thus primrosing the social path for the future mother of Doris Duke Cromwell. Charles S. Wayne, the managing editor to whom these missives were sent, testified that Mann's immunity list was prominently displayed on the office bulletin board. Only kind things, ruled Mann, must be said about General Russel A. Alger, James Hazen Hyde, Perry Belmont, James R. Keene, W. K. Vanderbilt, George J. Gould, J. Pierpont Morgan, A. J. Cassatt, Melville E. Stone, August Belmont, Senator W. A. Clark, George H. Daniels, Stuyvesant Fish, Henry M. Flagler, Abraham H. Hummel, E. Clarence Jones, Henry Lehr, John E. Madden, Creighton Webb, Charles T. Yerkes, Reginald Ward and Thomas W. Lawson.

Lawson, a parvenu from Boston, it seems had won immunity by heavy advertising lineage in *Town Topics*. Reginald Ward, concerning whom Mann had gathered a little dirt from his Boston correspondent, anted up 5,000 shares of Rice Syndicate to have some flattering comments about himself appear in 1904. Occasionally a name would be taken off the sacred list then put back on it when an "understanding" had been reached. Said Robert A. Irving, the colonel's man with the little black bag, when asked on the witness stand what had been his approach, "Well, I tell them that Colonel Mann is a great fellow to get in with distinguished people." None could claim fraud, for in June 1905 every one of the eighty-six subscribers to *Fads and Fancies of Representative Americans*—in addition to President Roosevelt, the Library of Congress, the New York Public Library and the British Museum—actually did receive the gilt-edged volume. It was as large as an atlas, three inches thick, bound in Russian leather, stamped in red and gold leaf, bearing an introduction by a Society stalwart, Mrs. Burton Harrison, and containing a nauseous debauchery of self-worshipping biographies, flattering portraits of the biographied— their houses, horses, dogs and yachts—treacle from cover to cover, not an unkind word. The lengthiest "biography," with a full-page portrait, was the eight-page sketch of railroader Collis P. Huntington. Although Huntington had died five years earlier, his widow gave Mann $10,000 in the belief that her husband as prime builder of the Golden West was entitled to make the biggest splash. Reading this impressive tome and noting the quality of its protagonists would make clear why subscribers cherished their copies of *Fads and Fancies*. Far more intriguing, however, might be a volume describing those episodes from their lives which Mann would use to blackmail them.

Shrewd public figures obey a familiar injunction: "Never sue a newspaper for libel; it's just likely to prove it." During all his shady career, only once was Mann sued for libel. When *Town Topics* printed some highly scurrilous comments about the private life of Solan Vlasto, publisher of the Greek-language newspaper *Atlantis,* Vlasto promptly hauled Mann into court and walked out counting five thousand dollars of Mann's money. For several years no other *Town Topics'* victim displayed anything matching this Greek's pugnacity. Many seethed, many complained, but none dared to act.

Withal, Colonel Mann's hour was approaching. One day *Town Topics* sniped at P. F. Collier as "a Bible salesman who had galloped into Society behind foxhounds." This did not amuse his son, Robert, owner of *Collier's Weekly*. Condé Nast, business manager, and several other of *Collier's* staff were devotees of the Society game and chose to laugh it off, but not *Collier's* Editor-in-Chief, Norman Hapgood, a wild-eyed, quick-on-the-draw crusader who was getting fed up with "a publishing business which should resemble the manufacture of corsets." When *Town Topics* made suggestive comments about President Roosevelt's daughter Alice, knight-errant Hapgood strapped on his armor, grabbed up his lance and leapt into the saddle. Actually what *Town Topics* said was that during Miss Roosevelt's visit to New York as guest of the Ogden Millses, "Princess Alice probably had conformed to the heavy drinking habits of that family."

For starters in *Collier's* for August 5th, Hapgood let go a salvo at Judge Deuel as "part owner and one of the editors of a paper of which the occupation is printing scandal about people who are not cowardly enough to pay for silence." Hapgood's thrust knocked the wind out of the *Town Topics* employees, and frightened some into coming up with hard evidence, including Judge Deuel's matchless memoranda urging his colleagues to "bag" certain well-known individuals, and "try to run down Marshall Field." Once to his Florida representative Deuel had written likening prospective victims to "Davy Crockett's coon—all you need to do is point your gun and every high-tone, desirable citizen of Palm Beach may tumble in your basket."

In a display of bravado, Mann filed suit against *Collier's.*

At first with great reluctance, now with a touch of pride, under cross examination Colonel Mann admitted he had borrowed a total of $184,500 from a substantial number, viz.: James R. Keene, $90,000; William K. Vanderbilt, $25,000; John W. Gates, $20,000; Dr. W. Seward Webb, $14,000; William C. Whitney, $10,000; Thomas F. Ryan (via Morton Trust Company), $10,000; Collis P. Huntington, $5,000; Roswell P. Flower, $3,000; J. Pierpont Morgan, $2,500; Howard Gould, $2,500; Grant B. Schley, $1,500; George S. Scott, $1,000.

James A. Burden, Jr., recent "mark" for a shakedown attempt, took the stand and gave damaging testimony. Edwin M. Post, Oliver Belmont, and, surprisingly, Harry Lehr, now followed. With quiet satisfaction District Attorney William Travers Jerome watched the libel action against *Collier's* turn into a scorching indictment of *Town Topics. Collier's* was promptly acquitted. Amos Pinchot sometime earlier had proposed that the most successful way to dispose of the colonel would be to shave off half his great moustache and parade him down Fifth Avenue in an open carriage. The idea now recruited volunteers but was abandoned either out of consideration for the colonel's bad heart or the fact that he always toted a gun. Never mind. With that jury's verdict Mann overnight became a has-been, a punched ticket. *Town Topics* advertisers, braver now, dropped out, and more than one New Yorker publicly wondered why no one had called the colonel's bluff years before. Vanquished but unbowed the colonel tried another low blow when *Town Topics* said that the name "Norman" had never occurred in the Hapgood family before; "a great friend of the mother of the *Collier's* editor was so named." At this readers were neither amused nor titillated. Mann then took a feeble swipe at President Roosevelt, accusing him of a social blooper in the wording of his daughter's wedding invitation. Again the same negative reader reaction. Colonel Mann now doubtless realized his day was done. For another fifteen years he would be seen on the streets of Manhattan, ghost-like in his shabby frock coat, "a bogey-man mothers might use to frighten strong-willed debutante daughters." But, as Dixon Wecter concludes, "From Lucifer he had fallen to Mrs. Grundy."

Colonel Mann's daughter endeavored to keep a chastened *Town Topics* afloat, in fact did so until the depression of 1931 when it breathed its last. Efforts to revive something similar—juicy bits of risqué gossip, vague innuendos of indiscretions—have reappeared from time to time but few survive. Most lacked wit. *Town Topics* was at best clever, at worst malicious, displaying both qualities in no predictable balance. In one debutante season it graded the season's buds as one might rate brood mares—Grade A: the debutante who had three generations of family with money and personal charm; Grade B: a potpourri which included young ladies with background but scant attractiveness along with reckless girls with money and position, and proper girls whose antecedents were tarnished by the wrong kind of divorces and financial scandal—in general, a class demoted by misbehavior, if not the young lady's, her parents'. Grade C included the *nouveaux riches* redolent with the aroma of stockyards, the burned carbon of steel mills, the pungent flow of crude oil and natural gas. Eligible young men often found these the most appealing because of their frank and unaffected manners, a keener spirit not yet submerged under stereotyped, pretended preference. This group socially was clearly on the make, and likely to be most hospitable.

Even the publication of spicy impertinences such as this, however, was not calculated to endear anyone to *Town Topics*. No one seems to have lamented its failure. Nor would Colonel Mann be missed at the Waldorf-Astoria, which in the palmier days of his career had been a favored rendezvous.

John Doyle, the assistant steward whose valiant services we may remember from the night of the Waldorf's opening, was friendly with Colonel Mann. At both the Waldorf and in his previous hotel employment Doyle had allowed Mann to buy his weekly supply of whiskey at wholesale prices, the subtle understanding being that *Town Topics* would have nothing unkind to say about the hotel's cuisine. One day busily at work in the hotel pantry, Doyle was descended upon by a furious George Boldt who came charging down the stairs waving a copy of *Town Topics.* "Look at this!" shouted Boldt. "It's disgraceful!"

Doyle took the paper from his boss's shaking grasp. Headlined was a story about the Waldorf, a pleasant, flattering bit of prose that praised its luxurious furnishings, lauded its tasteful decor, commended its fine service, but hidden behind this treacly gush a left hook: "But the oysters were hot and the soup was cold."

Nothing could be done short of writing a fat check, buying advertising in the publication or humoring Colonel Mann and hoping for the best. Boldt undertook this himself. For a while he won immunity by sending Colonel Mann a bottle of rare wines, a case of champagne, a couple of Virginia hams, a box of Beluga caviar. One day Mann sent Boldt a request for a loan of $200. He got the money and gave Boldt a note. A little later Mann requested another trifle, three hundred this time. Before long Mann was into Boldt for fifteen hundred dollars. There is no record that Boldt ever collected. Nor that his estate pressed the claim.

When Colonel Mann's infamous safe, that fearful Pandora's box, that murky "repository of the reputations of New York Society" was opened, guess what it contained?

Four bottles of brandy.

For another group of blackmailers, several wayward sons of the Fourth Estate called "We Boys," far bolder buccaneers than Mann, the Waldorf-Astoria provided a hunting ground. In fact for a while their headquarters as well.

Captain Smith's forces could adequately cope with gamblers, coin-matchers, thieves, hucksters of worthless oil stocks, professional market "tipsters," mashers, gigolos and prostitutes—even phoney cartoonists. Newspaper cartoons were fast coming in vogue. Those charlatans exploiting this would display an original unpublished drawing of some prominent figure, offer to make a flattering cartoon of it and have it published in any newspaper for $500—sometimes even a modest $200, up front, of course. The gullible guest usually salvaged nothing more from his investment than a poor sketch.

"We Boys" were more ruthless. One of their number might stop a guest, say that he represented the *World,* for example, then show him a news story, ready for publication, exposing some shadier recess of the guest's life. The dialogue would be brief and straight to the point:

VICTIM: "My God, you are not going to publish this! It would ruin my life! My wife would divorce me!

WE BOYS: "Well, it's the kind of story our readers enjoy. Our policy is to give them what they want."

VICTIM: "But for heaven's sake man! Who do you work for? The *World!* Doesn't Pulitzer own your paper? I've met him. I shall get in touch with him at once."

WE BOYS: "Don't do that. You'd accomplish just what you are trying to avoid. Mr. Pulitzer will say that if the story is accurate it is news, and if we don't publish it the competitors will; they would scoop us on our own story. What's more he will fire me for not having turned it in. No, I've a better idea. We Boys are taking up a subscription to pay hospital costs for sick and injured newspapermen, you know, the poor old guys who can't afford expensive medical treatment. What do you say, make a little contribution—shall we say $5,000—and We Boys will see to it that the story does not appear either in the *World* or any other newspaper."

VICTIM: "Five thousand dollars! God, man that's a lot of money . . ."

WE BOYS: "It's up to you. You say it would wreck your life, that your wife would sue for divorce. I don't know how much such consequences mean to you. For me they'd be worth much more than five grand. In fact, that is a bottom figure. What we really need, and what our Hospital Bed Committee asked me to get was $15,000."

For a number of years "We Boys" thrived. No, they were not regular members of the metropolitan press; many were experienced newspapermen at the moment unemployed—"free-lancing," or, as actors say, "between engagements."

"We Boys" were aggressive, resourceful and surprisingly convincing. If the cash "contribution" was slow to materialize their demand might be for new furnishings for the Newspapermen's Clubrooms, and club rooms they had. In fact, George Boldt provided them a Waldorf suite which for a while respectable members of the working press did frequent.

"They had the best grafting game I've ever run across," said Joe Smith. "And the only one I've ever fallen for. Before I got on to them I gave them an oil painting worth $500 for their clubroom."

The Inn of the Golden Dragon

*N*ot long after the proud Twenty-seventh Division, A. E. F., marched smartly up Fifth Avenue and saluted General Pershing on the Waldorf-Astoria balcony, another soldier of World War I came home. He was neither general, admiral, prince nor potentate but in preparation for his reception the entire Waldorf-Astoria staff turned handsprings of delight. Bellboys vied for the honor of carrying his duffel. Maids and housemen lingered for his smile. He was Alvin C. York, sergeant, infantry, an obscure farm boy from Pall Mall, Tennessee, and America's most decorated soldier—overnight her hero. Single-handed Alvin York had silenced thirty-five enemy machineguns, killed twenty-five of the enemy and brought back into Allied lines one hundred and thirty-five prisoners! A cheering Congress gratefully voted Sergeant York its Medal of Honor.

From the moment his transport had steamed through the Narrows, excited New York waited, arms outstretched. There would be parades, banquets, ceremonies, escorted celebrity tours, and, everywhere, throngs of adoring millions desperately wanting to see, to greet, to touch this man.

Officially in charge of welcoming arrangements was another soft-spoken Tennessean, a young Congressman from Alvin York's home district, and in the years ahead he, too, was destined to be the Waldorf's guest of honor as Secretary of State. His name was Cordell Hull.

As he did for the arrival of all illustrious guests, Oscar met Sergeant York and Congressman Hull at the red-carpeted entrance, proudly escorted them through Peacock Alley, across the lobby and up to a luxurious suite, next door to the one always held in readiness for the President of the United States. As he entered it Sergeant York's eyes fell at once upon a picture framed in silver and placed prominently in view. Slowly he picked it up, looked longingly at it, consumed for a moment with great emotion.

Swallowing apologetically, Sergeant York then turned to Congressman Hull. "That's the first picture I have seen of my mother in a long, long time."

Besides finding and placing that photograph there, Cordell Hull had also made arrangements for Sergeant York to talk with his mother—all so easy today but in 1919 long distance telephoning took an amount of doing. There was only one telephone in Pall Mall, Tennessee, at its general store, and waiting there for it to ring was a proud mother, doubtless experiencing those heart-rending emotions mothers the world over have known when their prayers have been answered and their sons are home safe from the wars.

Recalling this affecting scene the usually imperturbable Oscar remembers his own great emotion. The Waldorf-Astoria had entertained kings and queens, presidents, ministers of state, all ranks of nobility, the world's great in every field of human endeavor, but of all these remembered with the most affection by eight hundred men and women of its staff was Sergeant Alvin York. Because of his quiet, unassuming manner? Because of his genuine boyish wonderment at the splendor, the grandeur, the luxury of this great establishment? Because of his gratitude and humility? Yes, all of these, but mainly because he was one of them.

A long and distinguished list of guests had preceded this simple soldier; others would fill the years ahead. Indeed the hotel's register, treasured today by the New York Public Library, is one of the rarest collection of autographs in the world.

First to come had been titled Spaniards, great names such as Veragua, Aguilera, Barbolis, de la Corda; Princess Eulalie herself, Spain's Infanta, came to linger and captivate New York with her charm. In April of 1896 appeared the Marquis Yamagata of Japan, the occasion for a great banquet, the Grand Ballroom bedecked with Stars and Stripes and Rising Suns.

And then there was Li Hung-Chang. . . .

He came to the United States on no official mission. He had so many titles the newspapers were uncertain how to identify him. Yet the arrival of Li Hung-Chang in August, 1896, thrilled New York as no event had before, as few have since. The city found the visit of an important, impressive Oriental absolutely irresistible.

[184]

Li was the Chinese equivalent of Gilbert and Sullivan's Pooh-Bah—an early ambassador extraordinary, prime minister, foreign minister, viceroy, Commander of the Army of the North, Lord High Admiral of the Fleet and Senior Guardian of the Heir Apparent.

Li had been to St. Petersburg, Russia, for the coronation of Czar Nicholas II and was on his way home. More important to New Yorkers was the fact that he traveled with eighteen aides and twenty-two servants, wore robes of rainbow-hued silk, brought three hundred pieces of luggage, a golden sedan chair, several cases of songbirds, two noisy parrots, many beautifully plumaged chickens and a supply of one hundred-year-old eggs. Overwhelmed by such exotic cargo and faced with such a personage, New York went all out.

On August 28, soon after daybreak, people were headed for lower Manhattan. By eleven o'clock packed humanity lined streets, thronged piers and rooftops, hung from windows, tree limbs and lampposts and overloaded every available boat. Besides the North Atlantic Squadron of ten gleaming-white battleships, two cruisers, a monitor and a ram, the Sixth U. S. Cavalry Regiment—America's finest horsemen and their mounted band—had been ordered up from Fort Myer, Virginia, to serve as Li's escort. President Grover Cleveland left his fishing tackle on the banks of Buzzard's Bay and hurried down to New York to insure the warmth of America's welcome.

Fire Islanders first sighted Li's ship. Guests of the Surf Hotel had spent days in special preparations. Since dawn William Temple had been up in the Marine Observatory scanning the horizon through his glass. In the distance he saw a whiff of smoke. Moments later it took the shape of a steamer coming fast. Temple shouted, and crowds rushed to the hotel's windows. In the yard Captain Charles Weeks and his life-saving corpsmen had a small howitzer, primed to fire the first American salute to Li Hung-Chang. *Boom!* went the cannon, and from the Observatory a great American flag unfurled. Solemnly the ship dipped her colors in answer to the salute.

In Chinatown, balconies and windows blazed with color, and chains of lanterns united the thoroughfare. Four "portals" draped with American and Chinese banners formed a background for thousands of minor ornaments. Despite special permission to shoot off firecrackers in Chinatown until September 5, most had been saved for the great day of Li's arrival.

New York's reporters went down the bay aboard the *Dolphin,* which carried General Thomas H. Ruger, military commander of the Department of the East, and his party to welcome Li for President Cleveland.

The official party and press mounted a ship's gangway and were ushered forward to the Ladies' Salon. Li was already on hand, borne in his chair by four seamen. He had seated himself on a divan under a skylight, a 74-year-old six-footer with a white goatee and a braided queue that fell to his hips. The American Line vice-president, James A. Wright, did the introductions. Li stood to greet General Ruger and invited him to sit on his left. The Chinese minister sat on the viceroy's right. Directly in front of Li stood interpreter Lo Fing-Luh, a skilled linguist in German and French as well as English. Between Li and Lo there seemed to be complete and total communication, often without so much as a word being uttered. Lo intently watched his master's lips move when he spoke and made sure that he understood precisely what was said. Observers soon noted that Lo roared with laughter anytime Li said anything having the barest flavor of wit.

With General Ruger were two aides; a State Department representative, Assistant Secretary W. W. Rockhill, fluent in Chinese, and General James Wilson, who had known Li in China. Li seemed amused by the reporters and photographers. With sly little winks he conveyed to them the impression that understood English and used an interpreter only to give him more time to ponder vexing questions. With General Ruger he displayed an astonishing lack of tact, pointing out that generals seemed to be everywhere, producing roars of laughter among the Chinese.

When the time came for Li to get in his chair and be borne down the gangplank, Colonel Frederick Grant rushed up and introduced himself. Li was delighted to see the son of his old friend, President Grant. He asked after Mrs. Grant and wanted to insure that he would have a chance to visit Grant's Tomb. Li had been one of the early subscribers to the fund for building it.

Several thousand people lined the Fulton Street pier. Directly in front of the American Line wharf the police had cleared a square. As people poured in from the side streets it looked as though they would overflow the barriers. Time and again the police charged the crowds with sudden and assumed ferocity. Many people had brought lunches; others sent messengers for sandwiches. The arrival of the Sixth Cavalry and the maneuvers of the naval militia kept everyone entertained, even those who had already been patiently waiting for five long hours.

In front of the lower gangplank, a space of a hundred feet or more was guarded with a stout, clothbound railing. Within this enclosure was the Chinese consul and his wife, members of the Celestial diplomatic family and Chinese merchants. The merchants did not hobnob with the consul and his party; everything was governed by caste. The hats they wore, and the buttons on top of them, represented the 19 grades in the Chinese social scale. Those who wore a white button on the crown were of the fifth grade, highest represented in the merchants' associations. Lesser grades wore blue, purple and gold buttons. He who wore no button at all was obviously of the lowest rank. Li's was a jeweled button of red agate or jade, indicating the highest rank.

Leading from the gangplank was a strip of red carpet, resplendent against the battered planking. Along this the Chinese gentlemen were lined up in a picturesque pattern. But the march-past of the Naval Reserve put them out of plumb, and Consul Szo ran down the ranks tapping one man on the nose with his fan, gently kicking another in the shins, unceremoniously treading on the toes of another, to remind them they were out of alignment.

As the ship finally approached, the crowd jammed up against the railing and hung from beams up and down the length of the pier, while in the street outside the police were almost bowled over. As the gangplank was swung aboard, the Naval Reserve presented arms and their band played a fanfare. The cavalry swayed into a sinuous line. At their bugler's "Attention!" the horses plunged and the crowd scampered from under the hooves.

"There he is!" screamed a boy and everyone craned forward. At the top of the gangplank stood China's great man, smiling benevolently. From right to left Li looked, and seemed pleased. The tradesmen of Mott Street whom the consul had trained so well bent double in salutation. The crowd surged and cheered. First out of the pier was a carriage-load of secretaries from the consulate. The crowd mistook them for Li and started to cheer.

Li's carriage then appeared, the coachmen fingering his lines nervously. The viceroy still smiled and carried an umbrella as he entered New York.

"Never had one individual been more highly honored by the people of this metropolis," observed the *Herald*. "It was a unique display for New York," noted the *World*, "where the Chinese have always stood for less then nothing; a despised race. . . ."

What did His Excellency eat? At 5 a.m. a rice gruel; at 6 a.m. hard-boiled eggs in vinegar, curry and rice, and a rice custard; at 11:30 a.m. braised fish and sauce, braised pork and onions with sauce, pork livers chopped fine, fried potatoes and gravy, curry and rice; at 3:30 p.m. broiled fish and onion sauce, braised turkey chopped in pieces, pork with brown sauce, potatoes and gravy, curry and rice. Li's own cooks prepared his meals. A choice selection of sauces and vegetables was carried in cans and the ship's commissary provided chicken, turkey, pork and pork livers.

After Li's procession left the pier, reporters scampered about interviewing other passengers about the great man. Had Li been a good sailor? Yes, or at least he had appeared regularly on deck. The crossing had been uncommonly smooth. Did his fellow passengers speak informally with him? Well, yes, if they spoke at all. Most of the time they were answering Li's questions. Whose company did the Grand Old Man of China seem most to enjoy? The children's! He would spend hours talking with them. Especially Bessie Gattle, age 11, who had recited for him. What had she recited? "The Pride of Battery B." Li had given her a medal with his picture on it. He had also enjoyed meeting the Abbott Sisters, a music hall act, returning to Broadway after a successful London run. These two beauties had given an informal performance in his staterooms and Li had presented them with an autographed picture of himself. He had also talked ships with shipbuilder Theodore W. Cramp of Philadelphia and politics with Virginia Senator John W. Daniel.

At the Waldorf everything was ready. For several weeks, since that familiar telegram from the State Department saying simply "Mr. Nye will arrive from Washington in the morning," the hotel had known it would have another important state guest. That it should turn out to be the viceroy from China and not another South American dictator or European prince made little difference to anyone except the housekeeper. Finding Chinese flags and decorations might present a problem.

"We'll go down to Chinatown," said George Boldt to Oscar. "We will copy everything they have . . . banners and things like that. We'll make them five times as large and ornate."

They headed for Mott Street and bought pennons and lanterns. Oscar spied a great triangular banner with scalloped sides. It was bright yellow with the fiercest of dragons, one that breathed fire. "That would be the Imperial flag of China," explained an attentive shopkeeper.

They bought several of each and hurried back to the Waldorf where seamstresses went to work. Soon the hotel looked like a Chinese inn with flags and bunting of every color of the rainbow displayed at every vantage point. The largest flag hung from the Fifth Avenue flagstaff.

Boldt knew that Li Hung-Chang traveled with his own chef, bakers, valets, guards, footmen, secretaries, interpreters and physician. He even had three men to help him smoke: one to carry the pipe, one the tobacco or cigarettes, one the fire. His cooks brought his food and bowed, waiting for his appraisal of each dish—not because he feared poison, but because he was accustomed to living that way. He also carried his own wines, tea and supplies of mineral water.

For the diplomatic banquet Saturday night Oscar planned a splendid menu. Several waiters, those serving nearest Li, would be Secret Service men. Oscar would conduct Li to the Grand Ballroom (converted for dining) down his secret passageway which led to a curtained door behind the head table.

George Boldt inspected the second floor reserved for royal guests. Li Hung-Chang would have the State Suite, a great bedchamber furnished in the style of the fifteenth century. Everyone admired its superbly carved bedstead, its canopy of figured mahogany, and the room's fine Gobelin tapestries. When the Duke of Veragua had occupied this suite, he, being very religious, had desired a small chapel. So Boldt supplied a tiny prayer alcove with an altar, closed off with draperies from the rest of the surroundings. Veragua's prayer nook would be an ideal place to store Li's valued coffin, which he usually took with him. Fearful of dying beyond the Middle Kingdom, he wanted to make sure that his remains would be shipped there immediately to be buried with his ancestors.

George Boldt looked at his great gold watch and hurried downstairs. One elevator was reserved exclusively for Li and his party. Guards would insure that no one came on this floor. Crossing the lobby, Boldt quickly appraised a platoon of bellboys. He noted several new faces behind the desks: more Secret Service men. Masses of luggage were being brought in through the freight entrance: cages with birds, tea caddies, bundles bound with hemp, European strapped portmanteaus, even bundles tied with bandannas as though just fetched up from steerage. He paused to admire the robed celestials sorting them out. Li had five servants concerned only with luggage; one, a very old retainer, sat atop a trunk, giving instructions.

As the *Times* man said, the Waldorf had become the Inn of the Golden Dragon.

Boldt looked again at his watch, snapped shut its cover and returned to the lobby. The Hungarian orchestra was tuning up. State Department officials had arrived. The crowd outside was restive. Would Inspector Monahan's men be able to restrain them? Guests filled every chair in the lobby—guests and plainclothesmen. Already ejected was one curiously dressed individual who wanted to sell fans. *Japanese* fans!

Boldt hurried to Oscar's post on the red carpet, just outside the 33rd Street entrance. He heard cheers billowing up Fifth Avenue. Police bicycle corpsmen passed; mounted police were nudging people back to the curbs. The cheers grew louder. Now the bright flash of trumpets, the boom of drums. Boldt darted out under the canopy. The marching column wheeled smartly in from Fifth Avenue, the plumed cavalry dressing their gleaming sabers. Now came the carriage. Above Boldt's head the great blue dragon stirred and swayed contentedly in New York's bright afternoon sun.

New York's next arrival from the inscrutable East was the Crown Prince of Siam, not at all Anna's gruff protagonist in *The King and I,* but a serious, intelligent monarch whose passion was tennis. The year 1902 was when a remarkably scrutable European, Prince Henry of Prussia, appeared. It seems that his brother, the Kaiser, had been making outrageous boasts about his new fleet, had even dared interpose some of it between Dewey's warships and the Spanish enemy at Manila. Germany's mercurial stock with Americans was at the moment on the downside. This affable prince had come hoping to improve matters and at the same time take delivery on the Kaiser's new yacht, *Meteor,* poised on the ways of a Staten Island shipyard awaiting His Highness and Alice Roosevelt to smash the ritual bottle. Meanwhile, Prince Henry would sight-see, ride the Sixth Avenue "El," hear "Prosits!" and endless post-strudel speeches.

As always, the Waldorf sought to do its best; preparations for Prince Henry were detailed and lavish. Only minutes after Boldt and Oscar together had proudly escorted the prince to his royal suite Boldt's phone rang. It was the prince's equerry. "Could we have a little hot water, please? His Highness would like to take a bath."

"Certainly!" Boldt, red-faced, hung up the phone. "Damn those plumbers! Hurry! Every available hand—a bucket brigade!"

It coursed up backstairs, down the length of a corridor, passed from hand to hand into the royal suite. Thus in the most modern hotel of the century Prince Henry got his bath water, brought by hand, and at a temperature that pleased him.

That evening he also got a splendid feast. The German-language newspaper *The New York Staats-Zeitung* was host. Well scrubbed and soaked, the royal Prussian appetite proved prodigious. Consumed, not by the prince alone of course, were 200 quarts of soup, 7,200 oysters, 500 chickens, 50 pounds of fish, a ton of beef and 600 ducks. How much beer? How much *sekt*? Who counts? The royal visit proved a success. Once more fragile German-American relations were safely cemented—or at least Scotch-taped.

Just as the Spanish-American War had brought Admiral Dewey to the Waldorf, and the *Titanic* disaster had filled its lobby with distressed survivors who'd been plucked from the sea, and World War I put General Pershing on its balcony and Sergeant York in a state suite, the year 1919 became the Waldorf's year for Presidents, America's Wilson, DeValera from the Sinn Fein Republic, Mexico's Diaz. Coming now was an avalanche of state visitors. Victory in Europe had focused the world's attention on this vigorous young world power; the center of gravity in world politics had shifted westward across the Atlantic. America was the "in" place; all the world's great wanted to come. And all roads led to New York, to its hospitable, handsome Waldorf. For passersby not to see at least one foreign flag flying over Fifth Avenue from the Waldorf would be rare indeed. Usually there were several.

The telegram from the State Department signalled that the estimable Nye, Washington's security-protocol expert, was coming once again to help make New York's welcome sumptuous and safe for an official guest of the United States. Usually the hotel might depend on at least a week for its special preparations, for re-decorating, touching up, moving furniture about to get pieces pleasing to the particular guest. Not all preparations were cosmetic. In advance the Waldorf learned what the honoree's favorite dishes were, often mobilizing corps of special cooks for each monarch. Waiters, maids and other help were designated who spoke the honored guest's language, a Boldt cardinal requirement which once meant changing dining room help three times in a single week. Private entrances would be opened up, private elevators designated, direct private telephone lines installed. During his stay the Prince of Wales kept open a direct line from the Waldorf to *H. M. S. Renown* anchored in the Hudson off Eighty-sixth Street. When President Taft came the Waldorf knew not to serve him rich desserts but remembered his great fondness for baked apples. Admiral Dewey, quite in character, enjoyed seafoods. President Teddy Roosevelt—an old Waldorf patron even before that wintry night when he stood out in the cold and protected it against anarchists' attacks—not unlike Presidents Wilson, Harding and Coolidge usually enjoyed eating whatever the hotel's own epicurean royalty deemed tasty. Just as the new Waldorf-Astoria on Park Avenue would later set something of a record by simultaneously serving 4,000 of New York's Finest at a breakfast, the old Waldorf-Astoria reached peak performance in 1924 with its lavish banquet for one of the plainest, surely the quietest of all American presidents, Calvin Coolidge. For that gala occasion 2,430 covers were laid, utilizing all seven dining rooms, an army of 323 waiters reinforced by another 1,000 busboys, pantrymen and kitchen helpers. Guests that evening consumed a ton of chicken (roughly one thousand birds aflying), enough sea bass to overpopulate the old Battery Park Aquarium, 500 young lambs, 600 quarts of ice cream, 150 gallons of soup, half an acre of asparagus, 2,000 square feet of potatoes, an acre of lettuce, a small mountain of mayonnaise, and enough Apolonaris, White Rock and coffee to float a carrier, plus uncountable quantities of celery, olives, cakes and anchovies. Such logistical statistics as these neither agitate nor excite a great innkeeper. They produce yawns. In the Waldorf's golden book of great achievements the Coolidge banquet stands out for quite another reason—the speed with which 820 ballroom tables were cleared, the rooms readied for dancing.

Two hundred housemen did it in less than twelve minutes!

To entertain visiting royalty or anyone else in New York has never posed a great problem. Whatever one fancies is available, from the Emperor of Japan's fascination for sea shells to Arab potentates' predilection for belly-dancers. Edward Prince of Wales's special delights were jazz, Long

Li Hung-Chang, Viceroy of China, the Waldorf's most eminent guest, August, 1896. (Courtesy Waldorf-Astoria Hotel)

Li Hung-Chang leaving the Waldorf at the 33rd Street entrance, August, 1896. (Courtesy Waldor-Astoria Hotel)

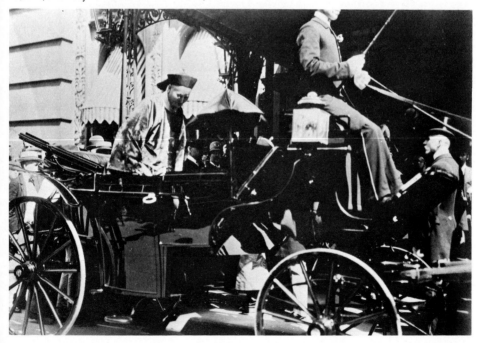

Three beautifully engraved, full-color covers from Oscar of the Waldorf's menu collection, for dinners honoring General John J. Pershing of the U.S.A., Governor General Earl Grey of Canada, and Grand Prince Albert of Hungary. (Courtesy Waldorf-Astoria Hotel)

Colonel William D'Alton Mann,
jovial publisher of the scandalous
Town Topics, and part-time
blackmailer.

The Sixth Avenue elevated ran from the Battery to Central Park. Here
is the station stop at 42nd Street. The view is to the east, with the
walls of the Croton reservoir on the right, and the mansard roof of the
old Grand Central Station on the left. (*Harper's Weekly,* July 25, 1868)

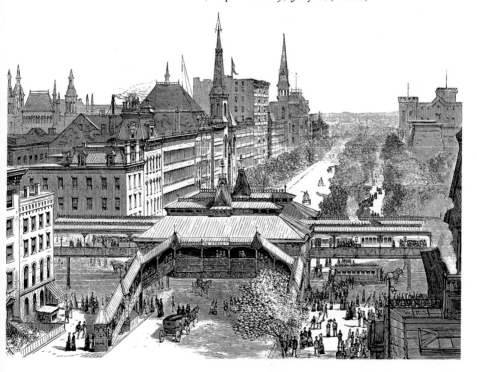

Fifth Avenue at 23rd Street (Madison Square), 1898. The view is to the
north, with the entrance to the Fifth Avenue Hotel at the left.
Photograph by Byron. (The Byron Collection, Museum of the City of
New York)

Fifth Avenue looking south from
34th Street. The Waldorf would
be on the immediate right. Wash
drawing by Corwin Knapp Lins
(Museum of the City of New Yo

Fifth Avenue omnibus drawn by three horses at Fifth Avenue and 42nd Street, 1899. (Museum of the City of New York)

Bicycling on Fifth Avenue, 1897. Looking north from 124th Street. (Museum of the City of New York)

WHEN LIFE IS VERY STRENUOUS AND SPIRITS ARE WAY DOWN
YOU'D BETTER GO TO POLLYS IN LITTLE GREENWICH TOWN
FOR THERE THE CLANS ARE GATHERED - ITS THERE YOU'LL FIND 'EM ALL
THE ARTISTS AND THE WRITERS RANGED ALONG THE WALL.
MISS POLLY TAKES THE MONEY AND MIKE SAYS HE JUST CAN'T
WAIT ANY FASTER ON THE FOLKS IN POLLY'S RES TAU-RANT.
J.T.B.
GREENWICH VILLAGE - NEW YORK
JESSIE TARBOX B

Polly's Restaurant, Greenwich Village. Photographic postcard by Jessie Tarbox Beals. (Museum of the City of New York)

The Waldorf's Roof Garden, used during the winter as a skating rink and during the spring and summer as an elegant area for dining and dancing under the stars. (Courtesy Waldorf-Astoria Hotel)

The Waldorf Roof Garden towards the end of its era, being used as a children's playground. (Courtesy Waldorf-Astoria Hotel)

The end of an era, May, 1929. Peacock Alley is demolished as preparations begin for the construction of the new Empire State Building. (Courtesy Waldorf-Astoria Hotel)

The grand old building comes down, November 7, 1929. (Courtesy Waldorf-Astoria Hotel)

Island's horsey set, and a dazzling girl reporter from the *Daily News* who helped him close up bistros along 52nd Street. Albert, King of the Belgians, when not making aerial flights above the city, seemed most fascinated by telephones, the ease with which long-distance calls were completed; indeed, when his itinerary took the king off to San Francisco he could not resist calling up the Waldorf-Astoria just to say hello. As the first hotel to install a telephone in every room the Waldorf's reputation in this communications area was considerable.

Contributing to this great inn's reputation as the Palace of New York came Prince Carol of Rumania (travelling incognito but readily recognized by his red-haired mistress), the Maharajah of Kapurthala, Prince Poniatowsky of Russia, Prince of Tallyrand-Perigord, Prince Masimir Lubomirski of Poland, Marshal Foch, Presidents Bessca of Brazil and Diaz of Mexico, Sir Thomas Lipton, Lord and Lady Dacies, Cardinal Mercier, Canada's Premier Sir Robert Borden, Premiers Calderon of Bolivia, Chamorro of Nicaragua, Mathieu of Chile; Lloyd George and Lord Balfour, Marconi of Italy and the telegraph, the Duke of Veragua, the Count de Castellane, France's Viviani and Jusserand.

Time marches on. A second generation of Siam's rulers came in 1931 reminding the Elegant Inn of their father's visit in 1902; today a third and fourth generation periodically visits. But for all its regal aspect, unique among hotels of the world, in the hearts and minds of tens of thousands of Americans the Waldorf's special meaning is one's own bar mitzvah, graduation dance, debutante ball, testimonial dinner or silver anniversary. The world around, honeymooners by the thousands become wistfully sentimental remembering the felicitous setting it furnished for that cherished juncture in their lives. The Waldorf loves honeymooners; indeed Hollywood once made a film about these. To honeymooners the hotel presents a bronze replica of their registration card.

Oscar's recorded career uncovers events more memorable than royal visits: the arrival of the Oberamergau Passion Players who walked Gotham's streets in biblical costumes, the day when Barnum and Bailey's Circus— animals, clowns and calliopes—performed in the Grand Ballroom. The oldest social function on the Waldorf calendar is New York's Annual Charity Ball, whose proud celebrants are traditionally the First Families of New York, an event having its beginnings at the old Academy of Music in 1857; it was the community's single legitimate Society event for raising funds for charity—"legitimate" as opposed to many "charity" promotions with other purposes often leaving charity a poor second as beneficiary.

The Annual Charity Ball came to the Waldorf-Astoria in 1900 and there it has remained. Rigidly formal, its traditional Grand March presents a pageant of the city's social history. Always led by New York's governor, scions of oldest families follow in strict order of precedence. The evening of the Annual Charity Ball always found an S.R.O. sign on the Waldorf; every suite, every room, every broom closet reserved with scores of private receptions and dinners taking place. Inextricably the Charity Ball was part of this city's history, its patrons and patronesses those proud families responsible for this community's world eminence. "Names," reminded Oscar, "are part of the Waldorf's psyche, the viable part that makes Waldorf-Astoria a famous name in itself."

In the spring of 1905 an urgent meeting took place in George Boldt's office. Wearying of complaints about the condition of the rooms, Boldt had summoned the head housekeeper, a gregarious type whose fondness for large functions caused her to concentrate on supervision of the ballrooms and reception parlors to the exclusion of individual guestrooms. Present also were the head houseman and William A. McCusker, Boldt's senior assistant. When all were seated Boldt spread the complaints out across his desk like a fan. Turning to the housekeeper he asked what she had to say. The woman was indignant. The reports were unfounded! The rooms were in tiptop condition! The head houseman, under her command, took a similar stand.

Boldt turned to McCusker. "What do you have to say?"

"Mr. Boldt, your house is rotten."

"Rotten?" Boldt's neck crimsoned. "Why, what do you mean!"

"It's filthy," said McCusker. "Go up and see for yourself. Take any room, say number five-twenty."

Furious, Boldt stalked out to the front desk, McCusker following. Selecting a random room key, up they went. Boldt walked in first. One look and he wheeled on McCusker. "You are in charge. Fire that houseman! Get this hotel cleaned up!"

McCusker sacked the houseman and the housekeeper. Then he went to work. Room-by-room he put the hotel through a cleanup, paintup and plumbing modernization program. It proved expensive and would do little towards bringing back the dissatisfied. In fact, most never returned. Across the next decade the great hotel struggled to hold its own financially. By 1915 it was actually operating in the red. Luckily, the First World War intervened, bringing with it an increase in activity and patronage. This would not save it, only postpone its demise. Fickle fashion never again favored the old Waldorf. This once-dazzling princess had now become a tawdry old dowager; she had seen her day. Under Boldt's guidance a younger man, someone of energy, imagination and ability, might have saved it. But Boldt stubbornly held the reins in his own hands and these, alas, were now enfeebled. Illness, grief over the loss of his beloved Louise, physically and spiritually depleted him. On December 5, 1916, George Boldt died.

More serious than its arteriosclerosis, the Waldorf-Astoria had become a victim of the Statler Syndrome; it no longer enjoyed the benefits of prime location. New York had rapidly moved farther uptown. Additionally, tastes had changed; during the first decade of this century hundreds of thousands of Americans were regularly travelling to London, Rome, Vienna, Paris, the Riviera, increasingly under the influence of César Ritz's type hostelery, elegant but modest, tastefully appointed, smaller hotels, surroundings in which every guest would be known to every servitor. Ritz also required that from the lowliest dishwasher to the most resplendent headwaiter, each employee be kept ever mindful that the sole reason for his existence was the individual guest's comfort. In any large inn, one of Waldorf proportions, host-guest relationships are fragile at best. Even without constant employment turnover inherent in its size, it is all but impossible for a Waldorf-Astoria to sustain personal rapport with the one thousand guests who every three days empty and refill its rooms. Requirements of American travelers were shifting to tastes characteristic of second-generation wealth. These being more secure in social, business and professional status, disdained the ostentation, the splash and plather their more gregarious, *nouveau-riche* parents once delighted in. That earlier rancher or lonely prospector, back from the desolate western expanse, rolling in money, longed for the glamor, the nepenthian cheer of the Men's Cafe, the cultured elegance of the Grand Ballroom, the sensuous glamor of Peacock Alley. Not so his educated, widely traveled, more sophisticated progeny. These candidly preferred the smaller inns now proliferating north and east of the Waldorf.

First to appear was the new Manhattan at 42nd Street and Madison Avenue which opened in 1896. So far as New Yorkers were concerned the Manhattan never became fashionable, but it attracted a prosperous class of guests, upstate New Yorkers, mostly travelers from other points along the New York Central. President William McKinley and Dr. Booker T. Washington, the eminent Black educator, both patronized the Manhattan. Incidentally, in that day had Dr. Washington or any other Black strode through the lobby of an eastern hotel chances are southern guests would have packed up and moved. To the Manhattan's credit its enlightened management invited Booker T. Washington to be its guest, and to Dr. Washington's credit he always used the hotel's private, lower floor entry. His New York visits were frequent. Robert Odgen, John Wanamaker's partner, a founder of Hampton Institute, was his staunch friend; in the Odgen home first convened those influential and caring New Yorkers most concerned with the welfare of the South's ten million unassimilated Blacks.

Following the Manhattan came the Netherland at Fifty-ninth and Fifth Avenue, with the Savoy soon to rise on the corner opposite, both to enjoy substantial partronage. Oddly, it was John Jacob Astor III who grasped the idea that wealthy Americans now crowding into New York comprised a breed eager for something different. This was the inspiration for another Astor hotel further uptown, one to be much smaller than the Waldorf but of such luxury and quiet refinement to rank it among the most exclusive in the world. With conformity to the skyline profile it would be a modest skyscraper, but have a small lobby, a few handsome, paneled public rooms and fair-sized private rooms, but great suites, all lavishly appointed yet within the discrete confines of good taste. Thus it was Astor's new St. Regis, opening in 1904, which loosed the first barrage against the Waldorf-Astoria, at once targeting several of Boldt's wealthiest patrons. R. N. Haan, a Hungarian, then operating several successful New York restaurants, was selected to operate the new inn. Haan quickly went to Paris and brought back Edmond Bailly, among the greatest chefs Europe could boast. Across the land word of

Bailly's culinary marvels quickly spread, intriguing America's more influential hosts and hostesses to come and savor dishes from his own hand at the stylish St. Regis.

Across Fifth Avenue directly opposite the St. Regis, in 1905 the Gotham appeared; not so prestigious as the St. Regis but another to siphon off Waldorf patronage. So rapidly was new wealth accumulating all over America, several years might elapse before Boldt would actually feel the effect of these raids on his house count. By then, 1906, the Belmont had opened on 42nd Street with B. L. M. Bates as proprietor. Bates, who had trained in the old Brunswick on Madison Square, the inn favored by Yale and Harvard undergraduates, had made a small fortune with the Murray Hill, a block below the new Belmont, which he would continue to run as well. Among Bates's early guests, also proselyted from Boldt, was Senator Stephen B. Elkins of West Virginia.

Also in 1906 along Forty-second Street appeared the Knickerbocker, another John Jacob Astor property. It too may not have lured away many of Boldt's permanent guests but it did offer the hungry and the thirsty gratifying new distractions. Many revelers in what was soon called "the Forty-second Street Country Club" would admire Maxfield Parrish's "Old King Cole," a celebrated painting which today hangs in the St. Regis's King Cole Room. In the new Knickerbocker was incorporated an idea borrowed from London's Carleton House, the step-and-stage grillroom entrance which provided women's faces, figures and gowns a chance for admiring display. A third John Jacob Astor property, the Hotel Astor, which had opened further up Broadway two years earlier, was destined to compete for the Waldorf's banquet income.

But the old Waldorf-Astoria's most formidable competitor proved to be the Plaza, which came along in the fall of 1907 at Fifth Avenue's southeast entrance to Central Park. First to decamp from the Waldorf, his home for eight years, was John W. Gates, now a Plaza stockholder for whose coming a luxurious apartment had been especially constructed. Others who had known the personable Plaza manager, Fred Terry, from hotels he had managed in Palm Beach and Hot Springs quickly followed. Among these were John Drake, a Gates associate; Hermann Frisch, "the Sulphur King," remembered as a durable member of those Waldorf poker parties; Adolphus Busch, the St. Louis brewer with his large family; and

Alvah C. Dinkey, Andrew Carnegie's associate. Then one explosive day the dike seemed to burst when thirty-two families packed up and left the old Waldorf to join this northward migration to the Plaza. These were the very core of the Waldorf's prominent social and political patronage from Chicago, Baltimore, Cleveland and Pittsburgh. If Boldt's income had not yet suffered, the great hotel's prestige was mortally struck, its peacocks had found a new alley, pristine precincts where bright-plumaged wealth and fashion might preen and strut. These newer inns epitomized good taste in quiet restraint. Public and private rooms of the Plaza reflected American predilection for European motifs but shunned ostentation and assiduously respected the guest's wish for privacy. Before very long the Belmont, the St. Regis and the Plaza would raid the Waldorf's most jealously guarded monopoly, its unique status as exclusive residence for distinguished foreigners. In this battle competitors could not sustain their attack; undisputedly the new Waldorf is again the "Palace of New York."

Let's glance back for a moment at what else was taking place as New York and the nation ushered in the twentieth century. Frederick Lewis Allen provides a memorable sketch of that New Year's Day:

> On the morning of January 1, 1900, there was skating in Van Cortlandt Park and presently it began to snow. But the sharp cold had not chilled the enthusiasm of the crowds who the night before had assembled in Lower Broadway to celebrate. The cable cars were jammed with people. Broadway in front of Trinity Church was well-nigh impassable, the crowds were dense in Wall Street as far down as the Subtreasury steps, and there was a great din of tin horns punctuated from time to time by firecrackers. It had been a good year and another one was coming. . . . Uptown in the mahogany-paneled library of the big brownstone house at the corner of Madison Avenue and Thirty-sixth Street, John Pierpont Morgan, head of the mightiest banking house in the world, the most powerful man in all American business, sat playing solitaire. During the next twelve months he would buy paintings and rare books and manuscripts in immense profusion for his townhouse to accommodate twenty-four hundred guests at his daughter's wedding, and would begin negotiations with Andrew Carnegie, the twinkling little steelmaster whose personal income in 1900 would be over twenty-three million dollars, for the formation of the United States Steel Corporation, the biggest corporation that the world has ever seen.

From that elysian view Allen plummets us into the squalor of another
quarter:

> On the lower East Side were poverty, filth, wretchedness on a scale
> which to us today would seem incredible. And in many other cities and
> industrial towns of America the immigrant families were living under com-
> parable conditions, or worse; for at a time when the average wage-earner
> got hardly five hundred dollars in a year, most of these newcomers to the
> country scrabbled for less. . . . No one either knew or cared—why not?
> Because it was a time of complacency. After the depression of the mid-
> Nineties the voices of protest at the disparities of fortune in the United
> States had weakened. Populism was dead; the free silver agitation had pe-
> tered out; the once angry farmers of the Plains States were making out so
> well a traveler commented that every barn in Kansas and Nebraska has
> had a new coat of paint. Not yet had the oncoming group of journalists
> whom Theodore Roosevelt, in a burst of irritation, labeled "muckrakers,"
> begun to publish their remorseless studies of the seamy sides of American
> life.

American literature, like American journalism, was going through
what Ambrose Bierce called "a weak and fluffy period"; Dreiser's *Sister
Carrie,* published in 1900, went almost unnoticed and then was withdrawn
from circulation as too sordid or pornographic.* "The best journals and
the best people," notes Allen, "concerned themselves very little with fortunes of the average man, and very much with the fortunes of ladies and
gentlemen, with the pomp and circumstance of Society, with the furthering
of a polite and very proper culture for the elect."

Those New Year's merrymakers delighted in leaving that century
behind. They'd good and ample reasons. True, the Nineties brought New
Yorkers prosperity. They had brought to bud America's Magic Era of
Science. They had buried many haunting, deeply-rooted superstitions.
But ended was the bloody era which had seen the Union tested on the
battlefield. The United States was one people.

*Thirty years later Dreiser's *An American Tragedy* was a forbidden publication by edict of
the Massachusetts Supreme Court, a retrograde movement not to continue, for in 1966
the U.S. Supreme Court held that the government could not suppress a book as obscene
as long as it had merit as literature. Two-thirds of a century—one-third of America's
national existence—was consumed in judicial deliberations before arriving at this decision,
deep-rooted to the Constitution's First Amendment.

Behavior and Bohemianism

With the end of the nineteenth century New Yorkers put away their childish things. Or many of them. No longer did they cling to barbaric superstitions about infant care, the therapeutic powers of blue window glass. If lingering in *U.S. Pharmacopoeia* was one prescription beginning, "Take a tenpenny weight of wax from the ear of a dog . . ." at least doctors no longer thought tuberculosis was caused by allowing candlewicks to burn too low.

The medley of races in this crowded polyglot community had brought other Old World superstitions not to be quickly uprooted. When the night wind wailed through East Side gorges many trembled in the belief that this was the restless cry from the souls of children unbaptized. Among those tenement multitudes charms and carved fetishes hung above the beds of the sick; mystic spells were woven that differed little from those whispered centuries gone in the forests of Northern Europe. Seldom did it attract the attention of the law, but the black art of witchcraft had not been banished.

It was once relatively easy for tenement dwellers to track down that sinister Slav who was in league with the devil, to locate the seer who made children immune to poison by writing magic words in blood upon their foreheads, or to find love-philters. Through the congestion north of Grand Street ghosts were widely reported, tales of demonology were common to Chinatown. Almshouse dwellers sitting in the sun, watching the surging tide and the glistening river, spoke believably of spirits and banshees and fays. In Essex and Ludlow Streets and along East Broadway lingered a belief in Lilith, the legendary first wife of Adam—not the fabulously beautiful, eternally young Lilith of Rossetti who ensnared the souls of men in her enchanted hair. The Lilith whom these East Side women chanted incantations against personified evil; she lurked unseen, she would kidnap or injure a newborn child.

Other races in other neighborhoods knowing nothing of Eve's predecessor clung to a belief that newborn children were likely to be stolen away; that their abductors were fairies who'd leave behind changelings, deformed children, the offspring of gnomes. In consequence of this some mothers cruelly tortured the "changelings" foisted upon them in the belief that the kidnappers, out of pity for the gnomes' offspring, would be induced to bring back their stolen child. Sociologists speculate whether inexplicable cases today of fiendish wrath toward children by sullen and reticent parents may not be rooted in this grim pagan belief. In 1905 throughout East Side tenements a certain textbook on necromancy was widely read; its sequels still find readers. It told how to make oneself invisible or impervious to bullets, how to cure diseases. To learn difficult incantations the book recommended the services of a Wise Woman. Lest you be some gunman's target you must say "O Josophat, O Tomosath, O Plasorath!" and quickly pronounce Jarot backwards three times. Our "low-vaulted past"? High on the list of popular requests in many libraries today are books on witchcraft, according to librarian reports.

Nor were superstitions exclusively the property of New York's poor. The rich dreaded thirteen at table. Many buildings, notably hotels, had no thirteenth floor (except the Waldorf, remember?). In his painting of the *Last Supper* Da Vinci illustrates a gaffe which many still acknowledge; has not Judas upset the salt! Until recently men warded off rheumatism, now known as arthritis, by carrying horse chestnuts in their pockets. Wall Streeters, including J. Pierpont Morgan, regularly engaged spiritualists. Another broker's day was doomed if his barber did not shave his right cheek first, "and the first stroke must be up." Many New Yorkers in moving their households would not carry away the broom and others would not bring the family cat with them lest bad luck be theirs. Many still put horseshoes over their doors to ward off evil, a superstition that some believe arose from the horseshoe-shaped blood splash of the Passover. Broadway performers before stepping onstage are traditionally wished "Break a leg!" by fellow performers. Race track devotees, like today's professional baseball players, have an entire liturgy of superstitions; for example, you are sure to win if on the way to the track you accidentally meet a cross-eyed man. Mariners know that to whistle aboard ship will call up turbulent storms and a storm at sea the first day out means that some miscreant seaman had sneaked out of a harlot's bed without paying her. The idea of placing objects into the cornerstones of New York's structures harkens back to times when it was thought strengthening to put human bones in the underpinnings of bridges; in 1892 the Chinese made certain that the Czar of Russia's proposed Trans-Siberian railroad included these safeguards.

The "evil eye," a hex from Italy thought to be possessed by many along Roosevelt and Elizabeth Streets, and at Mulberry Bend, later had many believers in Harlem. With late summer the Romany women, dark-eyed, mysterious gypsies in beads, loose-fitting blouses and sandals, would appear at every tenement door possessing an array of useful charms for warding off evil, beginning with the stringing of certain shapes of coral about the necks of children. Novitiates knew that by holding your fingers a certain way you can immunize yourself against the evil eye: folding the two middle fingers into the palm leaving others projecting like prongs (this has quite different meanings for Texas Longhorns and Italians, by the way). With threats of evil spells the gypsy women sold fetishes, extorting a good portion of what might have otherwise found its way into Christian offerings; more than one poor Catholic priest welcomed the approach of winter for sending these Romany women south. Around the outbreak of World War I schools of the East Side experienced a prolonged epidemic of "devil frights"; great numbers of children were kept at home because of the belief that the Evil Being whom Petrus Stuyvesant shot with a silver bullet at Hell Gate now haunted their schoolhouse. Those few children brave enough to show up time and again would rush from the classroom shouting "The devil is at the window!" In several settlement schools Hebrew parents were convinced that Christians were striving by spells and branding marks to seduce their children away from their faith.

Not to be overlooked is the fact that in 1900 New York's foreign born, with their children, comprised 76 percent of its inhabitants; the majority of the student body of its free colleges. If its superstitions seem absurd consider for a moment precepts of old New York's quaint etiquette, "the barrier which Society draws around itself, its shield against the impertinent, the improper and the vulgar." No nation on earth has become more conscious of its manners nor subscribed more heavily to books of etiquette. Earlier British visitors such as Mrs. Trollope, Captain Basil

Hall, James Silk Buckingham, Charles Dickens, Oscar Wilde, Bernard Shaw, Paul Bourget, Rudyard Kipling, G. Lewis Dickinson, once safely returned home, had variously loosed stinging barbs at America's social behavior, the manners, or want of them, they'd observed. As each patronizing pronouncement winged back across the seas and landed in the press Yankee hackles went up, and America's displeasure with the British mounted. Many English yet patronized America as a wayward colony.

Not all visitors had been uncharitable. Dickens complimented the American male's unfailing chivalry towards women, a vanishing gallantry Europe scarce remembered. Others noted behavior which, in their view, was more eccentric than ill-mannered, such as the great importance in American family life occupied by children; how daughters of sixteen could preside over a dinner table with the poise and grace of their mothers— and frequently did. Only Sir Philip Gibbs saw America as a "nation of nobodies."

Said Lord Bryce, speaking of America in 1888: "The manners of the best people are exactly those of England, with a thought more of consideration towards inferiors and of frankness towards equals."

"People are the same the world over; only their customs make them different." A great body of codified social behavior was published in the United States between 1840 and 1900. Many were highly successful. All prove how customs make us different, even among ourselves.

Perhaps because medieval houses were built with overhanging stories from which slops were thrown into the street, and passing vehicles splashed mud, etiquette decreed that a gentleman walk nearest the curb; and a gentleman walking two ladies must never sandwich himself between them. Tobacco, regarded in the Civil War years as "a loathesome indulgence of the male, scarcely within the pale of tolerance," by the end of the century had a better reputation. In that earlier day, according to Cecil Hartley's *Gentleman's Book of Etiquette,* one must never smoke in the presence of clergymen, and one must never offer a cigar to an ecclesiastic. After smoking a gentleman must change his clothes, rinse his mouth, and brush his teeth before joining the ladies. Frontier American women may have had a predilection for their menfolk's clay pipe or Duffy's snuff but these were regarded as too rustic by the gentry. Women did not often smoke in public until the first decade of this century. Mrs. Frederick Lewisohn seems to have been the pioneer. Asking her to throw her cigarette away at Sherry's precipitated a social crisis of dramatic proportions—at least for the editors of the *Herald*. Long after World War I the ladies of Charleston who smoked ordered their cigarettes from out-of-town suppliers rather than be embarrassed by the disclosure of local patronage.

Society, like freemasonry or other cults of exclusion had its marks of identification—its own passwords, phrases, inflections, and gestures. As stringent as its sanctions were its taboos: a butler who takes a card in his fingers, a center light in the drawing-room, a rocking-chair, a maid who removes more than one place at a time, a high handshake, ready-tied bow ties, the word "tux" for dinner jacket, or such locutions as "Meet Mrs. Blank" and "Pardon my glove." Only the self-consciously genteel live in "residences," sign their letters "cordially yours," fear to say "go to bed" and not "retire" or put their elbows on the table when they choose. The Victorian and the Opulent Era saw stature and character in their symbols; corset-straightened dignity and unbending rectitude. The huge crinoline hoop skirt literally commanded social space, trailing garments, too impractical for walking, but implying a carriage waiting at the door. Today only heavily lacquered mandarin fingernails remain to pretend the owner's unfamiliarity with dishpan—and keyboard.

Miss Leslier's *Behavior Book,* which first appeared in 1853, admonishes: "While at table all allusions to dyspepsia, indigestion or other disorders of the stomach are vulgar and disgusting. The word 'stomach' should never be uttered at any table, or indeed anywhere else, except to your physician or in private conversation with a female friend interested in your health. And," reminds Miss Leslie, "the fashion of wearing black silk mittens at breakfast is now obsolete."

Fashion, which Dr. C. W. Cunnington defines as "a taste shared by a large number of people for a short space of time," experienced rapid mutations following the Civil War along with customs and rules of etiquette. Robert Tome's *Bazar Book of Decorum* asserts, "When you salute a lady or gentleman in the street to whom you wish to show particular respect, you should take your hat entirely off and cause it to describe a circle of at least ninety degrees from its original resting place." Such gyrations would naturally encourage the invention of an automatic hat-tipping device, an ingenious spring inside the hat responding to slight inclination of the wearer's head to raise the hat without the assistance of his hand. Tome's book, with a nod to Cyrano, offers this counsel: "The nose should not be fondled before company, or, in fact, touched at any time unless absolutely necessary. The nose, like other organs, augments in size by handling, so we recommend that every person keep his own fingers, as well as those of his friends or enemies, away from it."

Mrs. John Sherwood's *Manners and Social Usage,* appearing in 1884, with numerous revisions up to the eve of the new century, tells us "that gentlemen now wear pearl colored gloves embroidered in black to dinner and do not remove them until they sit down to table." With the waltz and other dances which couples would perform alone, the need for placing his arm about his partner's waist also demanded that the gentleman's hand be gloved or that he at least have a handkerchief covering his palm. Ward McAllister, Society's Elsa Maxwell of the early Waldorf era, says, in all solemnity, "A dinner invitation once accepted is a sacred obligation. If you die before the dinner takes place your executor must attend the dinner."

Under pressure of new life styles old rules of etiquette gave way releasing women from traditional bondage of "Kinde, Kirche, Kuche." New freedoms vis-à-vis the opposite sex were invoked in their behalf. Chaperones, long thought immovably anchored in any gathering of young people, began to diminish. In the Eighties Mrs. John Sherwood had decreed, "She must accompany her young lady everywhere; she must sit in the parlor when she receives gentlemen; she must go with her to the skating rink, the balls, the parties, the races, the dinners, especially to theater parties; she must preside at the table and act the part of the mother so far as she can; she must watch the characters of the men who approach her charge and endeavor to save the inexperienced girl from the dangers of a bad marriage, if possible." Edith Wharton's mother numbered all the families in due order who comprised the world to which her daughter was born, ". . . and there her world stopped short. Make no mistake about it," writes Michael Millgate.

The term "chaperoning" New Yorkers changed to "matronizing." A society belle's invitation to dinner with a bachelor contained the phrase, "Mrs. Brockholst Cutting will kindly matronize the party." In a 1900 edition of Mrs. Sherwood's book a readiness for change is apparent: "Although in some circles an unmarried woman of increasing years is thought to be exempt from vigilance, an elderly girl of thirty-five is very unwise to visit an artist's studio alone, even though there is in art an enobling and purifying influence which should be a protection." Betrothal meant not a relaxation but tightening of chaperonage in startling contrast to eighteenth century America when in a burst of freedom from suffocating puritanism, morals were considerably relaxed. In that era Harvard theologians debated with fervor "whether it be fornication to lye with one's Sweetheart before marriage." Church records indicate that many young lovers of the 1700's did not consider sexual intercourse between engaged people a sin.

Not so their stuffier grandchildren: "Nothing is more vulgar in the eyes of our modern society than for an engaged couple to travel together or to go to the theater unaccompanied, as was the primitive custom. Society allows an engaged girl to drive with her fiancé in an open carriage but it does not approve of his taking her in a closed carriage to an evening party." Glancing back across two decades of the Victorian mores reflected in Henry James's *A London Life,* we find one rational young woman who expected a man to marry her and save her reputation because the two had been left alone in a box at the opera. Chaperones were insisted upon by many conservative American families well into the first half of this century; before World War II, patrons of the Metropolitan Dancing Class still had their chaperones, "maids or professionals hired from an agency like Miss Dignum's at $10 an evening, who sat and read in the lobby or dressing rooms of the Waldorf until 'Home, Sweet Home' brought their imprecise duties to an end."

Serving notice upon the world that a daughter has become nubile is a rite belonging to Society alone, or at least those ambitious for its cachets. Southern belles of the eighteenth century "came out" at an appreciably earlier stage than their northern cousins—Margaret Herbert of Alexandria, Virginia, granddaughter of Washington's kinsmen, the Carys, was presented to Society at fourteen. Débuts at fifteen and sixteen were common. In the mid- and late-nineteenth century the coming-out party might be an elaborate dance but more typically an afternoon reception at which the debutante received with her parents, relatives and a few of her close girl friends, welcoming not only young men but a generous assortment of dowagers and elderly gentlemen. After the reception had thinned, an informal dinner might follow, to end with a dancing or a theater party. The debutante's conventional age, then as today, was eighteen. In New York a young lady might make her bow at any time during the season which began officially in mid-November with the Horse Show and closed at the start of Lent. The really hectic season is briefer. This begins with the Tuxedo Autumn Ball, or after the opening of the Metropolitan Opera, and by New Year's Day the bloom is off the peach, which means a massive congestion of activity around Thanksgiving, Christmas and January First, intensified by the holiday inrush from colleges and schools. In New York Society there are approximately 300 debutantes each year, producing an aggregate seasonal expenditure between fifteen and twenty million dollars, an average hotel catering bill for food, drink, service, music and flowers of $20,000 to $30,000. Among hotels angling for this trade there is a keen rivalry. At first it belonged exclusively to the Waldorf, with the new Sherry's and Delmonico's sharing modestly. Then it shifted to the Ritz-Carlton during the meteoric eminence of that grand Madison Avenue establishment, now back to the new Waldorf with the Pierre and the Plaza competing. Voguish today in New York as elsewhere are balls and festive dinners in art museums and great public galleries. Excessive spending which transformed ballrooms into southern gardens and tropical jungles in December with tons of gardenias, orchids, monkeys, parrots and palms—fantasies costing from $75,000 to $100,000—peaked during the season 1928–29 then began to diminish. Tribal pomp of this kind, those extravagant introductions to Society of such young ladies as Charlotte Dorrance, Eleanor Post Close, Gloria Gould, Barbara Hutton or Helen Lee Doherty have now ceased to be considered acceptable form, if, in fact, they ever were.

A few footnotes to the nineteenth century before laying the era of America's adolescence to rest. During that century the spoon came into our lives to join the fork and knife as a useful table utensil. Tomatoes, called "love apples," were still believed to be poisonous, years away from being a generally acceptable food staple; Europeans stared aghast at mid-century American travelers actually eating tomatoes. Early into that era Shakespeare, banned at Harvard as obscene, gained permissive respectability; he now could be privately read though had not yet penetrated Harvard's curriculum. Akin to rugby, football appeared but very shyly. When Frank Hering arrived at Notre Dame in 1896 to coach it he had a hard time working up enough enthusiasm to get an eleven-man squad on the field. Lynchings, if thought only vestigial aberrations of Reconstruction which would abate in the new century did not in fact do so. In 1900 there were 115 lynchings recorded but in 1901 the number rose to

130, which is to say that on average ten times each month somewhere in the Home of the Brave armed citizens took the law into their own hands, overwhelmed legitimate officers of the law, seized some other un-armed and helpless citizen, subjected him to cruel torture and mutilation, then savagely murdered him.

Examination of these penumbrial areas in American social order sug-gests taking a look at other social mutations. What was the new Bohe-mianism? One early manifestation of it was the much publicized Seely Dinner at Sherry's, remembered for the near nude belly dance of a Coney Island nymph named Little Egypt and a highly publicized police raid by Captain Chapman. Curiously, popular indignation did not drive this host into exile. On the other hand, when James Hazen Hyde gave his famous Versailles Ball and was hounded out of the country, it was not because the party was disreputable, the costumes vulgar, the entertainment ob-scene, but rather because of its extravagance; Hyde had spent upwards of $100,000 on food alone. Public judgments in such matters are highly unpredictable. Much the same was true in that great scandal of the nine-teenth century, the Reverend Henry Ward Beecher's flagrant hanky-panky with Elizabeth Tilton, wife of a prominent parishoner, all of which a vengeful Victoria Woodhull exposed in a lurid muck-drenched court trial. What resulted? The cockolded husband became the lover of Victoria Woodhull, she became a candidate for president of the United States, and the Reverend Beecher's pastorate prospered as he preached to ever larger congregations. Despite Elizabeth Cady Stanton's minor involvement in that scandal, under her leadership women sought and won a measure of equal rights.

An early manifestation of this was the Waldorf-Astoria's announce-ment that women dining alone would be served at any hour in all of its restaurants, an accommodation which hotels here and abroad promptly followed. Twice the number of divorces were granted in 1898 upon the wife's complaints than in 1878. But those thousands of hapless females still swept into divorce courts with their figures structured in whalebone, with wire "forms" resembling two inverted sieves molding their bosoms and steel scaffolding shaping their behinds. Not until 1893 did an avant-garde *Ladies Home Journal* beseech ladies not to put their daughters into corsets at the age of twelve and hope "that they themselves would find the courage to do without them." Many Americans of that day were born, lived and died never knowing the existence of homosexuality, preferring perpetually to remain innocently perplexed at the strange behavior of Oscar Wilde and Walt Whitman.

We lament with Allen Churchill that "There are many things the world will never see again. One of these is the fine, free spirit of Greenwich Village in the years between 1912–1930, its Bohemian heyday."

If anything has transpired to dim that spirit after 1930 one would be scarcely aware of it. Social patterns, music, art, the dance, tastes in behavior, manners of speech and dress seldom have their origins at the upper strata. Just the opposite. While wealthy Americans may have imported the liberality of the new Bohemianism from Europeans, what was happening to that fine free spirit once it arrived was peculiarly American, singularly original, the creation of poor, not rich, Americans. A sad fact is that today many Americans conscious of Greenwich Village—New York below Fourteenth Street, the West Side from Chelsea to Van Dam—regard its Bohemian delineations and many of its inhabitants as a community of cop-outs, young persons congealed by artificialities who pretend that libertarianism and lax morals are a requisite to artistic achievement. Sightseers in buses come away with this impression because ready exhibits of this are precisely what puts tourists in buses.

The Village had venerable beginnings. Thomas Jefferson dined there wearing red waistcoat and red knee breeches to match his red hair. "To quaint old Greenwich Village," long years later wrote O. Henry, "the art people soon came prowling, hunting for north windows and eighteenth century gables and Dutch attics and low rents. Then they imported some pewter mugs and a Waldorf chafing dish or two from Sixth Avenue and became a 'colony.' "

Fifty years ago old-time mumming was still existent in Greenwich Village, a fascinating survival of some venerable custom in an ancient European community. Children of the Village went about the streets on holidays, particularly Thanksgiving Day, singly or in groups of from half a dozen to a dozen, some with masks and fantastically dressed in simple home-made costumes. Huge street bonfires on election night, another ancient New York tradition that was outlawed when the streets became asphalt, persisted in Greenwich Village to become an annual battle of wits between watchful police and Villagers. The latter could conspiratorily hide combustible junk, packing boxes and old furniture until the secret hour for bringing it out and setting it ablaze.

True, today as yesterday, much of the Village's population displays neither artistic talent nor the integrity essential to its development; nevertheless, Greenwich Village in this century has been the Parnassus of America. It has been "home" for Willa Cather, Eugene O'Neill, Sherwood Anderson, Theodore Dreiser, Edna St. Vincent Millay, Malcolm Cowley, Hart Crane, Hendrik Willem Van Loon, Thorne Smith, Harold Stearns, Van Wyck Brooks, Burton Rascoe, Ben Hecht, Louis Untermeyer, Floyd Dell, Max Eastman, Max Bodenheim, Edward Weeks, John Reed, Walter Lippman, Harry Kemp, and George Cram Cook, and many newer ones.

The Village nurtured as well sculptors Jo Davidson and Gertrude Vanderbilt Whitney; playwrights, stage designers of the calibre of Robert Edmond Jones; painters Maurice and Charles Prendergast, John Sloan, William Glackens, George Luks, Everett Shinn, Art Young, Reginald Marsh, Jerome Bloom, Maurice Becker, Kenneth Hays Miller, Hans Stengel, William Auerbach Levy, Guy Pene du Bois and Peter Arno; choreographer Agnes De Mille; composers George Antheil and Edgar Varese, and actors Noel Coward, an actor named Archie Leach who became Cary Grant, and a politician-songwriter named James J. Walker who became mayor. Its publishers-in-residence were Donald Friede and Horace Liveright. These were by no means the first Bohemians to discover America's "Left Bank." Edgar Allen Poe once lived there as did that stalwart leader of independent thought and action, Thomas Paine, in a cottage on Henry Street between Christopher and Jones, which present day names translate Bleecker between Grove and Barrow.

"There was quietness and quaintness, there were neighbors who knew each other, there was sauntering in the streets," wrote Max Eastman. "It is hard to believe any section of Manhattan Island quiet but so narrow and twisted are Village streets—West Fourth Street actually crosses West Eleventh—heavy traffic keeps its distance. And so green are its shaded parks and walled gardens, so picturesque its intimate little monuments and historic markers, its gambrel roofs and dormer windows, old fanlights and pillared doorways, the artistic iron newell posts, one has the sensation of being of another age in a pleasant, refreshing, ageless American village."

"After all," adds Robert Shackelton, "one finds in any Latin Quarter pretty much what he takes there; if he takes youth and ambition and happiness he finds happiness and ambition and youth. If he takes a cynical mind and a doubting heart he sees only doubts and cynicisms. Greenwich Village stands for unrest, but it also stands for happiness. It gives an outlook upon life. It gives music and conversation and touches of restaurant happiness to those who cannot afford the extravagance of uptown. It gives color to many a life that would otherwise be but drab. And it is interesting to see and hear Greenwich Village working, and talking, eating, drinking, dancing and making merry, or taking life seriously. In the studios and in the restaurants you see some who are thrilled and some who are amused; you hear eager discussions of everything on earth or below or above the earth; you are yourself amused or interested, you feel tolerant or critical. When you must find your way by dim lamplight through a covered passage and across a littered yard you find it difficult to take Greenwich Village seriously; but somehow it must be taken with a good deal of seriousness because it takes itself so seriously. . . ."

How seriously?

It is recorded that in the years 1920–1925 one half of all the literature published in the United States was created in Greenwich Village.

Eleven

Yesterday

$\mathcal{W}$hat were they like, this new breed, this second generation of pioneer wealth, these siblings of great miners, ranchers, drovers, oil prospectors, steel makers, railroad builders, ship owners, land speculators, revered geniuses of science and financial wizardry? They had a strong predilection for opera, as well as for painting and sculpture, European manners and the French language. "Many society ladies," writes Mary Cable in *American Manners and Morals,* "spoke English with a slight French accent, much as New York debutantes today cultivate languorous, sultry speech that begins in the depths of their throats and comes out with no movement of their lips." Dixon Wecter believes the zenith of European influence upon American society was during this period, from 1895 to the Great War. Those wishing to remain socially in evidence had to be seen annually on both sides of the Atlantic, especially in Paris, London and the German spas. "And wherever they went they took their own bed linen and towels, as well as a few personal servants," Mrs. Cable adds.

"Since for the very rich to live was to acquire," volunteers an *American Heritage* editor, "they no sooner set foot in Europe than they began to buy things. From Worth gowns and Savile Row suits they branched out to jewels, dogs, horses, wines, dinner services, *objets de vertú,* and soon the world of art." They also brought back servants; America's great residences demanded these, the butler with an English accent remains a status symbol. To do it right meant a display of London tailored livery, for no native American would be found dead in livery. All through this Gilded Age, princes, dukes and other noblemen continued to be a popular import. In 1909 someone calculated that upwards of 500 American heiresses had married titled foreigners resulting in a major flight of capital. Now besides England's, titles of Italy, France and Germany were acceptably significant. While most upper crust Americans seemed happy to prosper

[217]

in a classless republic they began to display an inordinate interest in genealogy, when possible to unearth a coat of arms in their ancestries they were quick to have it engraved on their letter paper or silver, have it painted on their carriage doors, wear it on jewelry. Genealogists assert that not fifty colonial families have a right to armorial bearings yet in the late nineteenth century so remarkably had their descendants proliferated Tiffany's set up a department "blazoning, marshalling, and designing arms complete." Notes Mrs. Cable, "An Office of Heraldry" did a flourishing business in New York and numerous books to aid self-styled genealogists soon appeared. One went so far as to assure its readers, "Christ was a gentleman, as to the flesh, by the part of his mother, and might have borne coat-armor." Persons of distinction began organizing themselves into clubs, many of which still exist; to name a few: the Colonial Dames, the Descendants of the Signers of the Declaration of Independence, the Society of Descendants of the Continental Congress, the Huguenot Society of America, the Order of Colonial Lords of Manors in America, the Society of Mayflower Descendants, and the Daughters of the American Revolution. Some had great social cachet, while others, like the D.A.R. were open to too many people to remain for long exclusive. Similarly many secret societies flourished dating back to the Know Nothings of 1840, parent of the Ku Klux Klan—masonic orders, Woodmen, Eagles, Pythians, Odd Fellows, Elks, Moose. So popular did secret fraternal orders become in the United States by the Twenties it is estimated that one out of every three American adults knew some secret password, wore some identifying button and once a week dressed up in special regalia to share arcane incantations with his or her fellow knights, nobles, ladies, sisters or brothers. "Lodge Night" in the average American home held as fixed a place on the family calendar as Sunday worship.

From different but no less arcane gestation, the Black Hand Society, today recognized as the Mafia, early transplanted itself from Sicily to New Orleans, thence New York. This cult of the vendetta of strictly "mezzogiorno" Italian origins exerted little influence outside that ethnic community until the ambitious second decade of this century when gambling, vice and prohibition law led to its expansion as a nationwide consortium of organized crime.

One saw in the ending of the nineteenth century vigorous revolt against Victorian morals. Ever in cycle, by 1905, observers note, Americans of wealth seem committed to the double standard, another concept imported from Europe where unfailingly this banner has waved. In cozy London West End flats behind the Royal Savoy chapel numerous Americans regularly installed their mistresses during summer visits to England, excepting those few ladies who demanded shelter in fashionable hotels commensurate with that occupied by their lover's wife and family; if wife and family were at the Carlton this meant nothing less than Claridges or the Berkeley for the girlfriend.

By 1905 the pace of life in New York had accelerated to a tempo that expatriates returning after twelve years abroad would hardly recognize. Gaiety, high living and chorus girls had come into their own. Automobiles began to jam traffic on Fifth Avenue; roads leading out from the city had been paved and widened. Roadhouses thrived, being now accessible by other means than coaches-and-four or hired carriages and long hours of driving. Back in those years when coaches had been running from the Waldorf and other Fifth Avenue hotels to such favored spots as the Woodmansten Inn, newcomers to Manhattan might boast that they had made the trip behind so famous a driver as Hungarian-born Aurel Batonyl, otherwise distinguished for having married Society's glamorous Mrs. Burke Roche. Motor car spins to sylvan retreats became popular, enhancing romantic possibilities never feasible in public conveyances.

No saga of the city would be complete without mention of its love affair with its river and the romantic excursion boats that breasted its waves in overnight voyages to Albany. Countless courtships began with promenades along their spacious decks. The night boat to Albany, the Hudson River Day Line Excursions, for nearly a century became as intimately a part of New York as Battery Park and Broadway as well as inspiration for songwriters and stage skits. Travel with Isabel and Basil March on *Their Wedding Journey,* by William Dean Howells, a honeymoon which nearly became a maritime disaster when their love boat rammed and sank another ship. When the two ships collided Isabel was sound asleep. Luckily, only the bride's sensibilities were damaged. Rushing out of her cabin she found "a world of dishabille, a world wildly unbuttoned and unlaced, where ladies wore their hair down their backs, walked about in stockings and spoke to each other without introduction." Properly Isabel

[219]

and Basil restrain their disapproval at the steamboat's lavish appointments: "Good heavens, Isabel, does it take all this to get us plain republicans to Albany in comfort? Or are we really a nation of princes in disguise!" They despair at finding "no interval between disgraceful squalor and ludicrous splendor aboard ship; the owners catering to the taste of the richest and most extravagant plebeian amongst us. He unhappily minds danger and oppression as little as he minds money so long as he has a spectacle and a sensation, and it is this ruthless imbecile who will have lace curtains cloistering the stateroom berth into which he climbs with his pantaloons on, and out of which he may be blown by an exploding boiler at any moment. . . ." From Albany the young couple go by train to Rochester where they made the acquaintance "of a traditionally obnoxious being, the American hotel clerk." This front desk dandy displayed "a neat moustache and well-brushed hair; jeweled studs sparkled on his shirt front and rings on his white fingers. He did not lift his haughty head to look at the wayfarer who meekly wrote his name in the register; he did not answer him when he begged for a cool room. 'Upstairs!' " Basil learns that for daring to ask for a cool room the clerk had assigned them one into which the sun had been shining the whole afternoon; but since their luggage had already been put into it it seemed useless to protest. "And like a true American he shrank from asserting himself."

Hotel men may not recognize that shrinking true American too timid to complain, but only practiced managerial myopia would prevent their recognizing the jaundiced front desk type. Once a traveler journeyed beyond the assiduously cultivated professionalism of Fifth Avenue's famous inns, attitudes toward the guests often changed with the landscape.

Twelve

Hail and Farewell!

$\mathcal{G}$eorge Boldt's death almost cost the Waldorf its own life. Boldt enjoyed a wide acquaintance; he was an individual who valued old friends and sought new ones, a hotel's most valuable asset. For scores, nay hundreds, of Waldorf-Astoria arrivals George Boldt's welcome meant they were "home." George Boldt, Jr., held the reins for three years after his father's death but young Boldt never pretended to any great desire to be an hotel operator and was happy when that role was taken over by Augustus Nulle, once private secretary to George Boldt then successively chief steward, purchasing agent, managing director, and secretary-treasurer of the Waldorf.

The Nulle interregnum showed a want of drive, a sense of purpose. The hotel survived in the way most great industries do when the prime mover dies and lawyers or bankers are thrust into command, when the skipper is gone from the bridge and the chief steward is at the helm. No great disaster or spectacular success results, but one or the other is not long in coming. Luckily, the sharp upsurge in travel with World War I brought substantial business to the Waldorf; even more once America had entered that conflict.

A block west of the Waldorf-Astoria at 34th Street and Sixth Avenue had appeared a great new hotel called the McAlpin. Charles P. Taft of Cincinnati, one of the larger McAlpin investors, owner of the Hotel Taft in New Haven, brought from New Haven to the McAlpin's management a competent professional named Lucius M. Boomer. Boomer, a native of Poughkeepsie, had all Boldt's capabilities for wooing success coupled with a highly cultivated taste in furnishings, a keen sense of organization, and innovative methods of cost-accounting that eliminated waste in the kitchens, an enormous expense in hotels the size of the McAlpin or the Waldorf-

Astoria. Among those fascinating statistics identified with a great hotel—
that it annually buys fifty miles of towels or dispenses enough coffee each
year to fill Lake Champlain—should be a statistic showing that the waste
from its kitchens could sustain x number of hogs, laying Leghorns or
trout hatcheries. Until Boomer came along kitchen waste was waste. Cor-
recting this and adapting other money-saving and money-making opportunities at the McAlpin impressed a number of his admirers. Among
these was Coleman du Pont, one of the more strenuous members of the
illustrious Delaware clan. "I'll buy the Waldorf-Astoria if you will run
it," said a telegram one day from du Pont to Boomer vacationing in Florida.
The two soon got together and formed the Boomer-du Pont Properties
Corporation which soon took possession not only of the Waldorf but Boldt's
old Bellevue-Stratford in Philadelphia; the Claridge, a fine Times Square
Hotel; Washington's famous Willard Hotel; and the Windsor Hotel in
Montreal. Boomer eventually would head Louis Sherry's, Inc., and become
president of the Sherry-Netherland Hotel opposite the Plaza on Fifth Avenue, and the Savarin restaurant chain which was destined to bloom at
the towering new Waldorf-Astoria which the world knows today.

What in fact the Boomer-du Pont combine purchased was neither
the Waldorf structure nor the land on which it sat. These remained Astor
possessions. From Boldt's estate for $500,000 they bought only Boldt's
lease and the Waldorf-Astoria's furnishings. A gratifying surprise to
Boomer when he took command was the loyal attachment of Waldorf
employees; Oscar and Nulle remained as did other veteran department
heads and more than one hundred faithful workers who for three decades
had been identified proudly with the great institution. In jig time Boomer
crystalized this ésprit by his own vigorous example. He also made structural
alterations to the lower floors to improve revenue and cut waste; Peacock
Alley was widened and more brilliantly illuminated, the Bradley-Martin
Ballroom would vanish to be reborn as the Jade Room, which proved an
immensely popular restaurant.

Wartime prosperity bequeaths no annuity. With victory came a
mortal blow for saloon keepers, many restaurants and for a wide segment
of the hotel industry. Believing that Americans could be legislated into
a state of grace, Congress now passed the Volstead Act, making it unlawful
to import, manufacture, transport or sell alcoholic beverages. Because of
high profits from wines and spirits, hotels customarily had put lower

prices on food and service. Consequently America's hotels now confronted both loss of income and sharply higher operating costs.

At midnight June 30, 1919, the famous rectangular mahogany bar in the Men's Cafe served its last drink, and then was ceremoniously axed apart, its fragments distributed as souvenirs. Chief Engineer Ezra Bingham tells of hundreds of misty-eyed old friends standing silently by, wincing and groaning with each blow of the ax. Replacing the Men's Cafe came a candy shop, a delightful smelling one down the length of which stretched a gleaming onyx soda fountain with shining nickle-plated soft drink and whipped cream dispensers.

Somehow it just wasn't the same.

Another Boomer innovation was the roof garden. Boldt had always been leery of roof gardens but finally, under pressure, had given in, opening one of a summer's night to the delight of everyone. When one evening scores of patrons caught in a sudden rain squall ran for cover without paying their bill, Boldt's objections prevailed and the Waldorf's erstwhile roof garden became a skating rink. During the garden's existence it had proved that hundreds preferred *al fresco* dining; at least one newsman waxed postively rhapsodic with descriptions of the romantic setting, the mellifluous music, the twinkling heavens, the cooling breezes from the faraway Orange Mountains and the breathtaking view—all from the dizzying height of 17 stories. Oscar Hammerstein's Olympia Roof and the Grand Central Palace's Roof Garden both did good business. In 1896, said Stephen Crane, describing the former in terms of an experience everyone has shared: "Roof entertaining had probably been invented by some Arab or Moor in a long gone century but the American has only recently seized upon the idea. The people who swarm to the Olympia are conveyed by two elevators to where the cool and steady night wind insults the straw hat and the scene here during the popular part of the evening is perhaps more gaudy and dazzling than any in New York. It has an exuberance which reminds one of the Union Depot train sheds of some western city. The steel arches of the roof make a wide and splendid sweep, and over in the corner there are some real swans swimming in real water. The whole structure glares like a conflagration with countless electric lights. Oscar has caused the execution of decorative paintings upon the walls. They appear to have been painted with a nozzle; if he'd caused the execution of the decorative painters he'd have done much better.

"One of the features of the roof garden is the waiter who stands directly in front of you whenever anything interesting transpires on the stage. The waiter is 300 feet high and 72 feet wide. His little finger can block your view of the golden-haired soubrette, and when he waves his arm the stage disappears as if by miracle. Someday there may be a wholesale massacre of roof garden waiters but they will die with astonished faces and with questions on their lips. Skulls so steadfastly opaque defy axes or any other method which the populace occasionally uses to such colossal stupidity."

Boomer succeeded where Boldt had failed by simply putting the Astor half rooftop under glass to create several dining and dancing places. All became instantly popular.

What pre-war northward population shifts and new uptown competition had earlier begun, hastening the old establishment's demise, Prohibition would now complete. With declining income came fresh pressures to build a great new skyscraper on the ground the hotel occupied. By 1924 rumors were rife that the great hotel would close. One day came the discreet announcement that the Waldorf-Astoria Realty Corporation had been formed to *purchase* the property from *the Astors;* the buyers, dominantly Coleman du Pont, included W. W. Atterbury, Leroy W. Baldwin, M. C. Brush, Robert K. Cassatt, L. I. Dunham, Percy H. Johnston, William C. Sproul, E. T. Stotesbury, John R. Todd, and Lucius Boomer. Sharply increased taxation demanded new revenues; much of the hotel's Thirty-fourth Street frontage was converted into shops, with stockbrokers' boards and travel offices imploding into the stately old lobby itself. In flowed offers for the Fifth Avenue frontings; one at a tempting annual lease of $300,000 would have meant eliminating both the Rose Room and the Empire Room. Proper land use, that uncompromising evaluator of all real estate, was telling the Waldorf's owners that the old lodging house sat on a piece of ground that would yield vastly greater sums were it not there. They got the message. Finally plans for the magnificent new Empire State Building and destruction of the Waldorf-Astoria Hotel were formally announced. "But," Boomer took pains to make clear, "we retain the rights to the name 'Waldorf-Astoria Hotel' for future use." New Years Eve 1929, ending a year Wall Street would never forget, was roisterously celebrated with one of the greatest revels of the old hotel's glamorous history.

Hail and Farewell!

On May 1st all thirty-eight New York organizations who had made Waldorf-Astoria their regular gathering place were invited to a banquet in the Grand Ballroom. "The most glorious testimony to a departing friend that New York has ever witnessed," said the *New York Evening World*. "Every phase of New York life was represented: university men, military men, bankers, brokers, philanthropists, politicians, manufacturers, merchants, churchmen, writers and newspapermen." Billed as "The Final Dinner," this nostalgic assemblage was presided over by Dr. Nicholas Murray Butler, Columbia University's eupeptic president, with effulgent George T. Wilson as toastmaster. Along the flower-banked head table as honored guests were the heads of organizations that had known the Waldorf-Astoria as home. These included Rotary Club president H. Dykes; George A. Zabriskie, Sons of the American Revolution; Colonel Franklin Q. Brown representing the Army and Navy Club; Michael Friedsam, the Fifth Avenue Association; Thomas Ewing, the Patent Law Association; George E. Fahys, the Church Club; William Fellowes Morgan, League for Industrial Rights; Herbert C. Green, the Ohio Society; New York's former mayor, John F. Hyland; John McGlynn of the Hotel Association; Bertram Borden of the New England Society; Philip C. Meon, the Oil Trades Association; Charles P. McClellan, the St. Andrew's Society; Stephen Callaghan, St. Patrick's Society of Brooklyn; Percival Wilde, Lake Champlain Association; Dr. Marcel Knecht, *Le Matin;* Adolph S. Ochs, *The New York Times;* Leonard F. Loree, the Chamber of Commerce; United States Senator Royal S. Copeland; the Episcopal Bishop of New York, the Rt. Rev. William T. Manning, and William A. Prendergast, chairman of the Public Service Commission.

After the banquet those who for years had been Waldorf residents returned for the last time to their suites. These included the William Rogers Chapmans, Harry Stevens and that venerable dean emeritus of culture who had done the most to initiate New York Society into the exalted world of music, Albert Morris Bagby. It also included Colonel E. H. R. Green, son of Wall Street wizard Hetty Green, who among other idiosyncracies had bequeathed a goodly sum to a mongrel pooch named Cupid Dewey "because he loves me and doesn't know how rich I am."

May 3rd, its final operating day, was designated "Employees' Day" when every dollar taken in would go into a benefit fund to assist those workers who were leaving the hotel's employ, many incorrectly believed, forever.

Now the auction, the sale of the furniture, fixtures and *objets d'art* to restore to Boomer-du Pont corporate coffers the $500,000 paid Boldt's estate. On May 4th, 1929, in its thirty-second year, the august Waldorf-Astoria Hotel shuddered and collapsed under the shattering blows of the wrecking crew's massive, two-ton ball. In a spectacular 242 days, as though magically dropped into place from heaven, where once nobly stood The Elegant Inn majestically appeared the towering Empire State Building, the world's tallest structure, a marble sculptured stalactite whose cloud-crested 104 stories was crowned by an airship mooring mast, whose 25,000 offices would soon search for tenants. The Great Depression by now having settled in, these would not materialize quickly. Indeed, for several years the dollars collected from sightseers for a thrilling meteoric spurt upward to its cloud-bathed parapet paid the Empire State Building's taxes.

Some share Juliet's sentiment that "parting is such sweet sorrow," others Tennyson's "every parting means to die a little." From across America, from around the world, still other millions reading of the old Waldorf's passing sensed the poignant nostalgia of Byron:

Farewell!
    For in that word, that fatal word, however
    We promise—hope—believe,
    There breathes despair.

Bibliography

Bibliography

Allen, Frederick Lewis. *Only Yesterday*. New York: Harper & Brothers, 1932.

Brown, Henry Collins. *In the Golden Nineties*. Reproduction of 1927 edition. New York: Arno Press, 1971.

Churchill, Allen. *Park Row*. Reproduction of 1958 edition. Westport, Conn.: Greenwood Press, 1973.

Crockett, Albert Stevens. *Peacocks on Parade: A Narrative of a Unique Period in American Social History and Its Most Colorful Figures*. Reproduction of 1931 edition. New York, Arno Press, 1975.

Grafton, John. *New York in the Nineteenth Century*. New York: Dover Publications, 1980.

Morris, Lloyd. *Incredible New York: High Life and Low Life of the Last Hundred Years*. Reproduction of 1951 edition. New York: Arno Press, 1975.

Shackleton, Robert. *The Book of New York*. New York: Gordon Press, 1977.

Wecter, Dixon. *The Hero in America: A Chronicle of Hero-Worship*. Reproduction of 1942 edition. New York: Irvington Publications, 1972.

Index

Index

Although not a "hotel man," Albin Pasteur Dearing has been consultant to both The Pierre in New York and the Stevens (the present Conrad Hilton) in Chicago. He was also the original promoter of Aspen in Colorado. He was wounded twice in World War II and decorated for combat actions as leader of parachute commands. In Korea he headed psychological warfare operations, and in Vietnam was attached to the French High Command before the American involvement there (which he opposed as a member of the Pentagon's Special Staff). Dearing attended Southern universities (Sewanee and Florida) and did graduate work at Grenoble and Strasbourg. He writes for several newspapers and magazines, including *Reader's Digest*. He lives in Perugia, Italy.